Being a Writer™

Funding for Developmental Studies Center has been generously provided by:

The Annenberg Foundation, Inc.

The Atlantic Philanthropies (USA) Inc.

Booth Ferris Foundation

The Robert Bowne Foundation, Inc.

The Annie E. Casey Foundation

Center for Substance Abuse Prevention
    U.S. Department of Health and Human Services

The Danforth Foundation

The DuBarry Foundation

The Ford Foundation

Google Inc.

William T. Grant Foundation

Evelyn and Walter Haas, Jr. Fund

Walter and Elise Haas Fund

The Horace Hagedorn Foundation

J. David and Pamela Hakman Family Foundation

Hasbro Children's Foundation

Charles Hayden Foundation

The William Randolph Hearst Foundations

Clarence E. Heller Charitable Foundation

The William and Flora Hewlett Foundation

The James Irvine Foundation

The Robert Wood Johnson Foundation

Walter S. Johnson Foundation

Ewing Marion Kauffman Foundation

W.K. Kellogg Foundation

John S. and James L. Knight Foundation

Lilly Endowment, Inc.

Longview Foundation

Louis R. Lurie Foundation

The John D. and Catherine T. MacArthur Foundation

A.L. Mailman Family Foundation, Inc.

The MBK Foundation

Mr. and Mrs. Sanford N. McDonnell

Mendelson Family Fund

MetLife Foundation

Charles Stewart Mott Foundation

National Institute on Drug Abuse,
    National Institutes of Health

National Science Foundation

New York Life Foundation

Nippon Life Insurance Foundation

Karen and Christopher Payne Foundation

The Pew Charitable Trusts

The Pinkerton Foundation

The Rockefeller Foundation

Louise and Claude Rosenberg, Jr. Family Foundation

The San Francisco Foundation

Shinnyo-en Foundation

Silver Giving Foundation

The Spencer Foundation

Spunk Fund, Inc.

Stephen Bechtel Fund

W. Clement and Jessie V. Stone Foundation

Stuart Foundation

The Stupski Family Foundation

The Sulzberger Foundation, Inc.

Surdna Foundation, Inc.

John Templeton Foundation

U.S. Department of Education

The Wallace Foundation

Wells Fargo Bank

Grade 3

VOLUME **1**
TEACHER'S MANUAL

Being a Writer™

Last summer I
zoo for my tenth
got their. I s
monkey!. The
Then the lion
scared. I saw a
to sit on it's
want to but
huge hippo hip
a girl but
s it
onn,
after

First edition published 2007.

Being a Writer is a trademark of Developmental Studies Center.

Page ii of volume 2 constitutes an extension of the copyright page.

Developmental Studies Center wishes to thank the following authors, agents, and publishers for their permission to reprint materials included in this program. Many people went out of their way to help us secure these rights and we are very grateful for their support. Every effort has been made to trace the ownership of copyrighted material and to make full acknowledgment of its use. If errors or omissions have occurred, they will be corrected in subsequent editions, provided that notification is submitted in writing to the publisher.

Excerpt from "Meet the Author: Eloise Greenfield" from the Houghton Mifflin Education Place® website (http://www.eduplace.com/kids/hmr/mtai/greenfield.html). Copyright © Houghton Mifflin Company. Reprinted by permission of Houghton Mifflin Company. All rights reserved. Excerpt from www.judyblume.com, copyright © 2007 by Judy Blume. Reprinted by permission of William Morris Agency, LLC on behalf of the Author. "Eloise Greenfield" reprinted by permission from *The Big Book of Picture-Book Authors & Illustrators* by James Preller. Scholastic Inc./ Teaching Resources. Copyright © 2001 by James Preller. Excerpts from *In November*, text copyright © 2001 by Cynthia Rylant, reprinted by permission of Harcourt, Inc. "Judy Blume" excerpts from *Author Talk* by Leonard S. Marcus, copyright © 2000 Leonard S. Marcus, reproduced by permission. Excerpts from *Childtimes: A Three-Generation Memoir* copyright © 1979 by Eloise Greenfield and Lessie Jones Little. Used by permission of HarperCollins Publishers and the Herman Agency. "First Day of School" from *Kids Write Through It: Essays from Kids Who Have Triumphed over Trouble*. Copyright © 1998 Fairview Press. Reprinted with permission of Fairview Press. "Believing in Myself" from *Kids Write Through It: Essays from Kids Who Have Triumphed over Trouble*. Copyright © 1998 Fairview Press. Reprinted with permission of Fairview Press. "How I Saved a Dog's Life" from *Kids Write Through It: Essays from Kids Who Have Triumphed over Trouble*. Copyright © 1998 Fairview Press. Reprinted with permission of Fairview Press. Excerpts from *If You Were a Writer* by Joan Lowery Nixon. Text copyright © 1988 Joan Lowery Nixon. Reprinted with the permission of Simon & Schuster Books for Young Readers, an imprint of Simon & Schuster Children's Publishing Division. Excerpts from *Cherries and Cherry Pits* by Vera Williams. Text copyright © 1986 Vera Williams. Used by permission of HarperCollins Publishers. Excerpts from *The Paper Bag Princess* by Robert Munsch. Copyright © by Robert Munsch. Published by Annick Press Ltd. 1980. Reprinted with permission. Excerpts from "Meet Kevin Henkes!" from www.kevinhenkes.com, copyright © Kevin Henkes. Used by permission of HarperCollins Publishers. Excerpts from *Julius, the Baby of the World* Copyright © 1990 by Kevin Henkes. Used by permission of HarperCollins Publishers. Excerpt from *Tacky the Penguin* by Helen Lester. Text copyright © 1988 by Helen Lester. Reprinted by permission of Houghton Mifflin Company. All rights reserved. Excerpt from *Grandma's Records* by Eric Velasquez copyright © 2001. Reprinted by permission of Walker & Co.

A special thanks to Donald Murray (who passed away December 30, 2006) for the wonderful assortment of author quotations that he gathered in his book *shoptalk: learning to write* published by Boynton/Cook Publishers in 1990.

Developmental Studies Center
2000 Embarcadero, Suite 305
Oakland, CA 94606-5300
(800) 666-7270, fax: (510) 464-3670
www.devstu.org

ISBN: 978-1-59892-316-2

Printed in the United States of America

4 5 6 7 8 9 10 MLY 16 15 14 13 12

TABLE OF CONTENTS

continues

TABLE OF CONTENTS *continued*

Acknowledgments

Many people were involved in the development of the *Being a Writer* program, and we are grateful for their time, expertise, suggestions, and encouragement. First, we wish to thank the members of our Teacher Advisory Board, who piloted the lessons during our development year, giving us expert feedback to help shape the format and content of the program and collaborating with us in numerous invaluable ways:

Albany Unified School District
Ali Gooding
Nancy Johnson
April Stewart
Christiane Zmich

Hayward Unified School District
Andrea Richards
Jill Rosenthal
Melanie Tirrell

Newark Unified School District
Jennifer Boyd
Patrick Brose
Hemawatie Dindial
Gail Fay
Midge Fuller
Michelle Leipelt
Karen Stevenson
Katherine Jones
Anjuna Wagner
Lilia Woo

Oakland Unified School District
Stephan Goyne
Lisa Lefrack
Kathy Wilson

West Contra Costa Unified School District
Jennifer Brock
Betty Buginas
Jeanie Hedeen
Nina Morita
Linda Takimoto

In addition, we wish to thank the teachers, principals, and district leaders who participated in the yearlong field testing of the program in the following school districts:

Albany Unified School District, Albany, California
Elgin Unified School District, Elgin, Illinois
Newark Unified School District, Newark, California
West Contra Costa Unified School District, El Cerrito, California

Acknowledgments

Finally, we wish to thank the many children's book publishers that assisted us during the development of this program and upon whose books these lessons are based.

Albert Whitman & Company
Annick Press Ltd.
Barron's Educational Series, Inc.
Bloomsbury USA Children's Books
Boyds Mills Press
Candlewick Press
Capstone Press
Charlesbridge Publishing
Chronicle Books
Compass Point Books
Crabtree Publishing Company
F & W Publications, Inc.
Farrar, Straus & Giroux
Firefly Books
Graphic Arts Center Publishing Company
Grolier Publishing Company
Harcourt Children's Books
HarperCollins Children's Books
Heinemann
Henry Holt & Company Books for Young Readers

Holiday House
Houghton Mifflin Children's Books
Hyperion Books for Children
Kids Can Press
Kingfisher Publications
Lee & Low Books
Lerner Publishers Group
Little Brown & Company
National Geographic Society
NorthSouth Books, Inc.
Penguin Putnam Books for Young Readers
Random House Children's Books
Richard C. Owen Publishers, Inc.
Sasquatch Books
Scholastic Inc.
Simon & Schuster
T&N Children's Publishing
Walker & Co.
Workman Publishing Company

This program was developed at Developmental Studies Center by:

Shaila Regan, *Director of Program Development*
Susie Alldredge, *Senior Program Advisor*
Dennis Binkley, *Assistant Director of Program Development*
Kenni Alden, *Curriculum Developer*
Jackie Jacobs, *Curriculum Developer*
Laurel Robertson, *Curriculum Developer*
Sarah Rosenthal, *Curriculum Developer*
Julie Contestable, *Consultant*
Annie Alcott, *Contributing Writer*

Pilar Beccar-Varela, *Contributing Writer*
Valerie Ruud, *Managing Editor*
Amy Bauman, *Editor*
Krista Faries, *Editor*
Ellen Toomey, *Designer*
Joslyn Hidalgo, *Production Manager*
Roberta Morris, *Art Director*
Scott Benoit, *Production Designer*
Renee Benoit, *Media Production Manager*
Jennie McDonald, *Manager of Publisher Relations and Rights*

Introduction

We all dream of sending our elementary school students on to middle and high school with a love of writing; an ability to write clearly, creatively, and purposefully for sustained periods of time; and a familiarity with the crafts and conventions of writing in the major genres. We want them to approach writing with confidence and understand that writing, first and foremost, is communication. In pursuing this dream, we ask ourselves: *What are the most important things for students to learn about writing during their elementary school years? What writing experiences are most important for students to have?* The *Being a Writer*™ program is our carefully researched, fully articulated answer to these key questions.

The *Being a Writer* program is a yearlong writing curriculum for kindergarten through grade 6, and the first program of its kind to bring together the latest research in teaching writing with support for students' social and ethical development. The program marries a writing process approach with guided instruction, providing a clear scope and sequence to ensure that your students learn the important elements of writing at their grade level. This all happens in the context of a caring classroom community—so crucial to motivating and inspiring students to grow as writers, thinkers, and principled people. As members of the community, the students learn and act on the values that govern the community (responsibility, respect, caring, fairness, and helpfulness). They practice the skills and dispositions they need to bring these values to life in their daily interactions.

Unique Features

The program's unique pedagogy grows out of years of research on writing and child development; a focus on character education and social and ethical development; and a desire to support teachers both as writers and as writing teachers.

Research Based/Classroom Tested

We drew on two decades of research in the areas of writing, motivation and learning theory, and social and ethical development to develop the *Being a Writer* program. In the 1980s, a major study of various modes of writing instruction showed that a writing process approach combined with clear objectives and opportunities for peer interaction produced an effect 22 times greater in students' pretest-posttest writing quality than approaches characterized by lecture, teacher-only feedback, and writing assignments imitating patterns or following rules. Interestingly, the study also found that positive feedback (commenting exclusively on what writers had done well, rather than on shortcomings) produced far greater effects in student writing than did negative feedback (Kelley 2002).

More recent work by researchers and leaders in the field, including Atwell, Calkins, Fletcher, and Graves,* supports the use of the following practices to improve students' writing practice and attitude:

- Teacher and peer conferences

- Classroom discussion

- Collaborative writing tasks

- Writing for real audiences and purposes

- Student self-assessment

- Regular periods of writing

- Choice of writing topics

- Models of good writing

The *Being a Writer* program was developed in consultation with an advisory board of teachers (of varied backgrounds and experience) who piloted the lessons and gave us extensive feedback to assure that the program addresses the needs of all students, is easily implemented, and fits into the normal classroom day.

Dual Focus: Academic and Social/Ethical Learning

Child development research tells us that children learn and grow best in environments where their basic psychological needs are met. Children need to feel physically and emotionally safe. They need to feel that they belong. They need to have a sense of themselves as autonomous and capable.* Studies indicate that when these basic needs are met at school by helping students experience a sense of community, the students do better academically (as measured over time by grades and test scores), exhibit more prosocial tendencies, and show greater resistance to problem behaviors such as drug use and violence (Resnick 1997; Schaps 2004).

The *Being a Writer* program helps you take deliberate steps to create a classroom writing community where your students feel empowered, supported in taking risks, and responsible to themselves and the group. The program weaves

To read more about the theoretical and research basis for the Being a Writer *program, please refer to the bibliography in volume 2.*

cooperative learning, social skill instruction, and discussion of values throughout the writing lessons.

Teacher Support

The program is designed to help teachers hone their skills both as teachers of writing and as writers themselves. Detailed, easy-to-follow lesson plans include suggestions for managing the writing process, facilitating discussions, assessing the class, and conferring with individual students. Teacher Notes throughout the lessons explain the underlying pedagogy of various activities and provide examples of what might happen in the classroom. The weekly Teacher as Writer section helps teachers cultivate their own writing voice while deepening their appreciation for what students are asked to do in the program.

Program at a Glance

The following sections describe the program components, writing development across the grades, and a typical daily lesson.

Program Components

The *Being a Writer* program includes:

- *Teacher's Manual*, two volumes per grade

- 20–30 children's trade books per grade to inspire and model good writing

- *Student Writing Handbook*, one for each student (at grades 2–6), containing excerpts, practice activities, a spelling word bank, and proofreading notes

- *Assessment Resource Book* (at grades 1–6), containing information and record sheets to assess writing and social skill development in individual students and the class

- *Skill Practice Teaching Guide* (at grades 2–6), containing mini-lessons to supplement grammar, usage, punctuation, and capitalization skill instruction in the program

- *Student Skill Practice Books*, one for each student (at grades 2–6), containing additional skill practice activities to be used in conjunction with the *Skill Practice Teaching Guide*

(At grades 2–6, you will need to provide each student with a writing notebook and a folder for loose pages. See Student Books, Notebooks, and Folders on page xxiv for further information.)

Development Across the Grades

The table below provides a snapshot of how learning in writing process, craft, and genre is developed over grades K–6. (See Skills and Conventions on page ix for how skill instruction develops across the grades.)

Writing Process and Craft	K	1	2	3	4	5	6
Write daily for various purposes and audiences	■	■	■	■	■	■	■
Generate ideas for writing	■	■	■	■	■	■	■
Choose their own writing topics	■	■	■	■	■	■	■
Extend writing to tell more	■	■	■	■	■	■	■
Confer with the teacher	■	■	■	■	■	■	■
Reread writing for sense	■	■	■	■	■	■	■
Learn about conventions from published works	■	■	■	■	■	■	■
Publish pieces in a variety of ways	■	■	■	■	■	■	■
Read and share published pieces with the class	■	■	■	■	■	■	■
Write for sustained periods of time	❑	❑	■	■	■	■	■
Learn about elements of craft from published works	❑	❑	■	■	■	■	■
Analyze drafts for specific elements and revise	❑	❑	■	■	■	■	■
Keep a writer's notebook for ideas and drafts		❑	❑	■	■	■	■
Develop relaxed, uninhibited attitudes about writing	❑	❑	❑	■	■	■	■
Cultivate creativity	❑	❑	❑	■	■	■	■
Confer in pairs	❑	❑	❑	■	■	■	■
Give and receive feedback	❑	❑	❑	■	■	■	■
Proofread and edit for spelling	❑	❑	❑	■	■	■	■
Proofread and edit for conventions (i.e., grammar, usage, punctuation)	❑	❑	❑	■	■	■	■
Revise based on partner feedback	❑	❑	❑	❑	■	■	■

■ formally taught　　❑ informally experienced

Writing Genres	K	1	2	3	4	5	6
Write and learn elements of fiction	☐	☐	■	■	■	■	■
Write and learn elements of expository nonfiction			■	■	■	■	■
Write and learn elements of letters			■	☐	☐	☐	☐
Write and learn elements of personal narratives	☐	☐	☐	■	■	■	■
Write and learn elements of functional nonfiction				☐	■	■	
Write and learn elements of poetry	☐	☐	☐	☐	■	■	■
Write and learn elements of persuasive essays					☐	■	■

■ formally taught   ☐ informally experienced

A Typical Daily Lesson

Lessons are generally divided into three sections: Getting Ready to Write, Writing Time, and Sharing and Reflecting. Some lessons also include an Extension that can be taught at another time; examples of Extensions include using technology to learn more about an author and writing in response to literature.

- **Getting Ready to Write.** Most direct instruction happens during this section of the lesson. The students gather to hear and discuss a read-aloud, brainstorm ideas for writing, participate in shared or modeled writing, do whole-class "quick-writes" (short, whole-class writing exercises), or discuss how they will work together.

- **Writing Time.** During this period of silent, sustained writing, you have the opportunity to write with the students, walk around and assess the class, and confer with individual students or pairs.

- **Sharing and Reflecting.** Students share and reflect on their writing and their social interactions in this section. They listen to one another's writing and express their appreciation. They discuss what's working as well as any problems that arose in their partner work and how to avoid those problems in the future.

Understanding the Program

The *Being a Writer* program helps students develop as writers *and* as caring, collaborative people. This dual focus is based on two beliefs: that students' academic learning flourishes when social learning is integrated into the curriculum and that we are called on as educators to help students develop as whole people—academically, socially, and ethically.

Focus on Writing

Students spend their first few, precious years as writers in our classrooms. As elementary students, they are at the very beginning of their lifelong careers as writers. Learning to write is like learning to master other means of communication; command of the written word, like command of the piano, oil paints, sign language, or mathematical symbols, relies less on innate talent than on years of steady practice and encouragement.

Motivation and Creativity

To get enough sheer practice writing during their elementary school years, the students need to really, *really* want to write. Thus, all instruction in writing processes, crafts, skills, and conventions in this program grows out of the need to tap into students' intrinsic desire to express themselves and to be understood.

Throughout the program, read-alouds of exemplary writing stimulate the students' imaginations and fuel their motivation to write. Reading about professional authors helps students learn that creativity can be gloriously messy and that writers write to satisfy themselves first. Students have a great deal of choice about what to write—even when writing about assigned topics, they draw on their unique experiences and interests to address those topics. Formal skill instruction is delayed in the units so that students can focus initially on just getting their ideas onto paper. However, basic writing mechanics and skills are taught early in grades K–1 (e.g., forming words, writing from left to right, spacing between words).

The Beginning of Writing (K–2)

Early writing develops on a foundation of drawing, oral language, and phonics. In grades K and 1 and at the beginning of grade 2, we create many opportunities for students to draw and tell their stories and to see writing modeled. The students see the teacher thinking aloud about what to write; drawing and writing letters, words, and sentences; using standard sentence punctuation; and rereading writing. We assume that the students are receiving separate phonics instruction alongside this writing program, including instruction about concepts of print (including letter names and upper/lower case), phoneme segmentation, sight words, and letter formation. Throughout the primary grades, we suggest that the teacher model writing using letter–sound relationships the students have learned in their phonics program. We include examples of how to model this writing using letter–sound relationships derived from the *SIPPS®* program (*Systematic Instruction in Phoneme Awareness, Phonics, and Sight Words*), developed by John Shefelbine and Developmental Studies Center.

The program structure at grades K–2 supports students in learning the basic skills they need to communicate in writing. Because this skill instruction is cumulative and builds on prior learning, the units at K–2 are designed to be taught sequentially.

Writing Process, Genre, and Craft

While students informally draft, revise, and publish their writing at grades K–2, it is not until grade 3 that the writing process becomes central to the program. After being formally introduced to the writing process at the beginning of the year, grade 3–6 students repeatedly engage in the cycle of prewriting, drafting, revising, proofreading, and publishing as they participate in the genre units.

The genre units—designed around personal narrative, fiction, expository nonfiction, functional nonfiction, persuasive writing, and poetry—immerse the students in each genre by having them hear, read, and discuss good examples of the genre. They learn about elements of the genre as they brainstorm ideas, do quick-writes, and write multiple drafts. After this immersion and drafting phase, they select a draft to develop and revise for publication in the class library. They spend the later weeks of the unit revising, proofreading, publishing, and sharing their pieces from the Author's Chair.

The genre units at grades 3–6 may be taught in any order, although we recommend that the expository nonfiction unit be taught later in the year due to its greater academic and social demands.

Writing Skills and Conventions	K	1	2	3	4	5	6
Write from left to right and top to bottom	■	■					
Put spaces between words	■	■					
Use a word wall to spell high-frequency sight words	■	■	■				
Use letter/sound relationships to approximate spellings	■	■	■	□	□	□	□
Capitalize the first word in a sentence	■	■	■	□	□	□	□
Use a period at the end of a sentence	■	■	■	□	□	□	□
Capitalize proper nouns and *I*		■	■	□	□	□	□
Use question marks and exclamation points		■	■	□	□	□	□
Use commas in greeting/closing of letters			■	□	□	□	□
Use an individual word bank and dictionaries to spell words			■	□	□	□	□
Use commas in dates			■	■	□	□	□
Recognize and use contractions (*isn't, aren't, can't, won't*)			■	■	□	□	□
Use commas in a series			■	■	□	□	□
Use apostrophes to show possession			■	■	□	□	□
Use quotation marks to punctuate speech			■	■	■	□	□
Use comparative and superlative adjectives				■	□	□	□
Correctly use commonly misused words (such as *they're, their, there; who's, whose*)				■	■	■	■
Recognize and use common parts of speech				■	■	■	■
Recognize and consistently use simple past, present, and future verb tenses					■	■	■
Use commas in direct quotations					■	■	■
Identify and indent paragraphs					■	■	■
Recognize and use prepositions and prepositional phrases					■	□	□
Recognize and consistently use point of view						■	■
Recognize and use conjunctions to connect ideas						■	■
Correctly cite books and magazines						■	■

■ skill taught   □ skill practiced

Skills and Conventions

Grammar, usage, punctuation, capitalization, and some spelling skills are taught in the program after the students have had ample time to draft their ideas. The initial stages of writing are always about inspiring good ideas and getting those ideas, in whatever form, onto paper. Students' motivation to learn the conventions of written English (beyond the basic writing skills discussed previously for K–2 students) grows out of their desire to communicate clearly with their readers in their published pieces. Thus, most skill instruction, particularly at grades 3–6, occurs in the revision and proofreading phases of the writing process.

At the upper grades, certain skills naturally lend themselves to particular genres (for example, the need to punctuate speech arises when writing fiction, while learning to use conjunctions seems appropriate for connecting ideas in nonfiction). Consequently, different skills and conventions are taught, as appropriate, in each genre unit. If a skill seems important to more than one genre, the instruction may be repeated.

Additional skill practice activities are provided in the *Skill Practice Teaching Guide* and *Student Skill Practice Book*. These activities can be taught anytime during the year to reinforce writing skills.

At all grades, we assume that there is a separate spelling program in place to provide students with formal instruction in spelling patterns, inflectional endings, roots, syllabication, and other aspects of spelling.

The table at left shows how instruction in skills and conventions develops across the grades. To see where skills are taught in grade 3, see the "Skill Development" chart in volume 2.

The 6+1 Traits and the *Being a Writer* Program

The goals of the *Being a Writer* program correlate closely to those of the 6+1 Traits Writing framework, developed by the Northwest Regional Educational Laboratory. In this widely used framework, student writing is formatively assessed through seven distinct characteristics of writing: ideas, organization, voice, word choice, sentence fluency, conventions, and presentation. The framework provides teachers and students with a common language to discuss good writing and rubrics to assess the quality of writing.

Examples of the 6+1 Traits in the *Being a Writer* Program

TRAITS	EXAMPLES
Ideas (the content or main theme in a piece)	• Students pick "feelings face cards" out of a bag and write about things that make them feel those emotions (e.g., happy, sad, surprised, angry). (Grade K, Unit 2) • Students write stories from the point of view of a toy. (Grade 2, Unit 3) • Students describe breakfast at their home using sensory details. (Grade 3, Personal Narrative) • Students choose topics they are curious about and research and write expository pieces about them. (Grade 5, Expository Nonfiction)
Organization (how meaning is structured in a piece)	• Students write the beginning, middle, and end of stories using three sheets of paper, and then go back to each section to tell more. (Grade 1, Unit 4) • Students explore strong opening sentences written by published authors. (Grade 3, Fiction) • Students write game rules and revise them for clarity, sequence, completeness, and accuracy. (Grade 4, Functional Nonfiction) • Students confer about plot in fiction by discussing the most important thing that happens to their character, what comes before, and what comes after. (Grade 6, Fiction)
Voice (how the writer's personal tone comes across)	• Students choose what they want to write about. (Grade 1, Unit 4) • Students write silly stories. (Grade 2, Unit 1) • Students use their imaginations and cultivate a relaxed, uninhibited attitude about writing. (Grade 4, Fiction) • Students think about who they are writing for in their persuasive essays. (Grade 5, Persuasive Essay)
Word Choice (the vocabulary the writer chooses to convey meaning)	• Students brainstorm words for scary stories. (Grade 2, Unit 1) • Students brainstorm alternatives for overused words such as *good*, *nice*, and *said*. (Grade 3, Unit 1) • Students select phrases or sentences that they think will intrigue their readers, and read them aloud to the class. (Grade 4, Expository Nonfiction)
Sentence Fluency (the rhythm, flow, and sound of the language)	• Students read their writing aloud. (Grade 1, Unit 2) • Students look for very long sentences, particularly those linked together with the words *and*, *so*, and *then*, to see if they should be broken into shorter sentences. (Grade 4, Fiction) • Students explore and use conjunctions to connect their ideas. (Grade 6, Expository Nonfiction)
Conventions (spelling, grammar, usage, capitalization, punctuation)	• Students approximate spelling using letter-sound relationships they have learned in their phonics instruction. (Grade K, Unit 2) • Students use a word wall to spell high-frequency sight words. (Grade 2, Unit 2) • Students use quotation marks to punctuate dialogue. (Grade 3, Fiction) • Students correctly use commonly misused words (such as *there/their/they're*). (Grade 5, Fiction)
Presentation (how the piece looks on the page)	• Students create books to be placed in the classroom library for other students to read. (Grade 2, Unit 3) • Students explore features of narrative books (e.g., dedication page, author's note, back cover blurb) and incorporate these into their published books. (Grade 3, Fiction) • Students explore features of expository text (e.g., diagrams, sidebars, maps, graphs) and incorporate these into their nonfiction reports. (Grade 5, Expository Nonfiction)

While the *Being a Writer* program uses its own language to help teachers and students understand and assess good writing, each of the 6+1 Traits is addressed in numerous ways. Examples from the program are described at left.

Focus on Social/Ethical Development

Research shows that building a safe and caring classroom community helps students perform better academically and become more motivated to achieve. It also helps them develop a sense of responsibility for their own learning and behavior, and empathy and motivation to help others (Schaps 2004). In the writing community, the students work in pairs, groups, and as a class to listen to and discuss writing, brainstorm ideas for writing, and share their writing.

Building Relationships

Caring, respectful relationships are the foundation of the writing community, and the teacher plays a key role in building a warm relationship with each of the students, as well as in facilitating and strengthening relationships among the students. The program creates opportunities to build these relationships deliberately. Early in the year, the students participate in teambuilders to get to know one another, and they learn procedures (such as gathering for sharing and using cooperative structures) in which they are responsible to one another. As the year goes on, they regularly plan for, discuss, and solve problems related to their work together. They cultivate empathy by imagining how others might feel, and they explore why it is important to treat others with care and respect. When they feel connected to others and cared for, students learn to relax, drop their fears, and take the risks necessary to grow academically, socially, and ethically.

Values and Social Skills

As you help build relationships, you also help the students understand the values that underlie these relationships. Across every year of the program, broad social goals help the students think about and act on the core values of responsibility, respect, caring, fairness, and helpfulness. They reflect on what it means to act on these values and their effects on the community. Lapses in applying the values are seen as normal learning experiences, rather than failures. In addition to the five core values, the students explore other values that arise in the read-alouds, such as courage, perseverance, gratitude, and compassion.

The social skills that students learn in the program help them to act on the values in a deliberate way. They learn basic social skills (such as listening to others and taking turns) early in the year, laying the foundation for the more sophisticated skills they learn later in the year, when both their academic work and resulting social interactions become more demanding. (For example, learning how to express appreciation for other people's writing early in the year prepares the students to give and receive specific feedback about their writing later in the year.)

The following table gives an idea of some of the social goals of the program, with their underlying values highlighted, the social skills taught in support of those goals, and the grade levels at which they are taught. Social skills are taught when developmentally appropriate; a skill that is formally taught in the primary grades will be reviewed and integrated in subsequent grades.

Examples of Social Goals (core values highlighted in green)	**Examples of Skills Taught to Support the Goal**	**K–1**	**2–3**	**4–6**
Students listen **respectfully** to the thinking of others and share their own.	Speak clearly.	■	❑	❑
	Listen to one another.	■	❑	❑
	Give their full attention to the person who is speaking.	■	❑	❑
	Share their partners' thinking with the class.	■	■	❑
Students work in a **responsible** way.	Handle materials responsibly.	■	■	❑
	Use writing and pair conference time responsibly.	■	■	■
Students express interest in and appreciation for one another's writing.	Ask one another questions about their writing.	■	■	❑
	Use the prompt "I found out" to express interest in one another's writing.	■	■	■
Students make decisions and solve problems **respectfully**.	Discuss and solve problems that arise in their work together.	■	■	■
	Reach agreement before making decisions.		■	■
Students act in **fair** and **caring** ways.	Share materials fairly.	■	■	■
	Act considerately toward others.		■	■
Students **help** one another improve their writing.	Ask for and receive feedback about their writing.		■	■
	Give feedback in a helpful way.		■	■

■ formally taught   ❑ reviewed and integrated

Random Pairing

We recommend that you randomly pair students at the beginning of each unit and have them stay together for the whole unit. (See Considerations for Pairing English Language Learners on page xxviii.) Working with the same partner over time helps students work through and learn from problems, build successful methods of interaction, and develop their writing skills together. Random pairing sends several positive messages to the students: there is no hidden agenda behind how you paired students (such as based on achievement); every student is considered a valuable partner; and everyone is expected to learn to work with everyone else. Random pairing also results in heterogeneous groupings over time, even though some pairs may be homogeneous in some way during any given unit (for example, both partners may be female). The box below suggests some methods for randomly pairing the students.

Some Random Pairing Methods

- Distribute playing cards and have the students pair up with someone with the same number or suit color.

- Place identical pairs of number or letter cards in a bag. Have each student pull a card out of a bag and find someone with the same number or letter.

- Cut magazine pictures in half. Give each student a picture half. Have each student pair up with the person who has the other half of the picture.

Cooperative Structures

Cooperative structures are taught and used at every grade level to increase students' engagement and accountability for participation. They help the students learn to work together, develop social skills, and take responsibility for their learning. Students talk about their thinking and hear about the thinking of others. Cooperative structures are suggested for specific questions throughout the lessons and are highlighted with an icon. In addition, you can use cooperative structures whenever you feel that not enough students are participating in a discussion, or, conversely, when many students want to talk at the same time.

In kindergarten, the students learn "Turn to Your Partner" and "Think, Pair, Share." Other structures are added as developmentally appropriate.

Teaching the Program

How the Grade 3 Program Is Organized

In the *Being a Writer* program at grade 3, there are 7 units, each varying in length from 1–6 weeks. Each week has four days of instruction. The first two units are meant to be taught in order, while the genre units may be taught interchangeably.

Units 1 and 2

These units are designed to be taught, in order, at the beginning of the year. Unit 1 builds the classroom community while inspiring the students to tap into their intrinsic motivation to write. Unit 2 introduces them to the writing process by having them select drafts for publication; and then revising, proofreading, and publishing them. During the first two units, the students learn the processes, procedures, cooperative structures, and social skills they need to be successful in the genre units throughout the year.

Genre Units

The genre units focus on personal narrative, fiction, expository nonfiction, and functional nonfiction. They may be taught in any order, although we recommend that you teach the nonfiction expository unit later in the year. Genre units begin by immersing the students in the genre; they hear and read many examples of the genre and try their hand at writing drafts in that genre. Mid-way through most genre units, the students select drafts to develop, revise, proofread, and publish for the classroom library.

Open Weeks

The program also provides open weeks to give you time in your curriculum to extend the units, finish units that go long, teach writing content not contained in the *Being a Writer* program, or allow free writing so students can practice what they have learned. Open weeks are also opportunities for you to confer with students in a way that is more general than is suggested in the units (see Teacher Conferences on page xxi). You can intersperse the open weeks throughout the year or combine them to use as a longer block of time.

what's happening? Am I confused at any point?" They learn to give feedback respectfully, and to receive it thoughtfully. Before and after each pair conference session, you facilitate discussions to help the students plan how they will interact and to discuss what went well, the problems they had and how they might be avoided, and how they acted responsibly. (For more about pair conferences, see Managing Pair Conferences on pages xxiv–xxv.)

Teaching the Program

How the Grade 3 Program Is Organized

In the *Being a Writer* program at grade 3, there are 7 units, each varying in length from 1–6 weeks. Each week has four days of instruction. The first two units are meant to be taught in order, while the genre units may be taught interchangeably.

Units 1 and 2

These units are designed to be taught, in order, at the beginning of the year. Unit 1 builds the classroom community while inspiring the students to tap into their intrinsic motivation to write. Unit 2 introduces them to the writing process by having them select drafts for publication; and then revising, proofreading, and publishing them. During the first two units, the students learn the processes, procedures, cooperative structures, and social skills they need to be successful in the genre units throughout the year.

Genre Units

The genre units focus on personal narrative, fiction, expository nonfiction, persuasive essay, and poetry. They may be taught in any order, although we recommend that you teach the nonfiction expository unit later in the year. Genre units begin by immersing the students in the genre; they hear and read many examples of the genre and try their hand at writing drafts in that genre. Mid-way through most genre units, the students select drafts to develop, revise, proofread, and publish for the classroom library.

Open Weeks

The program also provides open weeks to give you time in your curriculum to extend the units, finish units that go long, teach writing content not contained in the *Being a Writer* program, or allow free writing so students can practice what they have learned. Open weeks are also opportunities for you to confer with students in a way that is more general than is suggested in the units (see Teacher Conferences on page xxi). You can intersperse the open weeks throughout the year or combine them to use as a longer block of time.

Sample Calendar for Grade 3

	Unit		Length	Writing Focuses
FALL	**1**	The Writing Community	6 weeks	• Build a caring community and get to know one another • Get ideas for writing from read-alouds • Write freely
	2	The Writing Process	3 weeks	• Select a draft to develop and publish • Revise their drafts • Proofread for spelling and conventions using the word bank and proofreading notes • Write final versions and publish
	Genre Unit	Personal Narrative	4 weeks	• Write about significant topics from their own lives • Use sensory details and write engaging openings
		Open Week	1 week	
WINTER	**Genre Unit**	Fiction	6 weeks	• Develop characters through speech, thoughts, actions, and description • Use descriptive, sensory details to convey character • Use interesting verbs and adverbs
		Open Week	1 week	
	Genre Unit	Expository Nonfiction	6 weeks	• Research and write about an animal of choice • Explore text features such as illustrations and captions • Take research notes and organize them by subtopic
		Open Week	1 week	
SPRING	**Genre Unit**	Functional Nonfiction	3 weeks	• Write directions for drawings, crafts, how to care for things • Explore audience, purpose, sequence, clarity, accuracy, and completeness in directions
		Open Weeks	2 weeks	
	7	Revisiting the Writing Community	1 week	• Reflect on growth as writers and as community members • Plan summer writing

End-of-Year Unit

This last unit at each grade is meant to be taught at the end of the year to help the students reflect on their growth as writers and as members of the classroom writing community.

Sample Calendar for Grade 3

The sample calendar on the previous page shows the order of the units at each grade as well as how you might schedule the open weeks over the year. (If you are teaching the *Making Meaning* reading comprehension program alongside this program, see Use with the *Making Meaning* Program on page xxiii for information about integrating the two programs.)

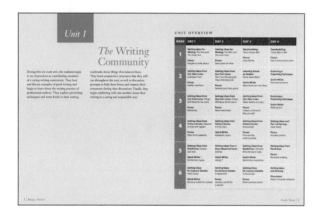

Planning and Teaching the Lessons

We offer the following considerations to help you plan and teach the *Being a Writer* lessons.

Unit and Week Overviews

To prepare to teach a unit, begin by reading the Unit Overview. The unit description and development tables will acquaint you with the goals and general outline of the unit, as well as development in a particular genre or area across grades.

Prepare for each week by reading the Week Overview and previewing the week. This will help you see how instruction supports the week's writing and social focuses as it flows from lesson to lesson. This will also alert you to any advance preparations or special requirements for the week.

Preparing the Daily Lessons

The lessons are generally divided into three sections: Getting Ready to Write, Writing Time, and Sharing and Reflecting. Each section has its own requirements in terms of student movement and teacher facilitation. Keep these in mind as you plan to teach the lesson. To prepare:

- Read the lesson purposes and keep them in mind as you read the entire lesson (including any *Student Writing Handbook* pages) and anticipate how your students will respond.

- Collect materials and anticipate room arrangement needs.

- Plan any teacher modeling required in the lesson.

- Review suggested discussion questions and decide which ones you will ask. Also review any Facilitation Tips to see if there will be opportunities in the lesson to use any facilitation techniques.

- Plan how you will pace the lesson to keep it moving. A lesson (including writing time) is designed to take, on average, 45 minutes at grades K–2 and 45–60 minutes at grades 3–6.

- If there is an extension, review it and decide if and when you want to do it with the class. Some may require additional materials or preparation.

Helpful Lesson Features

The lessons include a number of features to help you navigate them and provide background information and tips. These lesson features are listed in the table below.

Helpful Lesson Features

- **Teacher as Writer.** This weekly feature helps you cultivate your own skill and voice as a writer. It provides inspiring author quotes as well as prompts to stimulate your writing. We invite you to acquire a notebook and pen and enjoy the writing process along with your students this year.

- **Topic Notes.** These notes appear at the beginning of some lessons and provide background information about important aspects of the instruction, including lesson structure, purpose, pedagogy, and approach.

continues

Helpful Lesson Features *continued*

- **Teacher Notes.** These notes appear in the lesson margins and alert you to a variety of things, including the purposes of different activities, materials to be collected or saved, hints for managing the lesson, and ways to support struggling students.

- *Making Meaning®* **Teacher Notes.** These notes are written to the teacher who is teaching the *Making Meaning* reading comprehension program alongside the Being a Writer program. (See Use with the *Making Meaning* Program on page xxiii.)

- **"Students might say."** This feature gives you ideas of the kinds of responses you might expect from your students. If the students have difficulty answering a question you can always suggest some ideas in the "Students might say" note, then ask them to generate additional ideas.

- **Cooperative Structure Icons.** These icons indicate where in the lesson a cooperative structure, such as "Turn to Your Partner" or "Think, Pair, Share," is used.

- **Suggested Vocabulary.** This feature indicates which words in a read-aloud you might want to define for your students as you read. Vocabulary words are selected based on how crucial they are to understanding the text and the unlikeliness that students will be able to glean their meaning from the context. Words and definitions are provided.

- **English Language Learner Notes.** These notes suggest additional read-aloud vocabulary as well as various other strategies to support your English Language Learners during a lesson.

- **Teacher Conference Notes.** These notes help you confer with individual students during the writing time. (See Teacher Conferences at right.)

- **Class Assessment Notes.** These notes help you observe and assess the whole class during pair conferences and writing time. (See Assessments on page xxii.)

- **Chart Diagrams.** These diagrams illustrate charting techniques and examples of text generated by the class or by teacher modeling.

- **Facilitation Tips.** These notes suggest techniques you can use to facilitate class discussions among your students (for example, asking open-ended questions, using wait-time, and not paraphrasing or repeating students' responses).

Teacher Conferences

Early in the year, you begin conferring with individual students during the writing time. The purposes of these conferences are to assess and support individual students in their writing. You can keep an ongoing record of your conferences by documenting your observations and suggestions for each student on the "Conference Notes" record sheet (BLM1).

- **Conferring During the Units.** Your initial conferences focus on just getting to know the students as writers—their skills, motivation, and interests. As the year progresses, you focus more on particular aspects of writing that you have taught in the lessons. The Teacher Conference Notes suggest questions to guide your thinking as you read a student's writing and listen to him or her read and talk about it. This is followed in the note by suggestions for supporting the student based on what you noticed. The conferences during the units focus on reinforcing the teaching you have done so far in that unit. We encourage you to confer with each student at least once or twice per unit, if possible.

- **Conferring During Open Weeks.** We suggest that you continue to confer with individual students during the open weeks, broadening your focus to respond more generally to their writing. Point out and discuss things that you might otherwise skip over during a unit conference, such as misused words (for example, *there, their, they're*), missing punctuation, run-on sentences, or a tendency to "tell" rather than "show" (for example, *The dog was happy* versus *The dog wagged his tail and jumped in circles while barking happily*). In addition, you can discuss questions like:

Q *What are you writing?*

Q *Where did you get the idea for this piece?*

Q *What have you learned about good writing that you can use in this piece?*

Q *What is one question you want to ask me about your piece?*

Q *What do you want help with?*

In the conferences, it is helpful to use a tone of genuine interest and curiosity to foster students' confidence and a learning approach to writing. You can point out things you see them trying to do ("When I read the sentence 'I crunched my feet in the red leaves,' I could hear those dry, autumn leaves") and ask open-ended questions about their writing ("What other words can you include to help your reader imagine what it's like in this park?" "What were you thinking about when you changed the words in this sentence?"). When teaching directly, it helps to discuss the conventions in terms of how authors communicate with readers, ("Let me show you how writers let us know when one character stops talking and another one begins"), rather than simply following a rule ("All speech must have quotation marks").

Assessments

There are three kinds of assessment in the *Being a Writer* program—the Class Assessment, the Social Skills Assessment, and the Individual Student Assessment—and they are designed to help you see students' progress and make informed decisions about instruction as you move through the lessons. The expectation is that *all* of your students will develop at their own pace into competent, thinking writers and socially skilled community members.

The Class Assessment Note, which appears in the lessons at least once per week, is designed to help you assess the performance and needs of the whole class. During this assessment, we suggest that you walk around and observe students working individually or in pairs (perhaps selecting strong, average, and struggling writers to observe). Ask yourself the questions in the Class Assessment Note and follow up with the suggested interventions, if necessary. You can record your observations for each Class Assessment on the corresponding page in the *Assessment Resource Book*.

The *Assessment Resource Book* also contains the Social Skills Assessment and the Individual Student Assessment, both of which are recommended three times per year (at the beginning, middle, and end of the year). The Social Skills Assessment helps you note how well each student is learning and applying the social skills taught in the program. The Individual Student Assessment helps you see growth in each student's writing over the year. Please see the *Assessment Resource Book* for more information about these assessments.

Skill Instruction and Practice

Students learn the important writing skills for their grade in the *Being a Writer* units (see the "Skill Development" chart in the appendix in volume 2). If you feel that your students need additional practice with these skills, you can supplement the units with the skill mini-lessons in the *Skill Practice Teaching Guide*. This component, along with the *Student Skill Practice Book*, provides additional activities to help the students practice skills that are developmentally appropriate and consistent with prevailing standards of writing instruction at grade 3. The mini-lessons may be taught at any time in the year, and the practice activities can be assigned in class or for homework. Please see the *Skill Practice Teaching Guide* for more information.

Use with the *Making Meaning*® Program

The *Being a Writer* program can be taught alongside the *Making Meaning* program, a K–8 reading comprehension program also developed by Developmental Studies Center. This program teaches students comprehension strategies through read-alouds, guided and independent strategy practice, and Individualized Daily Reading. Some read-aloud books are used in both the *Making Meaning* and *Being a Writer* programs. This allows the students to explore a book from the points of view of both writers and readers.

If you are teaching both programs, we recommend that you start teaching them simultaneously at the beginning of the year. At grade 3, please teach the genre units in the order suggested in the "Sample Calendar for Grade 3" on page xvii. This will ensure that the books used in both programs are encountered first in the reading comprehension program, where the students can gain both surface-level and deeper understanding of them, before working with the books from the point of view of writers.

Throughout the writing program, *Making Meaning* Teacher Notes alert you to places where you can modify a lesson to avoid repeating content for your students. For example, if you are teaching a writing lesson with a book that was read aloud recently in a *Making Meaning* lesson, the *Making Meaning* Teacher Note might suggest that you simply review the book rather than read it aloud again, before moving on to the next step in the writing lesson. Also, because similar social skills and cooperative structures are taught early in the year in both programs, the notes will help you to reinforce the students' learning while avoiding a repetition of the instruction.

Tips for Managing the Program in Your Classroom

We offer the following tips to help you manage the *Being a Writer* program in your classroom.

Room Arrangement and Materials

- We recommend a classroom arrangement that allows for quiet individual writing at desks, regular partner work at desks, and whole-class gatherings and discussion. A rug or classroom library area is ideal for whole-class gathering. If this is not possible, think of a way to have the students face and sit close enough to you to hear and see the read-alouds and participate in discussions.

- Plan a place and a chair (sometimes two) to use for Author's Chair sharing.

- Free up wall space for a word wall (at K–2) and for displaying charts generated in the lessons. Write large enough so the charts can be read from a distance.

- Gather writing and publishing materials in a central location and make students responsible for maintaining this area neatly. Materials might include lined and unlined paper, pencils, pens, self-stick notes, highlighters, crayons or markers, construction paper, staplers, and any other desired materials for making books (such as hole punches and string).

Student Books, Notebooks, and Folders

- Students in grades 2–6 are responsible for maintaining a *Student Writing Handbook*, a *Student Skill Practice Book* (optional), a writing notebook, and a writing folder for loose papers and works-in-progress. Label the covers of all of these with the students' names, and encourage the students to be responsible for maintaining these in good shape in their desks. These materials should stay in the classroom during the year, rather than go home with the students.

- Because student writing notebooks are not included with the program, you will need to provide each student with a writing notebook at the beginning of the year (or have the students bring their own from home). We strongly recommend full-size notebooks (no smaller than a 7" x 9" composition book) with firmly bound pages, sturdy covers, and line spacing appropriate for your grade level.

- The writing folders can be file folders or pocket folders, or can be made out of folded construction paper or card stock.

Managing Work Flow

- Establish procedures to help the students move works-in-progress through the writing process. For example, when a student finishes her final version and makes it into a book, she might place it in a "Publication" basket in the corner of the class library to be read aloud during an upcoming Author's Chair sharing time.

Managing Pair Conferences

- When you have the whole class confer in pairs, you might have pairs spread out around the room so they can more easily focus and hear. (Students learn other specific procedures for pair conferences in the lessons.)

- In grades 3–6 lessons when students initiate their own pair conferences during the writing time (again, explained in the lessons), you might designate an area of the room where they may go to talk, away from other students who are working quietly.

Technology Use

- While we encourage the students to write their initial drafts by hand, double-spaced, in their notebooks, you may wish to have them type their pieces for revision and publication on computers, if they are available. Establish procedures and a schedule to ensure that students get fair access to computers, if not during a single unit, then over the year.

- Some units provide the option of having students research information or visit author websites online. Students might also be interested in publishing their writing online. You can find websites that publish student writing by searching by the keywords "publishing student writing online." Take time to provide students with a basic understanding of how to search for information and navigate the Internet.

- Consider enlisting parents or older students to help the students type their pieces and find information on the Internet.

Special Considerations

Teaching the Program in Combination-grade Classrooms

The *Being a Writer* program can be used effectively in combination-grade classrooms. Suggestions for combinations including your grade level are given below.

Grades 2/3 Classes

If you have a grades 2/3 combination, consider starting the year with the grade 2 program, carefully monitoring the students to see if the read-alouds engage them and inspire them to write. If your second graders are advanced, you can try teaching the personal narrative or fiction unit from grade 3 to see if the readings and writing tasks seem appropriate for them. If so, continue to teach the grade 3 program (with the exception of the nonfiction unit, which we recommend you teach from grade 2 for its additional support). If your second graders struggle with the grade 3 lessons, teach the grade 2 program to your whole class for the rest of the year. Schedule additional time to teach grade-appropriate skills to your third graders using the activities in the grade 3 *Skill Practice Teaching Guide*.

Grades 3/4 Classes

If you have a grades 3/4 combination, consider starting the year with the grade 3 program, carefully monitoring the students to see if the read-alouds engage them and inspire them to write. If your third graders are advanced, you can try teaching the personal narrative or fiction unit from grade 4 to see if the readings and writing tasks seem appropriate for them. If so, continue to teach the grade 4 program (with the exception of the expository nonfiction unit, which we recommend you teach from grade 3 for its additional support). If your third graders struggle with the grade 4 lessons, teach the grade 3 program to your whole class for the rest of the year. Schedule additional time to teach grade-appropriate skills to your fourth graders using the activities in the grade 4 *Skill Practice Teaching Guide*.

Supporting English Language Learners (ELLs)

The *Being a Writer* program helps teachers implement effective teaching strategies to meet the needs of all children, including English Language Learners (ELLs). English Language Development strategies are an inherent part of the program's design. In addition, the program provides suggestions for ways to modify the instruction to enhance the support for ELLs.

While the *Being a Writer* program is an effective tool in teaching writing to ELLs, it is not intended to stand alone as a comprehensive linguistic development program. It is assumed that additional support in second language acquisition is occurring for ELLs outside of this program.

About Teaching Writing to ELLs

One myth about teaching ELLs is that good teaching alone will meet their linguistic and academic needs, that they will simply "pick up" the language in the typical classroom context. While certainly "good teaching" (developmental, research-based instructional strategies) benefits English learners enormously, it is important to target their specific academic and linguistic strengths and needs. The first step is to develop an accurate picture of each child's English language proficiency level and previous academic experience.

Stages of Second Language Acquisition

Learning a new language is a developmental process. The following chart outlines the generally accepted stages of acquiring a second language, and characteristics of students at each stage. Progress from one stage to the next depends on a wide variety of factors, including cognitive and social development and maturity, previous academic experience, family education and home literacy practices, personality, cultural background, and individual learning styles.

Stages of Second Language Acquisition

Developmental Stages of Language Proficiency (under immersion)	Student Characteristics
Stage 1: Receptive or Preproduction (can last up to 6 months)	• Often "silent" during this period • Acquires receptive vocabulary (words and ideas that children "take in" or learn before they begin to produce words verbally) • Conveys understanding through drawing, writing, and gesturing • Gradually becomes more comfortable in the classroom
Stage 2: Early Production (can last up to 6 months)	• Uses one- to two-word answers • Verbally labels and categorizes • Listens more attentively • Writes words and some simple sentences
Stage 3: Speech Emergence (can last 6 months to 1 year)	• Speaks in phrases, short sentences • Sequences stories using words and pictures • Writes simple sentences
Stage 4: Intermediate Proficiency (can last 1 to 3 years)	• Uses increased vocabulary • Speaks, reads, and writes more complex sentences • Demonstrates higher order skills, such as analyzing, predicting, debating, etc.
Stage 5: Advanced Proficiency (can last 1 to 3 years)	• Demonstrates a high level of comprehension • Continues to develop academic vocabulary • Continues to speak, read, and write increasingly complex sentences

Considerations for Pairing ELLs

A key practice in the *Being a Writer* program is to have students work in unit-long partnerships. Random pairing is suggested as a way to ensure equity by reinforcing the value of each child in the classroom (see Random Pairing on page xiii). However, when considering the needs of English Language Learners, it may be advantageous to partner these students in a more strategic way. You might pair a beginning English speaker with a fluent English or bilingual speaker. It can be effective if the bilingual partner shares the ELL's native language, but we recommend prudence in asking the more fluent bilingual speaker to serve as translator. Another option is to place ELLs in trios with fluent English speakers to allow them more opportunity to hear the language spoken in conversation. In this case, it is important to make sure that all three students are participating and including one another in the work.

How the *Being a Writer* Program Supports ELLs

There are a number of effective English Language Development (ELD) instructional strategies integrated throughout the *Being a Writer* program. These strategies help make the content comprehensible, support students at their individual level of language proficiency, and help students see themselves as valuable members of the classroom community. They include the strategies shown in the chart below.

English Language Development (ELD) Strategies in the *Being a Writer* Program	
Emphasis on writing as meaningful expression	• Balanced approach to listening, speaking, reading, and writing • Teacher questioning • Explicit teacher modeling • Expository and narrative writing • Activating prior knowledge • Making connections (i.e. text-to-self) • Building intrinsic motivation through providing choice
Visual aids and engaging materials	• Rich, meaningful literature • Engaging book art • Emphasis on writing and illustration
Explicit vocabulary instruction	• Opportunities to preview and discuss read-alouds before lessons • Building academic vocabulary • Brainstorming words
Creating a respectful, safe, learning community	• Active, responsible learning • High expectations for classroom interactions • Explicit classroom procedures and routines • Explicit social skills instruction • Regular discussions to reflect on classroom values and community
Cooperative learning	• Cooperative structures such as "Turn to Your Partner" and "Think, Pair, Share" • Ongoing peer partnerships • Opportunities to express thinking orally and listen to others' thinking • Sharing work and reflecting

Additional Strategies for Supporting ELLs

In addition to the practices embedded in the *Being a Writer* lessons, the ELL Notes provide specific suggestions for adapting instruction to meet the needs of ELLs. In addition, you can implement a number of general strategies to help ELLs participate more fully in the program. These include:

- **Speaking slowly.** Beginning English speakers can miss a great deal when the language goes by too quickly. Modifying your rate of speech can make a big difference in helping them to understand you.

- **Using visual aids and technology.** Photographs, real objects, diagrams, and even quick sketches on the board can help to increase a student's comprehension. When giving directions, physically modeling the steps and writing the steps on the board while saying them aloud are effective ways to boost comprehension. Technology, such as books on tape or CD, can also be helpful.

- **Inviting expression through movement and art.** Having students express their thinking through movement and art can be enormously powerful. Drawing, painting, dancing, mimicking, role-playing, acting, singing, and chanting rhymes are effective ways for children to increase comprehension, build vocabulary, and convey understanding. The Total Physical Response (TPR) method, developed by James Asher, helps children build concepts and vocabulary by giving them increasingly complex verbal prompts (stand, sit, jump, etc.) that they act out physically and nonverbally (see the bibliography in volume 2).

- **Building vocabulary.** ELL vocabulary is highlighted for most read-alouds in the program, and we recommend that you introduce this vocabulary (discuss it, act it out, draw it, etc.) and define it during the reading. In addition, you might brainstorm words related to particular read-alouds or themes (see example below). The students can then illustrate each word and post the illustration next to the printed word, creating a visual chart to refer to as they write.

Ideas for "First Time" Stories		
tooth	broken bone	ocean
kindergarten	sleepover	birthday
baby brother	airplane	friend
apartment	bike	snow

- **Preteaching.** It is always a good idea to preteach concepts with ELLs, whenever possible. This could mean previewing vocabulary, doing a picture walk of a story, or looking at real objects or photographs before a lesson. Preteaching in a child's native language can be particularly effective—teachers, instructional aides, parents, or other community members can be enlisted to help.

- **Simplifying questions.** Open-ended questions are used throughout the *Being a Writer* program to elicit language and higher-order thinking from students. These questions are often more complex in structure than closed or one-word-answer questions. While all learners, including English Language Learners, benefit from the opportunity to consider such questions, you might periodically modify a complicated question into a simpler one to increase comprehension and participation by your ELLs. The chart below lists some suggestions for simplifying questions.

Suggestions for simplifying questions

Suggestion	Original Question	Simplified Question
Use the simple present tense.	What was happening at the beginning of the story?	What happens at the beginning of the story?
Use active rather than passive voice.	How was the window broken in the story?	Who broke the window in the story?
Ask *who/what/where/when* questions rather than *how/why* questions.	How are you and your partner working together?	What do you and your partner do to work well together?
Avoid the subjunctive.	If you were going to write about a family member, what might you write?	You will write a story about someone in your family. What will you write?
Provide definitions in the question.	Why is the old woman so reluctant to name the dog?	The old woman does not want to name the dog. She is reluctant. Why?
Provide context clues as part of the question.	What happens at the beginning of the story?	Peter wakes up and it is snowing. What else happens at the beginning of the story?
Elicit nonverbal responses.	What do you see in this picture that tells about the words?	This picture shows the sentence "I like to paint." Point to the paints. Point to the paintbrushes.
Elicit 1–2 word answer responses.	What do you think will happen when Peter puts the snowball in his pocket?	Peter puts the snowball in his pocket. Is that a good idea?

- **Assessing comprehension.** When students are in the preproduction and early production stages of language acquisition, it can be hard to assess exactly what they understand. It is important not to confuse lack of verbal response with lack of understanding. Rather than force ELLs to produce language before they are ready (which can raise anxiety and inhibit their progress), you can assess nonverbal responses while the students are actively engaged by asking yourself questions such as:

  Q *Do the student's drawings and written symbols communicate thinking or show evidence of my teaching (such as writing a frame sentence and illustrating it appropriately, or including a beginning, middle, and end in a story)?*

  Q *Does the student nod, laugh, or demonstrate engagement through other facial expressions?*

  Q *Does the student pick up academic and social cues from peers?*

  Q *Does the student follow classroom signals and routines?*

  Q *Does the student follow simple directions (such as "Please get out your writing notebooks and pencils")?*

  Q *Does the student utter, chant, or sing some familiar words or phrases?*

By carefully observing your English Language Learners and employing some of the strategies suggested above (as well as those in the ELL Notes in the lessons), you will be able to support your students' development as writers and as caring, collaborative participants in your writing community.

Building the Adult Writing Community at Your School

Being a writer yourself helps you understand the writing process and the joys and struggles that come with writing. Writing regularly informs both your instructional decisions and your interactions with individual students about their writing. We strongly encourage you to become part of an active writing community that will support you in your own development as a writer. Some particularly powerful activities for building a writing community are listed below.

Teacher as Writer

The Teacher as Writer section at the beginning of each week offers writing prompts and instructive quotes by well-known writers to inspire you to write. The prompts often relate to the writing focuses for the students that week.

We encourage you to start a writing notebook and write in it several times a week, both in school during the daily Writing Time and outside of school. Find opportunities to share the writing regularly with a writing partner or group.

Starting a Writers' Group at Your School

To start a writers' group at your school, find other adults (including teachers, administrators, parents, and other school staff) who are interested in writing regularly and supporting one another in writing. If there is a lot of interest, consider starting more than one writers' group to keep any one group from becoming too large. Schedule meetings at regular intervals (every month, every six weeks, or every other month) to share and discuss writing. Meetings can take place on or off school grounds, and the format can range from formal to informal. The Internet provides many sources of information about how to start and conduct a writers' group; search for this information using the keywords "starting a writers group."

Unit 1

The Writing Community

Unit 1

The Writing Community

Unit 1

The Writing Community

During this six-week unit, the students begin to see themselves as contributing members of a caring writing community. They hear and discuss examples of good writing and begin to learn about the writing practice of professional authors. They explore prewriting techniques and write freely in their writing notebooks about things that interest them. They learn cooperative structures that they will use throughout the year, as well as discussion prompts to help them listen and connect their comments during class discussions. Finally, they begin conferring with one another about their writing in a caring and responsible way.

UNIT OVERVIEW

WEEK	DAY 1	DAY 2	DAY 3	DAY 4
1	**Getting Ideas for Writing:** *The Pain and The Great One* **Focus:** People to write about	**Getting Ideas for Writing:** *The Pain and The Great One* **Focus:** Own point of view	**Teambuilding:** "Facts About Me" **Focus:** Judy Blume	**Teambuilding:** "Facts About Me" **Focus:** Get to know each other
2	**Getting Ideas from Our Own Lives:** *Grandpa's Face* **Focus:** Family members	**Getting Ideas from Our Own Lives:** *She Come Bringing Me That Little Baby Girl* **Focus:** Feeling bad, then good	**Learning About an Author:** Eloise Greenfield **Quick-Write:** Ideas from our own lives	**Exploring a Prewriting Technique** **Quick-Write:** Favorite sentence
3	**Getting Ideas from Our Own Lives:** *Things Will Never Be the Same* **Focus:** Memories	**Getting Ideas from Our Own Lives:** *Things Will Never Be the Same* **Focus:** More memories	**Getting Ideas from Our Own Lives:** *Oliver Button Is a Sissy* **Focus:** Create a character like yourself	**Exploring a Prewriting Technique** **Quick-Write:** Making lists
4	**Getting Ideas from Pattern Books:** *Alligator Arrived with Apples* **Focus:** Ideas from patterns	**Getting Ideas from Pattern Books:** *O is for Orca* **Quick-Write:** Alphabet topics	**Getting Ideas from Pattern Books:** *Fortunately* **Focus:** Fortunately, unfortunately	**Getting Ideas and Pair Conferring:** *Silver Seeds* **Focus:** Acrostic poems
5	**Getting Ideas from Nonfiction:** *Oceans and Seas* **Quick-Write:** Nonfiction topics	**Getting Ideas from a Story Based on Facts:** *Atlantic* **Quick-Write:** Using "I"	**Getting Ideas from Nonfiction:** *I Wonder Why the Sea Is Salty* **Quick-Write:** Nonfiction questions	**Getting Ideas from Nonfiction** **Focus:** Nonbook writing
6	**Getting Ideas for Sensory Details:** *Hello Ocean* **Quick-Write:** Sensory words for a place	**Getting Ideas for Sensory Details:** *In November* **Focus:** Sensory words for a month	**Getting Ideas for Sensory Details:** *In November* **Focus:** More sensory words	**Getting Ideas and Sharing** **Discussion:** Share a favorite sentence

UNIT 1: THE WRITING COMMUNITY

The Pain and The Great One
by Judy Blume, illustrated by Irene Trivas
(Dell Dragonfly, 2001)

She thinks her brother is a pain; he thinks she's a bossy know-it-all.

"About Judy Blume"
excerpted from the author's website,
www.judyblume.com (see page 21)

Judy Blume answers questions about her life.

Writing Focus

- Students hear and discuss good writing.

- Students generate ideas for writing.

- Students learn procedures for writing time.

- Students write freely about things in which they are interested.

- Students learn about a professional author's writing practice.

Social Focus

- Students build the writing community.

- Students learn procedures for working together.

- Students listen respectfully to the thinking of others and share their own.

- Students work in a responsible way.

DO AHEAD

- Plan a space in the classroom, such as a rug area, for the class to gather for read-alouds. The students should sit facing you, close enough to you to see the books you will share. If a rug area is not available, plan how the students will arrange their chairs so they can sit facing you.

- Collect enough lined writing notebooks so that each student in the class will have one.

- Prior to Day 4, write three interesting facts about yourself on a sheet of chart paper (for example, *I know how to make chocolate chip cookies*, *I have been white-water rafting*, and *I once found a spider under my pillow*).

TEACHER AS WRITER

"I write to find out what I'm thinking about."
— *Edward Albee*

Being a writer yourself can help you in teaching your students to write. In Teacher as Writer, we offer weekly prompts to help you in your own development as a writer, as well as instructive quotes by well-known writers. We encourage you to start a writing notebook and to write in it at least several times a week, and to share your writing regularly with colleagues who write. (See the front matter, page xxxii, for ideas about creating a writers' group at your school.)

In your notebook this week, describe yourself as a writer. What was writing like for you in school? What is it like for you now? How do you hope to develop as a writer?

Day 1

Materials

- *The Pain and The Great One*
- Chart paper and a marker
- Writing notebook and a pencil for each student
- Self-stick note for each student

Getting Ideas for Writing

In this lesson, the students:

- Hear and discuss a story
- Learn the procedure for gathering
- Gather in a responsible way
- Become familiar with their writing notebooks

About Writing Instruction Early in the Year

All growth and learning in the art and craft of writing depend on a solid foundation of abundant, uninhibited writing. To get enough sheer practice with the physical and mental act of writing during their elementary school years, students must tap into their intrinsic motivation to write. Unit 1 helps students develop this motivation by inspiring them to write freely and daily about things that interest them. Engaging read-alouds are used to stimulate creativity and as examples to inspire writing. In this unit, it is more important for the students to write generously, free from concerns about making it right or "good," than it is for them to write complete, correct pieces.

To support the students' writing practice in Unit 1, formal skills instruction is delayed until Unit 2. It continues in the "Revision, Proofreading, and Publishing" phase of all the genre units. For the time being, relax your expectations about the students' spelling and grammatical correctness, and encourage them to just write freely, getting their ideas down on paper.

GETTING READY TO WRITE

▶1 Introduce the Writing Community

Introduce the Being a Writer program by explaining that this year the students will be members of a classroom writing community. In the community, they will write about things that interest them, share and talk about their writing, learn about what professional authors do, and become stronger writers. Ask and briefly discuss as a class:

Q *What are some things you've written?*

Teacher Note

If the students have difficulty answering these questions, offer some examples like those in the "Students might say" note.

Q *What are some reasons that you write in or out of school?*

Students might say:

"I write when I leave my parents a note about where I'm going."

"I have to write a list of things to do for homework every week."

"I wrote a long story about a field trip we took in second grade."

Explain that writers constantly read examples of good writing to help them get ideas for their own writing and to give them a sense of the way good writing looks and sounds. This year the students will have many opportunities to hear, read, and discuss good writing.

2 Learn and Practice the Procedure for Gathering to Discuss Writing

Explain that the class will gather to hear a read-aloud. Explain that you would like the students to gather and sit facing you, either on a rug or in their seats. Before asking the students to move, state your expectations (for example, "I expect you to move quickly, quietly, and without bumping into one another"). Ask:

Q *What do you want to keep in mind to make moving go smoothly?*

Have the students move to their places. Ask:

Q *What did you do to move responsibly? What might you do differently when we try it again?*

Students might say:

"I made sure I didn't bump into anyone on my way to the rug."

"I came straight to the rug instead of doing something else first."

"Next time maybe we can try moving more quietly."

If necessary, have the students return to their desks and practice the procedure until they are able to gather in an orderly way. Explain that the students will use the same procedure every time they gather to talk about writing.

Explain that today you will read aloud an example of good writing. Invite the students to both enjoy the story and think about what it would be like to write such a story.

Making Meaning® Teacher

If you are teaching Developmental Studies Center's *Making Meaning* reading comprehension program, these notes are for you. They provide suggestions for linking the two programs.

If the students have already learned a procedure for gathering for a read-aloud, use the same one for gathering to discuss writing. Take this opportunity to remind the students of the procedure and your expectations.

3 ▸ **Read the First Part of *The Pain and The Great One* Aloud**

Show the cover of *The Pain and The Great One* and read the title and the author's name aloud. Explain that you will read the first part of the book today and the second part tomorrow.

Read "The Pain" on pages 3–18 aloud slowly and clearly, showing the illustrations as you read.

Teacher Note ▸

The pages of *The Pain and The Great One* are unnumbered. For easy reference, pencil in page numbers, beginning with the number 1 on the right-hand title page. (Page 3 says "The Pain" and page 5 begins, "My brother's a pain.") This system is used throughout the program for all read-alouds with unnumbered pages.

4 ▸ **Discuss the Story**

Ask and briefly discuss the questions that follow. Be ready to reread from the story to help the students recall what they heard.

Q *Who is telling this story? Who is "The Pain?"*

Q *What do you find out about the little brother in this story?*

Q *If you were going to write a funny story about someone you know, about whom might you write? What might you write about that person?*

Students might say:

"I would write about my baby sister. She can be a pain, too. She follows me all over the house."

"I would write about my uncle. He makes funny faces and always makes us laugh."

"I can write about my big brother. His hair is always a big mess when he gets out of bed!"

As the students offer ideas, record two or three of them as brief notes on a sheet of chart paper entitled "People We Can Write About."

People We Can Write About

baby sister — she follows me all over the house

uncle — makes funny faces

big brother — hair's a mess in the morning

WRITING TIME

5 ▶ Introduce Writing Notebooks

Distribute a writing notebook and a self-stick note to each student. Explain that this year the students will do all their *drafting*, or first-time writing, in their notebooks. They will also keep ongoing lists of writing ideas in the back of the notebooks. Have each student count back ten pages from the back of his notebook, mark that page with a self-stick note, and write "Writing Ideas" in big letters on that page. Explain that the students will list all of their ideas this year in this section of their notebooks.

On the first blank page of their writing ideas section, have the students write "People We Can Write About " at the top of the page. Have them copy ideas they like from the class chart and then add other ideas for fairy tales they could retell. Encourage them to talk to students sitting near them to get ideas.

After a few moments, call for the students' attention. Have the students share a few more ideas and add these to the chart.

Explain that the students will begin drafting in their notebooks tomorrow and that they may wish to use their ideas from today. Have each student write her name on her notebook, and explain that you will remind the students to bring their notebooks with them when they gather to talk about writing.

SHARING AND REFLECTING

 Reflect and Adjourn

Tell the students how you would like them to return to their seats. Have them return. Ask them to put their writing notebooks in their desks. If necessary, have them practice moving to their seats until they are able to move in an orderly way. Ask and briefly discuss:

Q *What did you do to be responsible as you moved back to your seat?*

Ask the students to put their writing notebooks in their desks until tomorrow.

Teacher Note

Save the "People We Can Write About" chart to use on Day 2 and in Week 2.

Day 2

Getting Ideas for Writing

In this lesson, the students:

- Hear and discuss a story
- Learn procedures for the writing period
- Write freely about things that interest them

GETTING READY TO WRITE

1 ▶ Gather and Briefly Review

Ask the students to gather on the rug, facing you. Remind them that they heard the first part of *The Pain and The Great One* and thought about people whom they know and about whom they could write. Explain that you will read the whole book aloud today. Invite the students to think about whether they might like to try writing a story like *The Pain and The Great One.*

2 ▶ Read *The Pain and The Great One* Aloud

Read the story aloud from the beginning, showing the illustrations as you read. Stop after:

> **p. 20** "My sister's a jerk."

Ask:

Q *What is the second part of this book going to be about? How do you know?*

Have a couple of volunteers share their thinking; then continue reading to the end of the story.

Materials

- *The Pain and The Great One*
- "People We Can Write About" chart from Day 1
- Pad of small (1½" × 2") self-stick notes for each student

3▶ Discuss the Story

Briefly discuss the story using the questions that follow. Be ready to reread from the story to help the students recall what they heard.

Q *What's funny about the way this story is written?*

Q *What do you find out about the big sister in this story?*

> **Students might say:**
>
> "The story is funny because both kids think their parents love the other one more."
>
> "The big sister can be just as much of a pain to her brother as he is to her."

Point out that each character tells the story from his or her point of view, and they have very different opinions about what life in their family is like. Explain that the students may also include their own opinions and points of view as they write.

Direct the students' attention to the "People We Can Write About" chart and ask:

Q *What other ideas do you have for people you could write about today? What might you write about them?*

As the students share, record several more ideas on the chart.

WRITING TIME

4▶ Learn Procedures for the Silent Writing Period

Have the students return to their seats. Explain that they will spend the next 5–10 minutes silently writing whatever they want to in their writing notebooks. They may add ideas to their writing ideas section or begin drafting a story at the front of their notebooks. Tell them that you would like them to double-space, or skip every other line, when they write in their notebooks.

Teacher Note

Double-spacing will give the students the necessary space to revise and edit pieces later on.

Explain that during writing time, you would like the class to work in silence, without talking, whispering, or walking around. Tell them that you will give them a signal when writing time is over. Explain that you will be writing along with them and ask that you not be interrupted. Give the students a moment to gather what they need, sharpen pencils, etc. Then have them write at their desks in silence for 10 minutes. Join them in writing, periodically scanning the room.

At the end of writing time, signal for the students' attention. Ask them to briefly review their writing from today; then ask:

Q *Do you think you might want to continue adding to this piece later?*

Explain that if they wish to add to this piece later they will need to save space in their notebooks to do so. Distribute a pad of self-stick notes to each student and tell them to place notes on the next two or three blank pages to remind them to save those pages to continue their piece. When they start a new piece of writing, they will skip the pages marked with self-stick notes. If they don't wish to continue this piece, they do not need to save any pages today. Ask:

Q *Did you remember to skip lines in your writing today?*

Explain that it is important to skip lines so there is space to add or make changes later. Tell the students that you will remind them to skip lines as they write.

SHARING AND REFLECTING

▶5 **Reflect on Writing as a Class**

Ask and briefly discuss:

Q *What did you write about today?*

Q *Was it hard or easy to start writing? Why?*

Q *What helped you focus on your writing today?*

Ask the students to put their notebooks and pads of self-stick notes in their desks for use again tomorrow.

◀ **Teacher Note**

A period of silent writing, during which you also write without interacting with the students, may feel new to you. We strongly encourage you to establish this routine early in the year. Students adapt to it quickly after a few reminders, and they learn to focus inward on their own thoughts during this time. By knowing that they are not to interrupt you or others, they come to rely on their own thinking and decisions as they write. As the writing period gradually lengthens over the coming weeks, you will begin conferring with students after writing yourself for 5–10 minutes.

Day 3

Materials

- "About Judy Blume" (see page 21)
- Paper and a pencil for each student

Teambuilding

In this lesson, the students:

- Learn about a professional author
- Write facts about themselves
- Speak clearly and listen to one another

GETTING READY TO WRITE

1 Read About Judy Blume

Remind the students that they heard *The Pain and The Great One* by Judy Blume and thought about people in their lives about whom they could write. Show the dedication page of the book and reread it aloud. Ask and briefly discuss:

Q *Who do you think "The original Pain and the Great One" might be? Why might Judy Blume have dedicated this book to them?*

Explain that Judy Blume answers some of her favorite questions from readers on her website and that you will share some of these with the students. Read "About Judy Blume" aloud slowly and clearly. Ask:

Q *What did you find out about Judy Blume?*

Have several volunteers share with the class. Ask the students to take responsibility for listening by raising their hand if they can't hear the person who is speaking.

2 Introduce "Facts About Me" Activity

Explain that this year the students will get to know many different authors. They will also get to know one another as authors, and this will help to build an atmosphere of trust in the writing community.

Today they will learn about one another by doing an activity called "Facts About Me." In this activity, they will write some interesting facts about themselves and discuss them with a partner.

Explain that you will ask the students some questions to help them think about interesting facts they might write. Emphasize that they do not need to remember all the questions or their answers; you are asking the questions just to get them thinking.

Ask the students to close their eyes and make mental pictures of their answers to the questions you ask. Give them time to visualize between the questions. Ask:

Q *Where and when were you born?*

Q *What is one thing you are really good at?*

Q *Where is an interesting place you have been?*

Q *What is something about you that you think might surprise other people?*

Q *What do you like to do when you're not in school?*

Q *What sport or game do you like?*

Q *What would you like to learn more about this year?*

After a few moments, ask the students to open their eyes.

WRITING TIME

3 ▶ **Write "Facts About Me"**

Distribute paper and have the students write their name at the top of their paper. Have the students silently write any three facts about themselves that they would like others to know.

When the students finish, collect their facts and explain that they will share the facts with a partner tomorrow.

Teacher Note

If the students have difficulty writing their facts, call for their attention and model writing a few facts about yourself on chart paper. (You might write *I know how to make chocolate chip cookies*, *I have been whitewater rafting*, and *I once found a spider under my pillow*.) Then have the students resume their own writing.

Teacher Note

Prior to Day 4, randomly assign partners and clip partners' facts together. (See the front matter, page xxviii, for considerations for pairing English Language Learners.) The students will find out who their partner is during the activity tomorrow. If you have an odd number of students, pair yourself with one of them for now.

Making Meaning® Teacher

Assign the students to work with their *Making Meaning* partner or assign new partners for the writing lessons.

SHARING AND REFLECTING

 Reflect on Working Together

Ask and briefly discuss:

Q *How might sharing facts about ourselves help us build our writing community?*

Remind the students that they are building a caring writing community in which they know and trust one another. Encourage them to find ways to get to know their classmates throughout the school day.

Day 4

Teambuilding

In this lesson, the students:

- Begin working with a partner
- Get to know one another
- Speak clearly and listen to one another
- Practice procedures for the writing period
- Write freely about things that interest them

GETTING READY TO WRITE

1 ▶ Prepare to Do the "Facts About Me" Activity

Remind the students that yesterday they wrote facts about themselves that they would like others to know. Explain that today partners will read each other's facts and then get together to talk about them. Before starting the activity, remind the students that they are building a caring writing community, and ask:

Q *When you meet your partner, how can you show that you're interested in getting to know him or her?*

Encourage the students to speak clearly and listen responsibly during the activity. Tell them that you will check in with them later to see how it went.

2 ▶ Model Writing Questions

Explain that, when you hand out the students' written facts, you will give each student his partner's facts. Before partners meet, they will read each other's facts and each write two or three questions they can ask the other.

Ask the students to watch as you model writing questions. Show your three charted facts and read them aloud.

Materials

- Your charted interesting facts (see "Do Ahead" on page 5)
- Students' paired fact sheets from Day 3
- *Assessment Resource Book*

◀ **Teacher Note**

The students will find out who their partner is during the activity (not before).

Ask:

Q *What questions can you ask me about my facts?*

As the students ask questions, record them below the facts on the chart.

Teacher Note ▶

If the students have difficulty generating questions, suggest some like those on the chart and ask, "What else can you ask me about my facts?"

Ms. Simon's "Facts About Me"

1. I know how to make chocolate chip cookies.
2. I have been white-water rafting.
3. I once found a spider under my pillow.

What did you do when you found the spider?

What's white-water rafting?

What do you put in chocolate chip cookies?

▶3 Read About Partners and Write Questions

Distribute the students' facts, so that partners receive each other's papers. Have the students silently read their partner's facts. Bring their attention back to you and ask:

Q *What questions can you ask your partner about the facts he or she wrote?*

Without sharing as a class, have the students think of two or three questions they can ask their partner and write those questions on their partner's paper. Give them a few moments to think and record their questions.

▶4 Have Partners Meet and Share Facts and Questions

When the students are finished writing, have them quietly move so partners are sitting together. Have partners talk about their facts and questions for a few minutes. After they have had a chance to talk, signal for their attention. Ask:

Q *What did you find out about your partner?*

Q *How did you and your partner make sure you both had a chance to share?*

Explain that partners will work together for the next several weeks and that they will begin by sharing their writing with each other later today.

WRITING TIME

5 ▶ Write Independently

Have the students return to their seats. Ask them to open their writing notebooks to the next blank page and spend the next 10–15 minutes silently writing whatever they want. Remind them to double-space their writing.

Emphasize that during the writing period there should be no talking, whispering, or walking around. Everyone (including you) will be writing silently. You will let them know when writing time is over.

Have the students write for 10–15 minutes. Join them in writing for 5–10 minutes; then walk around the room and observe them.

> ## CLASS ASSESSMENT NOTE
>
> As you write during the silent period, scan the class and ask yourself:
>
> - Are the students writing in silence?
> - Are they staying in their seats?
>
> If you notice the students having difficulty staying in their seats or writing in silence, call for the class's attention and remind them of your expectations before having them resume writing. Be aware that some students may need to just sit and think for a while before they start writing. Give them uninterrupted time to do this.
>
> Record your observations in the *Assessment Resource Book*.

Signal to let the students know that writing time is over.

Teacher Note

If necessary, remind the students to skip pages they have "saved" with self-stick notes in order to continue earlier writing.

Teacher Note

Remember, joining the students for a few minutes of silent writing demonstrates that writing is important and that you expect the students to work independently and tap into their own thinking and creativity during this time. As you write, scan the class periodically to monitor how the students are doing. If you notice off-task behavior, stop the class and restate your expectations.

SHARING AND REFLECTING

 ### Share Writing in Pairs

Have partners share their writing with each other. After all the students have had a chance to share, signal for their attention and ask:

Q *What did your partner write about today?*

Q *How do you know that your partner was listening to you as you shared your writing?*

EXTENSION

Read a Variety of Genres Aloud

One goal for the first few weeks of this program is to expose the students to a variety of genres through read-alouds. When you have time, read various types of fiction (such as realistic fiction, fantasy, mystery, and science fiction), nonfiction (such as memoir, biography, joke and riddle books, "how-to" books, magazine or newspaper articles, and other expository text), and poetry aloud.

About Judy Blume

Excerpted from www.judyblume.com

When were you born?

February 12, 1938

Where were you born?

Elizabeth, New Jersey

What were you like when you were growing up?

Small, skinny, a late developer. At first, very shy and fearful. Then, around fourth grade, much more outgoing. (I can't explain the change.) I enjoyed drama, dancing, singing, painting and performing. I loved to roller skate (we didn't have roller blades then). I also loved going to the movies and browsing at the public library. I was always reading something.

Are you married?

Yes. My husband's a writer, too. But he writes nonfiction books, about historic crimes!

How many kids do you have?

We have three grownup children between us, and one grandchild, whose first word was "book!"

Do you have any pets?

We had a wonderful Calico cat who lived sixteen years. Now our children have the pets and we get to visit them. Amanda has four horses and five cats. Randy has one cat, and another who sometimes stays over. My personal favorite is Mookie. She belongs to Larry, but she loves us, and we call her our grand-dog.

Is it fun to be a writer?

Not always. It's a solitary life and it can get lonely. You spend most of the day in a little room by yourself. But since I love to create characters and get to know them, I'm usually content.

continues

About Judy Blume

continued

About *The Pain and The Great One*, Judy says:
One rainy afternoon, when my children were about six and eight, and the house was filled with their friends, I suddenly got an idea. I sat right down and wrote [*The Pain and The Great One*]. The brother and sister in this book are based on my daughter Randy and son Larry. The cat is our first family pet…. It's my favorite of anything I've written for young children. Randy and Larry, who are grown now, still sometimes refer to each other as "The Pain" and "The Great One."

UNIT 1: THE WRITING COMMUNITY

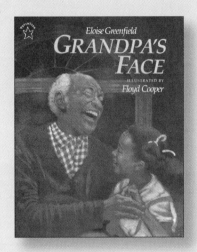

Grandpa's Face
by Eloise Greenfield, illustrated by Floyd Cooper
(Penguin, 1996)

Tamika loves her grandfather's face, but one expression scares her.

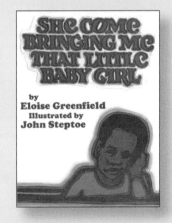

She Come Bringing Me That Little Baby Girl
by Eloise Greenfield, illustrated by John Steptoe
(HarperTrophy, 1993)

Kevin expects his mother to bring home a little brother, but she brings home a little baby girl instead.

"About Eloise Greenfield"
excerpted from *The Big Book of Picture-Book Authors & Illustrators* by James Preller (Scholastic, 2001) and www.eduplace.com

Eloise Greenfield talks about growing up and writing for children.

Writing Focus

- Students hear and discuss good writing.

- Students explore prewriting techniques.

- Students learn about how a professional author gets ideas from her own life.

- Students write freely about things that interest them.

Social Focus

- Students build the writing community.

- Students learn procedures for working together.

- Students express interest in and appreciation for one another's writing.

TEACHER AS WRITER

"I'm sure a beautiful empty notebook was the reason I wrote my first book. It was begging for filling."
— *Jacqueline Jackson*

In your writing notebook, start a section at the back called "Writing Ideas." Jot down events and ideas from your own life that you might want to write about. Think about:

- What is your earliest memory?

- When did something strange happen to you?

- When did you feel truly content or truly miserable?

- When did you realize something you didn't know before?

Day 1

Materials

- *Grandpa's Face*
- "People We Can Write About" chart from Week 1
- *Assessment Resource Book*

Getting Ideas from Our Own Lives

In this lesson, the students:

- Hear and discuss a story
- Begin working with a partner
- Learn "Turn to Your Partner"
- Write freely about things that interest them

GETTING READY TO WRITE

Teacher Note

The partners you assigned last week will stay together for Units 1 and 2. Take some time at the beginning of today's lesson to let them get to know each other by talking informally in a relaxed atmosphere. You might have them report to the class some interesting things they learn about each other.

▶1 Introduce "Turn to Your Partner"

Gather the class with partners sitting together, facing you. Explain that you will often ask partners to turn and talk to each other. The purpose is to give everyone a chance to think more about what they're learning by talking to another person. (For more information about the role of cooperative structures in social development, see the front matter on pages xiii–xiv.)

Explain the "Turn to Your Partner" procedure by saying, "Sometimes I will ask a question and say 'Turn to your partner.' When you hear this, you will turn to face your partner and start talking about the question. When I raise my hand, you will finish what you're saying, raise your own hand so others can see the signal, and turn back to face me."

Teacher Note

If your students are already familiar with "Turn to Your Partner," you do not need to model it here. Instead, take the opportunity to remind the students of your expectations for the procedure.

▶2 Model "Turn to Your Partner"

Have a student act as your partner and model turning to face each other and introducing yourselves by your full names. Then ask the students to turn to face each other and introduce themselves. After a moment, raise your hand and have them turn back to face you.

Practice again by asking:

Q *What are you interested in writing (or writing about) this year? Turn to your partner.*

Have partners discuss their thinking. After a moment, signal for their attention. Have a few volunteers briefly share what they discussed with the class.

Explain that you will read a story aloud. Say that you will stop during the reading for the students to use "Turn to Your Partner" to discuss a question. State that at the end of the lesson you will ask them to report how they did.

3▶ Read *Grandpa's Face* Aloud

Show the cover of *Grandpa's Face* and read the title and names of the author and illustrator. Read the story aloud slowly and clearly, showing the illustrations as you read.

> **ELL Vocabulary**
>
> English Language Learners may benefit from discussing the following vocabulary:
>
> **whined:** said in a crying voice (p. 16)
> **pretending:** making up something (p. 27)

Stop after:

> **p. 18**   "Her hand bumped her glass and knocked it over, sending green water spattering onto Grandpa's shirt and across the tablecloth."

Ask:

Q *What is happening in this story? Turn to your partner.*

Have the students discuss the question. After a moment, signal for their attention. Without sharing as a class, continue reading to the end of the book.

Teacher Note

A visual signal, such as a raised hand, allows the students to finish what they are saying before turning back to face you. Build accountability by reminding the students to raise their own hand when they turn to face you.

Teacher Note

You may find that some of the read-alouds are below the average reading level for your grade. This is intentional, as students will explore these texts as examples for writing. Students' writing development normally lags somewhat behind their reading ability.

4   Discuss the Story

Ask and briefly discuss the question that follows. Be ready to reread from the story to help the students recall what they heard.

Q   *What is this story about? Turn to your partner.*

Have partners discuss the question. Signal for the students' attention and have a few volunteers share their thinking with the class. Ask:

Q   *This story tells about a time when Tamika was upset about a family member. If you were going to write a story about a time you were upset about a family member, what might you write?*

Students might say:

"One time my brother wouldn't let me play with him. I was upset then."

"I was upset at my mom when she grounded me."

"It made me upset when my grandma went into the hospital. I wanted her to come home."

As the students offer ideas, add them to the "People We Can Write About" chart. Invite the students to write about some of these things today, if they wish. Ask and briefly discuss:

Q   *What did you do to be a responsible partner during "Turn to Your Partner?"*

Students might say:

"I listened to my partner during 'Turn to Your Partner.'"

"We talked about the question, and we didn't talk about anything else."

"We took turns and listened to each other."

WRITING TIME

5 ▶ Write Independently

Ask the students to return to their seats. Explain that they will write silently for 10–15 minutes. Write the following choices on the board as you explain what the students can do during this time:

- Choose an idea from your writing ideas section and write about it.

- Write about anything else in which you are interested.

Remind the students that they do not need to finish one piece of writing before starting a new one. Also review that during the writing period there should be no talking, whispering, or walking around. Everyone (including you) will be silently writing. You will let the students know when writing time is over.

Have the students write for 10–15 minutes. Join them in writing for 5–10 minutes; then walk around the room and observe them. If necessary, remind them to double-space their writing.

◀ **Teacher Note**

The purpose of this unit is to give the students practice writing freely about topics they choose. Read-alouds are intended solely to stimulate creativity; the students may or may not be inspired to write something related to a read-aloud. At this point, they are not expected to learn the features of genres or to write in any particular genre.

CLASS ASSESSMENT NOTE

Observe the students and ask yourself:

- Are the students writing in silence?

- Are they staying in their seats?

- Are they skipping lines in their notebooks?

- Are they writing rather than drawing?

continues

CLASS ASSESSMENT NOTE *continued*

If necessary, remind the class of your expectations for silent writing during this time. Note which students write easily and which ones have difficulty getting started. If you notice students drawing, gently remind them that it is time to write rather than draw. If you notice students struggling to start writing after 10 minutes, quietly pull those individuals aside and ask them questions, such as:

Q   *What are you thinking about right now?*

Q   *What interesting thing has happened in your life that you could write about? What could you write as a first sentence for that idea?*

Q   *What ideas have you written in your writing ideas section? Let's pick one and talk about what you might write.*

Record your observations in the *Assessment Resource Book.*

Signal to let the students know when writing time is over. Remind the students to use their self-stick notes to save blank pages in their notebooks for any unfinished pieces.

SHARING AND REFLECTING

▶ **6** **Briefly Share and Reflect on Writing**

Have the students put their pencils away and then have several volunteers share what they wrote about today. Ask:

Q   *Did you write about someone in your own life? Tell us about it.*

Q   *What other things did you write about today?*

Day 2

Getting Ideas from Our Own Lives

In this lesson, the students:

- Hear and discuss a story
- Practice "Turn to Your Partner"
- Write freely about things that interest them
- Take responsibility for themselves

GETTING READY TO WRITE

1 **Gather and Review "Turn to Your Partner"**

Gather the class with partners sitting together, facing you. Remind the students that they learned "Turn to Your Partner" yesterday. Briefly review the procedure and ask the students to be ready to talk in pairs again today.

Remind the students that they heard *Grandpa's Face* by Eloise Greenfield. Explain that you will read another story by this author and that the purpose of the read-alouds is to help the students get ideas for their own writing.

2 **Read *She Come Bringing Me That Little Baby Girl* Aloud**

Show the cover of *She Come Bringing Me That Little Baby Girl* and read the title aloud. Read the story aloud slowly and clearly, showing the illustrations as you read.

Stop after:

> **p. 14** "All she said was, 'Where's the baby? Where's the baby?'"

Materials

- *She Come Bringing Me That Little Baby Girl*

ELL Note

Cooperative structures like "Turn to Your Partner" support the language development of English Language Learners by providing frequent opportunities for them to talk about their thinking and listen to others.

Ask:

Q   *What's happening in this story so far? Turn to your partner.*

Have the students discuss the question. After a moment, signal for their attention. Without sharing as a class, continue reading to the end of the book.

▶3 Discuss the Story and Generate Writing Ideas

Facilitate a class discussion using the questions that follow. Encourage the students to listen responsibly to the discussion by turning to look at the people who are speaking (for example, "Shawn is going to speak now. Let's all turn and look at him"). Ask:

Q   *How does Kevin feel about his sister at the beginning of the story? At the end?*

Q   *If you were going to write a story about a time you felt bad and then ended up feeling good, what might you write? Turn to your partner.*

Have partners discuss the question. Signal for their attention and have a few volunteers share with the class.

> ***Students might say:***
>
> "One time I was crying because I didn't want to get a haircut. Then I got one, and it turned out okay."
>
> "In kindergarten I was afraid to come to school, but then I got used to it, and I liked it."
>
> "I felt bad when my cat got sick. Then it got well, and I felt happy again."

Invite the students to write about some of their ideas today, if they wish.

WRITING TIME

▶4 Write Independently

Ask the students to return to their seats. Explain that they will write silently for 10–15 minutes. Write the following choices on the board as you explain what the students can do during this time:

- Write about a time you felt bad and then good.

- Choose another idea from your writing ideas section and write about it.

- Write about anything else that interests you.

Remind the students that they do not need to finish pieces of writing before starting new ones. Also review that during the writing period everyone (including you) will be silently writing on their own. You will let them know when writing time is over. Join the students in writing for 5–10 minutes.

Signal to let the students know when writing time is over.

SHARING AND REFLECTING

▶5 Share and Reflect on Writing

Have the students put their pencils away; then have several volunteers share what they wrote about today. Ask:

Q *Did you write about a time you felt bad and then good? Tell us about it.*

Q *Did you add ideas to your writing ideas section? Tell us about them.*

Q *What other things did you write about today?*

◀ **Teacher Note**

The purpose of this unit is to give the students opportunities to write freely about topics they choose. Read-alouds are intended solely to stimulate creativity; the students may or may not be inspired to write something related to a read-aloud. At this point, they are not expected to learn the features of genres or to write in any particular genre.

◀ **Teacher Note**

If necessary, remind the students to use their self-stick notes to save blank pages in their notebooks for any unfinished pieces.

Day 3

Materials

- "About Eloise Greenfield" (see page 40)
- Chart paper and a marker

Learning About an Author

In this lesson, the students:

- Learn about a professional author
- Practice "Turn to Your Partner"
- Generate ideas from their own lives that they can write about
- Write freely about things that interest them

GETTING READY TO WRITE

 1 Learn About Eloise Greenfield

Gather the class with partners sitting together, facing you. Have them bring their writing notebooks and pencils with them.

Remind the students that they heard *Grandpa's Face* and *She Come Bringing Me That Little Baby Girl,* both by Eloise Greenfield. Explain that you will read aloud some information about Eloise Greenfield. Invite the students to think as they listen about how her childhood might have influenced the kind of stories she writes.

Read "About Eloise Greenfield" aloud; then discuss:

 Q *What did you learn about Eloise Greenfield from this reading? Turn to your partner.*

Have partners discuss the question. Signal for their attention and have a few volunteers share their thinking with the class.

> *Students might say:*
>
> "I learned that she grew up in Washington, D.C."
>
> "I found out that Eloise Greenfield played games like dodgeball and hide-and-seek."
>
> "I learned that she writes about African American families, like the one she grew up in."

 ELL Note

You might provide the prompt "I learned that…" to your English Language Learners to help them verbalize their answers to this question.

Point out that the students, like Eloise Greenfield, have been getting writing ideas from their own lives over the past week. On a sheet of chart paper titled "Writing Ideas," write *writing stories from your own life*. Explain that you will add other ideas to the chart over the coming weeks.

2 ▸ Introduce Quick-Writes

Explain that the students will do a quick-write to help them get ideas for their own writing. Explain that a quick-write is a 5-minute writing exercise that everyone will do together. It gives everyone a chance to practice a particular writing technique.

Write the questions that follow on the board and read them aloud.

- What is your earliest memory?

- When did something strange happen to you?

- When did you feel happy, sad, or afraid?

- When were you really, really surprised?

Ask the students to open to the next blank page in their writing notebooks and to pick one question to write quickly about for 5 minutes. Students who run out of things to say before the time is up should choose another question and keep writing. Encourage the students to keep their pencils moving and to write whatever comes to mind, without stopping to think too much about it.

After 5 minutes of silent writing, signal for the students' attention. Ask and briefly discuss:

Q *What was it like to try to keep your pencil moving for the whole time?*

Explain that the students will have more opportunities to practice writing quickly and continuously during quick-writes. Point out that this kind of writing can be very helpful in getting ideas for writing.

◀ **Teacher Note**

Quick-writes are short exercises that everyone participates in and discusses. They are an opportunity for the students to learn a technique together and to practice overcoming their "inner critic" by writing quickly, continuously, and without planning or deliberation.

WRITING TIME

▶ 3 Write Independently

Ask the students to return to their seats. Write the following choices on the board as you explain what the students can do during writing time:

- Continue the piece you started during the quick-write.

- Work on a piece you started earlier.

- Start a new piece of writing about anything that interests you.

Join the students in writing for 5–10 minutes; then walk around the room and observe.

Signal to let the students know when writing time is over.

SHARING AND REFLECTING

▶ 4 Share and Reflect on Writing

Have the students put their pencils away. Ask and discuss the questions that follow, inviting the students to read passages of their writing aloud to the class, if they wish.

Q *If you worked on the piece you started during the quick-write, tell us about it.*

Q *What else did you write about today? Tell us about it.*

EXTENSION

Learn More About Eloise Greenfield

Encourage the students to read more of Eloise Greenfield's books or learn more about her by searching her name on the Internet. Be aware that they will hear the essays, "Our House," "Chores," "Candy," and "John and the Snake," from her book *Childtimes* during the personal narrative genre unit.

ELL Note

English Language Learners may benefit from drawing their ideas before they write. Encourage them to draw what they want to write about and then talk quietly with you or a partner about their drawing. If necessary, support them by writing down key words or phrases they want to use so they can copy them into their writing.

Teacher Note

Save the "Writing Ideas" chart to use on Day 4 and throughout the unit.

Day 4

Exploring a Prewriting Technique

In this lesson, the students:

* Reflect on their writing
* Explore a prewriting technique
* Write freely about things that interest them
* Express interest in and appreciation for one another's writing

GETTING READY TO WRITE

1▶ Reflect on Writing Notebooks

Gather the class with partners sitting together, facing you. Remind them to bring their writing notebooks and pencils with them.

Explain that writers often get new ideas for writing from things they have written earlier. Today you will show them a technique that some authors use to help them come up with new ideas.

Ask the students to open their writing notebooks to their latest piece of writing and to read the piece silently. After a moment, ask the students to reread the piece and underline one or two sentences they particularly like.

When the students finish, ask several volunteers to read a sentence they underlined aloud and explain what they like about that sentence.

> **Students might say:**
>
> "I like this sentence because I used the words 'slurpy and slimy,' and I like those words."
>
> "I underlined this sentence because it tells what I pictured in my mind."
>
> "I like the way this sentence sounds, so I underlined it."

Materials

* "Writing Ideas" chart from Day 3

▶2 Quick-Write: Explore a Prewriting Technique

Ask the students to copy one of the sentences they just underlined onto the top of the next blank page of their writing notebook. Explain that the students will do a 5-minute quick-write today in which they will begin with the sentence they copied. Remind them to keep their pencils moving and to write whatever comes to mind without planning or thinking too hard about it.

Have the students write silently for 5 minutes. Signal for their attention and have partners turn to each other and share what they wrote. Call on several volunteers to read what they wrote to the class. Ask:

Q *Was it hard or easy to start writing from the sentence you wrote at the top of your page? Why?*

Q *When your partner read his or her writing to you, how did you show that you were interested?*

Explain that starting a new piece with a sentence from an earlier piece is a technique that the students can use whenever they feel stuck or when they don't know what to write about. On the "Writing Ideas" chart, add *starting with a good sentence from another piece*.

WRITING TIME

Teacher Note

The independent writing period is gradually getting longer. Observe the students carefully and increase the time more slowly, if necessary. The goal is to get the students writing independently for at least 30 minutes per day by the end of Unit 1.

▶ ## ▶3 Write Independently

Ask the students to return to their seats. Write the following choices on the board and ask the students to write silently for 15–20 minutes.

- Continue the piece you started during the quick-write.

- Work on a piece you started earlier.

- Start a new piece of writing.

Teacher Note

If necessary, remind the students to use their self-stick notes to save blank pages in their notebooks ▶ for any unfinished pieces.

Join the students in writing for 5–10 minutes; then walk around the room and observe them.

Signal to let the students know when writing time is over.

SHARING AND REFLECTING

4 ▶ Share Writing and Reflect on Interactions

Have several volunteers share what they wrote, and encourage the class to think about what they can do to express interest and appreciation as their classmates share. Ask:

Q *If you worked on the piece you started during the quick-write, tell us about it.*

Q *What questions or comments do you have for [Natalie] about the piece she just shared?*

Q *Why is it important that we show interest in and appreciation for one another's writing?*

FACILITATION TIP

Continue to prompt the students to **turn and look** at the person who will speak (for example, you might say, "Beth is going to speak now. Let's all turn and look at her"). During the discussion, scan the class to ensure that the students are looking at the person who is speaking. If necessary, interrupt the discussion to remind them of your expectations.

About Eloise Greenfield

Excerpted from *The Big Book of Picture-Book Authors & Illustrators* by James Preller (Scholastic, 2001)

Except for three months in Parmele, North Carolina, Eloise Greenfield has spent her entire life in Washington, D.C.... The second oldest of five children, Eloise looks back on her childhood in Washington, D.C., with fondness. "We didn't have much money, but my father always had a job and we were able to manage."... On her ninth birthday, Eloise and her family moved into a new housing project named Langston Terrace. For Eloise, it was love at first sight. She remembers, "It was built on a hill, a group of tan brick houses and apartments with a playground at its center.... There were so many games to play and things to do. We played hide-and-seek at the lamppost, paddle tennis and shuffleboard, dodge ball and jacks. We danced in fireplug showers; jumped rope to rhymes; played Bouncy Bouncy Bally, swinging one leg over a bouncing ball; played baseball on a nearby field; had parties in the social room and bus trips to the beach."

Although childhood was a magical time, it was also touched by racism. "There were a lot of things we couldn't do and places we couldn't go. Washington was a city for white people. But inside that city, there was another city. It didn't have a name and it wasn't all in one area, but it was where black people lived."

Excerpted from www.eduplace.com/kids/hmr/mtai/greenfield.html

Eloise Greenfield has been writing since she was in her early 20s and has published 38 children's books, including picture books, novels, poetry, and biographies. Her work often portrays strong, loving African American families and communities, such as the ones in which she grew up.... Mrs. Greenfield has a son, a daughter, and four grandchildren.

UNIT 1: THE WRITING COMMUNITY

Things Will Never Be the Same
by Tomie dePaola
(Puffin, 2003)

Author Tomie dePaola narrates his life in a diary.

Oliver Button Is a Sissy
by Tomie dePaola
(Voyager, 1979)

Oliver doesn't like to do the things that other boys do.

Writing Focus

- Students hear and discuss good writing.

- Students learn how a professional author gets writing ideas from his own life.

- Students explore prewriting techniques.

- Students write freely about things in which they are interested.

- Teacher begins to confer with students.

Social Focus

- Students build the writing community.

- Students learn procedures for working together.

- Students work in a responsible way.

DO AHEAD

Prior to Day 4, write this list on a sheet of chart paper entitled "List Topics":

- Ten exciting things

- Ten things that make me nervous

- Ten yellow things

- Ten people I'd like to meet

- Ten quiet things

- Ten small (or big) things

- Ten things I wonder about

TEACHER AS WRITER

"[The poet] is the tireless collector of the looks and sounds and shapes and feel of things."
— P. B. Shelley

Get your creative juices flowing by making lists. Select one of the following topics and list ten things that come to mind for it:

- Things that make me nervous

- Red things (blue, silver, black, etc.)

- Lonely things

- Things people have said to me that I remember

- Quiet things

- Small things with big meaning (or big things with small meaning)

Day 1

Materials

- *Things Will Never Be the Same*
- *Assessment Resource Book*

Getting Ideas from Our Own Lives

In this lesson, the students:

- Hear and discuss a story based on the author's life
- Generate ideas from their own lives that they can write about
- Learn "Think, Pair, Share"
- Write freely about things that interest them

GETTING READY TO WRITE

1 ▶ Gather and Teach "Think, Pair, Share"

Gather the class with partners sittings together, facing you. Have the students bring their writing notebooks and pencils with them.

> **Teacher Note ▶**
>
> If your students are already familiar with "Think, Pair, Share," simply remind them of your expectations.

Explain that today they will learn a cooperative structure called "Think, Pair, Share," in which they take a moment to think quietly before turning to a partner to talk. Explain that you will ask a question and wait a few moments for them to think. When you say "Turn to your partner," partners will turn to each other and begin talking. When you signal them, they will end their conversation and turn their attention back to you.

To have the students practice "Think, Pair, Share," ask:

> **Teacher Note ▶**
>
> During "Think, Pair, Share," pause for 10–15 seconds for students to think before saying "Turn to your partner."

 Q *What is one thing you want to keep in mind today to help your partner conversation go well?* [pause] *Turn to your partner.*

After a few moments, signal for the class's attention and then have a few pairs share with the whole class what they discussed.

Encourage the students to try the ideas they discussed as they use "Think, Pair, Share" during today's lesson.

2 ▶ Read from *Things Will Never Be the Same*

Show the cover of *Things Will Never Be the Same* and explain that the author, Tomie dePaola, based this book on some of the experiences he had growing up. Explain that you will read a chapter about something that happened to him as a child. Tell them that Miss Kiniry was his first-grade teacher, and Miss Gardner was his second-grade teacher.

Show the illustration on page 54 and read Tomie's diary entry; then read chapter eight (pages 54–61) aloud slowly and clearly, stopping as described on the next page. Clarify vocabulary when you encounter it in the text by reading the word, briefly defining it, rereading it, and continuing (for example, "'Instead I saw lots of arithmetic'—*arithmetic* is another word for *math*—'instead I saw lots of arithmetic charts up—all numbers'").

Suggested Vocabulary

arithmetic: math (p. 55)

diary key: small key used for the lock on a diary (p. 56)

skate key: a key-shaped tool for clamping old-fashioned roller skates to shoes (p. 56)

forbidden: not allowed (p. 57)

ELL Vocabulary

English Language Learners may benefit from discussing additional vocabulary, including:

fall leaves decorating the walls: leaf shapes hung up to make the room look prettier (p. 54)

copy: do the same thing that another person does (p. 59)

Stop after:

p. 57   "Miss Gardner saw them and said, 'Tommy, take those crayons home and leave them there.'"

Use "Think, Pair, Share" to have partners first think about and then discuss:

 **Q**   *What has Tomie told us so far about being in second grade?* [pause] *Turn to your partner.*

After partners discuss the question, signal for their attention. Without sharing as a class, reread the sentence and continue reading to the next stopping point:

p. 59   "'What's the matter now?' Miss Gardner asked."

Ask:

 Q *What else has Tomie told us about being in second grade?* [pause] *Turn to your partner.*

Have partners discuss the question, then signal for their attention. Without sharing as a class, reread the sentence and continue reading to the end of the chapter.

▶ 3 Discuss the Story and Generate Writing Ideas

Explain that authors often write about events or people from their own lives. Use "Think, Pair, Share" to have partners first think about and then discuss:

 Q *What memories do you have that you might be able to write about?* [pause] *Turn to your partner.*

After a few moments, signal for students' attention. Without sharing as a class, ask the students to open their writing notebooks to the writing ideas section and jot down some of their ideas.

After the students have had a chance to write, call for their attention and have several volunteers share what they wrote with the class.

Teacher Note ▶

If you notice many students having difficulty coming up with ideas, call for their attention and have several volunteers who have ideas read aloud what they have written. You might also model listing a few memories as the students suggest them. Then have the students go back to thinking and writing.

WRITING TIME

▶ 4 Write Independently

Ask the students to return to their seats. Explain that they will write silently for 15–20 minutes. Write the following choices on the board as you explain what the students can do during this time:

● Write about a memory.

- Choose another idea in your writing ideas section and write about it.

- Write something else that interests you.

Join the students in writing for 5–10 minutes; then walk around the room and observe them.

CLASS ASSESSMENT NOTE

Observe the students and ask yourself:

- Are the students writing in silence?

- Are they staying in their seats?

- Are they skipping lines in their notebooks?

- Are they writing rather than drawing?

If necessary, remind the class of your expectations for silent writing during this time. Continue to note which students write easily and which ones have difficulty getting started. If you notice students drawing, gently remind them that it is time to write rather than draw. If you notice students struggling to start writing after 10 minutes, quietly pull those individuals aside and ask them questions, such as:

Q　*What are you thinking about right now?*

Q　*What interesting thing has happened in your life that you could write about? What could you write as a first sentence for that idea?*

Q　*What ideas have you written in your writing ideas section? Let's pick one and talk about what you might write.*

Record your observations in the *Assessment Resource Book*.

Signal to let the students know when writing time is over.

SHARING AND REFLECTING

▶ **5 Briefly Share and Reflect on Writing**

Have the students put their pencils away and have several volunteers share what they wrote today. Ask:

Q *Did you write about a memory from your own life? Tell us about it.*

Q *Did you add ideas from your own life to your writing ideas section? Tell us about them.*

Q *What other things did you write about today?*

Day 2

Getting Ideas from Our Own Lives

Materials

- *Things Will Never Be the Same*
- "Conference Notes" record sheet for each student (BLM1)

In this lesson, the students:

- Hear and discuss a story based on the author's life
- Generate ideas from their own lives that they can write about
- Practice "Think, Pair, Share"
- Write freely about things that interest them

GETTING READY TO WRITE

1 ▶ Gather and Review "Think, Pair, Share"

Gather the class with partners sitting together, facing you. Have them bring their writing folders and pencils with them. Remind them that yesterday they learned a cooperative structure called "Think, Pair, Share," in which they take a moment to think quietly before turning to their partner to talk. Ask and briefly discuss:

Q *When we do "Think, Pair, Share," why is it helpful to take time to think before we start talking?*

Tell the students they will practice "Think, Pair, Share" again today.

2 ▶ Read from *Things Will Never Be the Same*

Remind the students that they heard a chapter from *Things Will Never Be the Same,* by Tomie dePaola, and that the author based this book on some of his memories of growing up. Explain that you will read another chapter aloud, and encourage the students to think about what they can write about from their own lives as they listen.

Show the illustration on page 36 and read Tomie's diary entry ("Y.B.F.I.T.W." stands for "Your best friend in the world."). Read chapter six (pages 36–43) aloud slowly and clearly, stopping as described below. Clarify vocabulary as you read, using the procedure you used on Day 1 (see page 45).

Suggested Vocabulary

recitals: dance shows or performances (p. 36)

tap: a kind of dancing in which the dancers make tapping sounds with their feet (p. 36)

the audience loved our number: the audience loved our dance piece (p. 41)

ELL Vocabulary

English Language Learners may benefit from discussing additional vocabulary, including:

audience: people watching a show (p. 39)

"specialty" number: a special dance (p. 41)

orchestra: a large group of musicians (p. 42)

Stop after:

p. 39   "Miss Leah said, 'I think the eye patch will be quite enough!'"

Ask:

 Q *What has Tomie told us so far about this memory?* [pause] *Turn to your partner.*

Without sharing as a class, reread the last sentence and continue reading to the end of the chapter:

p. 43   "Maybe Miss Leah would be my 'Judy.'"

Explain that this is a reference to Judy Garland, a famous actress and dancer in old movies.

3 ▶ Discuss the Story and Generate Writing Ideas

Ask and briefly discuss:

Q *What do we learn about Tomie dePaola from his childhood memories?*

Use "Think, Pair, Share" to have the students first think about and then discuss:

 Q *What other memories do you have that you might be able to write about?* [pause] *Turn to your partner.*

Ask the students to record any other memories they have in the writing ideas section of their writing notebook. Encourage them to select ideas from this list to write about during writing time today, if they wish.

WRITING TIME

4 ▶ Write Independently

Ask the students to return to their seats. Write the following choices on the board and have the students write silently for 15–20 minutes.

- Write about a memory or an idea from your own life.

- Continue a piece you started earlier.

- Start a new piece of writing.

Join the students in writing for 5–10 minutes; then begin conferring with individual students.

ELL Note

You might provide the prompt "We learned that…" to your English Language Learners to help them verbalize their answers to this question.

TEACHER CONFERENCE NOTE

Over the next two weeks, call individual students to a back table and confer quietly with them for 5–10 minutes each. To get a sense of their strengths and weaknesses as writers, ask each student to show you her writing, read some of it aloud to you, and talk with you about her ideas and feelings about writing. Some questions you might ask during these initial conferences include:

Q *Where did you get this idea?*

Q *What do you like about writing so far this year?*

Q *What kinds of things do you want to write, or write about, in the coming year?*

Q *How do you want to improve as a writer this year?*

Document your observations for each student using the "Conference Notes" record sheets (BLM1). Use the "Conference Notes" record sheets during conferences throughout the unit.

Signal to let the students know when writing time is over.

SHARING AND REFLECTING

5 ▶ **Briefly Share and Reflect on Writing**

Have the students put their pencils away and have several volunteers share what they wrote in their notebook today. Ask:

Q *Did you write about an idea from your own life? Tell us about it.*

Q *What other things did you write about today?*

Day 3

Getting Ideas from Our Own Lives

Materials

- *Oliver Button Is a Sissy*
- "Writing Ideas" chart from Week 2

In this lesson, the students:

- Hear and discuss a story based on the author's life
- Make up a character like themselves
- Practice "Think, Pair, Share"
- Write freely about things that interest them

GETTING READY TO WRITE

▶ **1** **Gather and Read *Oliver Button Is a Sissy* Aloud**

Gather the class with partners sitting together, facing you. Remind the students that you have been reading different kinds of texts to help them get ideas for writing from their own lives. Explain that today you will read another story by Tomie dePaola in which he makes up a character who is similar to himself. Encourage the students to think as they listen about whether they might like to make up a character who is similar to themselves.

Show the cover of *Oliver Button Is a Sissy* and read the title aloud. Read the story aloud slowly and clearly, showing the illustrations and clarifying vocabulary as you read.

> **Suggested Vocabulary**
>
> **routine:** dance steps (p. 25)
> **master of ceremonies:** the person who introduces the performers in a show (p. 35)

ELL Vocabulary

English Language Learners may benefit from discussing additional vocabulary, including:

attic: the room right under the roof of a building (p. 7)

tap shoes: special dancing shoes that make a tapping sound on the floor (p. 16)

talent show: performance where people do things they are good at, like singing or dancing or telling jokes (p. 24)

all the acts were performed: everyone did their part of the show (p. 28)

tapped: danced with tap shoes (p. 32)

 Discuss the Story and Make Up a Character

Use "Think, Pair, Share" to have the students first think about and then discuss:

 Q *If you were going to write a story about a character who is similar to you, what might you write?* [pause] *Turn to your partner.*

Have several volunteers share what they discussed with the class. Direct their attention to the "Writing Ideas" chart and add *creating a character like yourself* to it. Encourage the students to try writing a story about a character like themselves today, if they wish.

FACILITATION TIP

Continue to remind the students to **turn and look** at the person who will speak. Ask speakers to wait until they have the class's attention before starting to speak. Scan the class to ensure that all students are actively listening and participating in the discussion.

WRITING TIME

3 **Write Independently**

Ask the students to return to their seats. Write the following choices on the board and have the students write silently for 15–20 minutes.

- Make up a character like yourself and write a story about him or her.

- Write about a memory or an idea from your own life.

- Continue a piece you started earlier.

- Start a new piece of writing.

Join the students in writing for 5–10 minutes; then confer with individual students.

TEACHER CONFERENCE NOTE

Continue to call individual students to a back table and quietly confer with them for 5–10 minutes each. Ask each student to show you her writing, read some of it aloud to you, and talk with you about her ideas and feelings about writing. Some questions you might ask during these initial conferences include:

Q *Where did you get this idea?*

Q *What do you like about writing so far this year?*

Q *What kinds of things do you want to write, or write about, in the coming year?*

Q *How do you want to improve as a writer this year?*

Document your observations for each student using the "Conference Notes" record sheets (BLM1).

Signal to let the students know when writing time is over.

SHARING AND REFLECTING

▶ 4 **Briefly Share and Reflect on Writing**

Have the students put their pencils away and have several volunteers share what they wrote today. Ask:

Q *Did you create a character today? Tell us about it.*

Q *What other things did you write about?*

Q *Is it hard or easy to come up with ideas for writing? Why do you think so?*

EXTENSION

Write in Response to Literature

Briefly review *Oliver Button Is a Sissy* by discussing the following questions:

Q *How does Oliver feel about being called a "sissy?" What in the story tells you that?*

Q *What changes for Oliver at the end of the story?*

Have the students choose one of the following prompts and write about it in their notebooks:

- What do you admire about Oliver?
- Why do you think people tease others who are different from them?
- In what ways does Oliver show courage in this story?

Day 4

Exploring a Prewriting Technique

Materials

- "List Topics" chart, prepared ahead (see "Do Ahead" on page 43)
- "Writing Ideas" chart

In this lesson, the students:

- Reflect on their writing
- Explore making lists as a prewriting technique
- Write freely about things that interest them
- Work responsibly in pairs

GETTING READY TO WRITE

1 ▶ Reflect on Writing Notebooks

Gather the class with partners sitting together, facing you. Remind them to bring their writing notebooks and pencils with them.

Ask the students to spend a few minutes looking through their notebooks at the writing they have done so far this year. After a moment, use "Think, Pair, Share" to have partners first think about and then discuss:

 Q *What is one piece that you really enjoyed and what did you enjoy about writing it?* [pause] *Turn to your partner.*

Have several volunteers share what they discussed with the class.

2 ▶ Quick-Write: Making Lists

Explain that you will teach the students another quick technique for getting their creative ideas flowing in preparation for writing. Explain that writers sometimes make lists to help them think about a topic and to lead into longer pieces of writing.

Direct the students' attention to the "List Topics" chart and read the items aloud. As a class, select one of the topics on the chart and brainstorm ten things that could go on that list.

Teacher Note

"Ten exciting things" could be: birthdays, tetherball, first day of school, jumping off the high diving board, field trips, banana splits, author visits, finding a bird's nest, video games, and sleepovers.

ELL Note

You might invite English Language Learners to write their lists in their native language as well as in English.

Ask the students to open their writing notebooks to the next blank page in the writing ideas section. Explain that they will choose another topic on the "List Topics" chart, write that topic at the top of the page, and quickly jot down ten things that could go on that list. After 5 minutes, signal for their attention and have several volunteers share what they wrote. Invite the students to continue to work on lists today during writing time, if they wish.

WRITING TIME

 3 **Write Independently**

Ask the students to return to their seats. Write the following choices on the board and have students write silently for 15–20 minutes.

- Continue the list-making activity you started during the quick-write.

- Work on a piece you started earlier.

- Start a new piece of writing.

Join the students in writing for 5–10 minutes; then confer with individual students.

TEACHER CONFERENCE NOTE

Continue to call individual students to a back table and quietly confer with them for 5–10 minutes each. Have the students read their writing aloud to you. Discuss questions such as:

Q *Where did you get this idea?*

Q *What do you like about writing so far this year?*

Q *What kinds of things do you want to write, or write about, in the coming year?*

Q *How do you want to improve as a writer this year?*

Document your observations for each student using the "Conference Notes" record sheets (BLM1).

Signal to let the students know when writing time is over.

SHARING AND REFLECTING

4 ▶ Share Writing in Pairs and Reflect on Interactions

Explain that partners will spend a few minutes sharing their writing from today with each other. Ask and briefly discuss:

Q *What will you do to be a responsible partner as you share your writing?*

Scan the class as partners share their writing for 5–10 minutes. When it seems like most partners have shared, signal for their attention. Ask and briefly discuss:

Q *What did your partner write about today?*

Q *What did you do to be a responsible partner?*

◀ **Teacher Note**

If the students have difficulty answering these questions, point out some responsible behaviors you observed during the sharing. (You might say, "I noticed that partners were turned toward each other. I also noticed partners looking at each other and talking about their writing, rather than other topics. That was responsible.") Be aware that the students will become more thoughtful and perceptive about their own behavior and social interactions over time.

Week 4 Overview

UNIT 1: THE WRITING COMMUNITY

Alligator Arrived with Apples: A Potluck Alphabet Feast
by Crescent Dragonwagon, pictures by Jose Aruego
and Ariane Dewey
(Aladdin, 1992)

Animals bring alliterative goodies to an alphabet feast.

O Is for Orca: An Alphabet Book
by Andrea Helman, photographs by Art Wolfe
(Sasquatch Books, 1995)

Information about animals is organized by the ABCs.

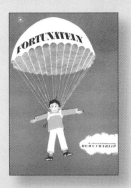

Fortunately
by Remy Charlip
(Aladdin, 1964)

Ned's luck keeps turning from bad to good in this pattern book.

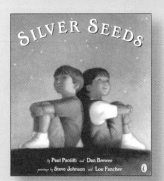

Silver Seeds
by Paul Paolilli and Dan Brewer, illustrated by Steve Johnson
and Lou Fancher
(Puffin Books, 2001)

Acrostic poems describe the natural world.

Writing Focus

- Students hear and discuss pattern books, alphabet books, and poems.

- Students explore prewriting techniques.

- Students write freely about things that interest them.

- Teacher begins to confer with students.

- Partners begin to confer with each other.

Social Focus

- Students build the writing community.

- Students learn procedures for pair conferences.

- Students work in a responsible way.

- Students listen respectfully to the thinking of others and share their own.

- Students express interest in and appreciation for one another's writing.

T E A C H E R
A S   W R I T E R

"Your writing is trying to tell you something. Just lend an ear."
     — *Joanne Greenberg*

This week select an idea from your notebook's writing ideas section and write for a few minutes. Reread what you wrote and underline one or two sentences that you really like. Ask yourself:

- What appeals to me about these sentences? What features of these sentences would I like to incorporate into more of my writing?

Choose one underlined sentence and use it as an opening sentence for a new piece.

Day 1

Materials

- *Alligator Arrived with Apples*

Getting Ideas from Pattern Books

In this lesson, the students:

- Hear and discuss a text that uses patterns
- Think about how they might use patterns in their writing
- Write freely about things that interest them
- Speak clearly and listen to one another
- Express interest in and appreciation for one another's writing

GETTING READY TO WRITE

1▶ Build the Writing Community

Gather the class with partners sitting together, facing you. Remind the students that they are building a writing community in which everyone feels safe, respected, and comfortable expressing their creativity through writing. Tell the students that because this is such an important goal, they will devote time periodically to talking about how they are doing building the community. Ask:

Q *What have you learned so far about being a member of our writing community?*

 Q *Why is it important that we all feel comfortable sharing our writing and thinking with one another? Turn to your partner.*

Have several volunteers share with the class. Ask follow-up questions such as:

Q *What might be scary about sharing our writing or thinking with others?*

Q *What can we do to help others feel that we respect and care about their thinking?*

FACILITATION TIP

Continue to remind the students to **turn and look** at the person who will speak. Ask speakers to wait until they have the class's attention before starting to speak. Scan the class to ensure that all students are actively listening and participating in the discussion.

Students might say:

"If we don't feel comfortable sharing our writing, we might keep it to ourselves and never get better at it."

"It could be scary to read something you wrote, because people might act bored or like they're not interested in it."

"We can listen when people are sharing their writing and tell them a part we liked."

Encourage the students to be aware of how they are showing interest in and respect for their classmates' thinking. Tell them you will check in with them to see how they are doing.

2　Read *Alligator Arrived with Apples* Aloud

Remind the students that you are reading various kinds of texts to help them get ideas for their own writing. Show the cover of *Alligator Arrived with Apples* and read the title and author's and illustrators' names aloud. Ask the students to think as they listen about whether they might like to try writing a book like this themselves.

Read the book aloud slowly and clearly, showing the illustrations and clarifying vocabulary as you read.

Suggested Vocabulary

elixir: a liquid used to flavor food (p. 15)

imparted: gave (p. 19)

kale, kohlrabi: cabbage-like vegetables (p. 21)

kasha: hot cereal made from buckwheat (p. 21)

quince: fruit similar to an apple (p. 27)

zaftig: plump (p. 35)

ELL Vocabulary

English Language Learners may benefit from discussing additional vocabulary, including:

diced: cut into small pieces (p. 13)

eclipsed: got in the way of (p. 15)

lugged: carried (p. 21)

violated tradition: didn't do things in the usual way (p. 31)

yielded: given (p. 35)

3▶ Discuss the Book

Ask and briefly discuss:

Q *What are some things that make this book fun to read?*

Q *What patterns do you notice in this book?*

Point out that for every letter of the alphabet there is an animal that brings foods that begin with the same letter. Reread a few pages and ask:

Q *If we were going to make up a page for the letter "s" in this book, what might it say?*

Teacher Note ▶

You might write, *Snake slithered in with spaghetti and soy sauce.*

As the students suggest ideas, write them where everyone can see them. Ask partners to choose another letter and to come up with ideas for what that page might say. After a few moments, signal for their attention and have a few pairs share their ideas with the class.

Invite the students to try writing an alphabet pattern book like *Alligator Arrived with Apples* during writing time today, if they wish.

WRITING TIME

4▶ Write Independently

Teacher Note ▶

Continue to gradually lengthen the independent writing period. Observe the students carefully and increase the time more slowly, if necessary. The goal is 30 minutes of independent writing per day by the end of Unit 1.

Ask the students to return to their seats. Write the following choices on the board and have the students write silently for 20–30 minutes.

- Try writing a pattern book.
- Work on a piece you started earlier.
- Start a new piece of writing.

Join the students in writing for 5–10 minutes; then confer with individual students.

TEACHER CONFERENCE NOTE

Continue to call individual students to a back table and quietly confer with them for 5–10 minutes each. Have the students read their writing aloud to you. Discuss questions such as:

Q *Where did you get this idea?*

Q *What do you like about writing so far this year?*

Q *What kinds of things do you want to write, or write about, in the coming year?*

Q *How do you want to improve as a writer this year?*

Document your observations for each student using the "Conference Notes" record sheets (BLM1).

Signal to let the students know when writing time is over.

SHARING AND REFLECTING

5 **Share Writing and Reflect on Interactions**

Have several volunteers share what they wrote and then use the questions that follow to encourage the students to express their interest and appreciation.

Q *What did [Carlos] write about today? What do you want to know more about?*

Q *What did you enjoy about [Mary Ellen's] story?*

Q *What do you want to ask or tell [Paula] about what she wrote?*

Help the students reflect on their interactions by briefly discussing:

Q *What did you do today to show interest in another person's thinking or writing?*

ELL Note

Questions like these help the students get to know one another, which in turn creates a sense of community that benefits everyone. English Language Learners, in particular, rely on having a supportive environment in which they can take the necessary risks to practice and grow in their second language.

Day 2

Materials

- *O Is for Orca*
- *Alligator Arrived with Apples*
- "Writing Ideas" chart

Getting Ideas from Pattern Books

In this lesson, the students:

- Hear and discuss an alphabet book
- Think about topics for alphabet books
- Write freely about things that interest them
- Use writing time responsibly

GETTING READY TO WRITE

▶1 Gather and Review "Writing Ideas" Chart

Gather the class with partners sitting together, facing you. Remind the students that they are focusing on listening carefully to one another and expressing interest in one another's writing and thinking. Explain that they will practice these skills today.

Briefly review the items on the "Writing Ideas" chart. Remind the students that yesterday they heard a pattern book; add *pattern books* to the chart. Explain that today they will hear another kind of pattern book, based on the alphabet, and that the students may wish to try writing alphabet books themselves. Add *alphabet books* to the chart.

▶2 Read *O Is for Orca* Aloud

Explain that today you will read *O Is for Orca,* another book organized around the alphabet. Show the cover and read the title and names of the author and photographer. Encourage the students to think as they listen about what it might be like to write a book like this themselves.

Read the book aloud slowly and clearly, showing the illustrations and clarifying vocabulary as you read.

Suggested Vocabulary

roost: sit to rest or sleep (p. 7)

master carvers: people very skilled in shaping wood (p. 10)

glaciers: giant rivers of ice that move very slowly down a mountain or valley (p. 12)

solitary cat: cat that lives by itself (p. 15)

coarse blades: long, flat, rough leaves of a plant (p. 29)

ELL Vocabulary

English Language Learners may benefit from discussing additional vocabulary, including:

propelling: pushing (p. 2)

sweet fragrance: nice smell (p. 8)

natural habitat: place where an animal or plant lives (p. 17)

affectionate peck: a friendly tap or kiss (p. 20)

continually reshapes the landscape: changes the shape of the land around it (p. 31)

3 Discuss the Book and Quick-Write Topics for Alphabet Books

Ask and briefly discuss:

Q *What are some things that make this book interesting to read?*

Use "Think, Pair, Share" to have the students first think about and then discuss:

 Q *If you wanted to write your own alphabet book, what topics could you write about?* [pause] *Turn to your partner.*

Have two or three students share their ideas with the class.

> *Students might say:*
>
> "Animals."
>
> "School."
>
> "Things I like."
>
> "Things I don't like."
>
> "Things that move."
>
> "Favorite foods."

◀ **Teacher Note**

If the students have difficulty coming up with topics, give some examples like the ones in the "Students might say" note.

Ask all of the students to open to the next blank page in the writing ideas section of their writing notebooks and to label it "ABC Book Topics." Have them do a 5-minute quick-write listing possible topics for alphabet books.

At the end of 5 minutes, signal for the students' attention and have a few more volunteers share an idea with the class.

4▶ Discuss Being Responsible During Writing Time

Explain that the students will write silently for 20–30 minutes today. Ask and briefly discuss:

Q *How will you act responsibly during writing time today?*

> ***Students might say:***
>
> "I will not walk around. I'll just sit and write."
>
> "I'm going to sharpen my pencil ahead of time so I won't have to do it during writing time."
>
> "I'm not going to talk to anyone at my table."

Encourage the students to keep these things in mind during writing time today. Explain that you will check in afterward to see how they did.

WRITING TIME

5▶ Write Independently

Ask the students to return to their seats. Write the following choices on the board and have the students write silently for 20–30 minutes.

- Try writing an alphabet book.
- Work on a piece you started earlier.
- Start a new piece of writing.

Join the students in writing for 5–10 minutes; then confer with individual students.

ELL Note

You might invite English Language Learners to write an alphabet (or character) book for their native language, if appropriate.

TEACHER CONFERENCE NOTE

Continue to call individual students to a back table and quietly confer with them for 5–10 minutes each. Have the students read their writing aloud to you, and discuss questions such as:

Q *Where did you get this idea?*

Q *What do you like about writing so far this year?*

Q *What kinds of things do you want to write, or write about, in the coming year?*

Q *How do you want to improve as a writer this year?*

Document your observations for each student using the "Conference Notes" record sheets (BLM1).

Signal to let the students know when writing time is over.

SHARING AND REFLECTING

6 ▶ Share Writing and Reflect

Have several volunteers share what they wrote. Encourage the class to express their interest and appreciation.

After the volunteers share, help the students reflect on their behavior and interactions by briefly discussing:

Q *What did you do during writing time that was responsible?*

Q *What did you do to behave responsibly during sharing time?*

EXTENSION

Research for Alphabet Books

Students may wish to research their alphabet book topic to help them find words for their book. Provide access to the Internet, class or school library, encyclopedias, and other resources. If many students are motivated to write alphabet books, consider scheduling additional time for them to work on that project. They might also work on their books at home.

Day 3

Getting Ideas from Pattern Books

In this lesson, the students:

- Hear and discuss a pattern book
- Write freely about things that interest them
- Use writing time responsibly
- Give their full attention to the person who is speaking

GETTING READY TO WRITE

1 ▶ Gather and Read *Fortunately* Aloud

Gather the class with partners sitting together, facing you. Remind the students that this week they heard two pattern books to help them get ideas for writing, *Alligator Arrived with Apples* and *O Is for Orca*. Explain that today you will read them a pattern book that is not organized around the alphabet. Encourage the students to think as they listen about whether they might like to try writing a story like this today.

Show the cover of *Fortunately* and read the title and the author's name aloud. Read the book aloud slowly and clearly, showing the illustrations as you read.

2 ▶ Generate Ideas for "Fortunately-Unfortunately" Pages

Ask and briefly discuss:

Q *What patterns do you notice in this book?*

Materials

- *Fortunately*

◀ **Teacher Note**

Remember that some of the read-alouds in this program are intentionally below the average reading level for your grade. The read-alouds are intended to inspire and provide models for students' writing, which normally lags somewhat behind their reading ability.

Use "Think, Pair, Share" to have the students first think about then discuss:

 Q *If we wanted to write a "fortunately-unfortunately" book, what could we say?* [pause] *Turn to your partner.*

Have a few pairs share their ideas with the class and record their ideas where everyone can see them.

Teacher Note ▶

If the students have difficulty coming up with ideas, give some examples like the ones in the "Students might say" note. Then ask, "What else could our 'fortunately-unfortunately' book say?"

> *Students might say:*
>
> "Fortunately, I caught the school bus this morning. Unfortunately, I was still in my pajamas."
>
> "Fortunately, I had a coat I could wear over my pajamas. Unfortunately, it had a gerbil in the pocket."
>
> "Fortunately, I had some peanuts to feed the gerbil. Unfortunately, the gerbil was allergic to peanuts."

Invite the students to try writing a "fortunately-unfortunately" book during writing time today, if they wish.

WRITING TIME

3 ▶ Write Independently

Ask the students to return to their seats. Write the following choices on the board and have students write silently for 20–30 minutes.

- Try writing a "fortunately-unfortunately" book.

- Work on a piece you started earlier.

- Start a new piece of writing.

Join the students in writing for 5–10 minutes; then confer with individual students.

TEACHER CONFERENCE NOTE

Continue to call individual students to a back table and quietly confer with them for 5–10 minutes each. Have the students read their writing aloud to you, and discuss questions such as:

Q *Where did you get this idea?*

Q *What do you like about writing so far this year?*

Q *What kinds of things do you want to write, or write about, in the coming year?*

Q *How do you want to improve as a writer this year?*

Document your observations for each student using the "Conference Notes" record sheets (BLM1).

Signal to let the students know when writing time is over.

SHARING AND REFLECTING

 Share Writing and Reflect on Interactions

Have the students put their pencils away. Have several volunteers share what they wrote. If necessary, remind them to give the student who is sharing their full attention.

After they share, help the students reflect on their interactions by briefly discussing:

Q *What did you do that was responsible during writing time?*

Q *How did we do giving our full attention to the person who was sharing?*

Q *Why is it important to give our full attention to the person who is sharing?*

Day 4

Materials

- *Silver Seeds*
- "Writing Ideas" chart
- *Assessment Resource Book*

Getting Ideas and Pair Conferring

In this lesson, the students

- Hear and discuss acrostic poems
- Think about acrostic poems they could write
- Write about things that interest them
- Learn procedures for pair conferences
- Express interest in and appreciation for one another's writing

GETTING READY TO WRITE

1 Gather and Read *Silver Seeds* Aloud

Gather the class with partners sitting together, facing you. Explain that today you will read some poems aloud. Encourage the students to think about whether they might like to try writing poems like these.

Show the cover of *Silver Seeds* and read the title and the authors' and illustrators' names aloud. Read the first four poems, "Dawn," "Sun," "Shadow," and "Hills," by saying the name of each poem and reading the poem slowly and clearly, showing the illustration. Tell the students you will reread the poems while they look at the pages. Ask them to look carefully at the poems and see what they notice. Reread the four poems; then ask:

 Q *What do you notice about these poems? Turn to your partner.*

Have a few volunteers share with the class.

> **Students might say:**
>
> "The letters going down spell a word."
>
> "The whole poem is about the word.'"
>
> "Sometimes there is one word for the letter and sometimes more than one."

Point out that in each poem, the first letters of the lines, read together, spell the name of the poem. Read the remaining poems in the book, slowly and clearly, showing the illustrations as you read.

2 ▶ Write an Acrostic Poem as a Class

Pick a short word and write it vertically where everyone can see it (for example, *cat*). Point to the first letter and ask:

Q *What are some words that start with [c] that you might use in a poem about [a cat]?*

Using the students' suggestions, write a line that begins with the first letter. Repeat the process for each letter until the poem is complete.

Point out that poems like these are called *acrostic poems*. Invite the students to try writing more poems like this today. Direct the students' attention to the "Writing Ideas" chart and add *acrostic poems* to it.

◀ **Teacher Note**

If the students have difficulty coming up with ideas, suggest some yourself (for example, for the letter *c* in the word *cat* you might suggest "cute," "cuddly," "curled up," or "chasing a mouse").

An acrostic poem for the word *cat* is:

Curled up in the window
Asleep in the sun,
Taking an afternoon nap.

WRITING TIME

3 ▶ Write Independently

Ask the students to return to their seats. Write the following choices on the board and have the students write silently for 20–30 minutes.

- Try writing an acrostic poem, or any poem.

- Work on a piece you started earlier.

- Start a new piece of writing.

- Add ideas to your writing ideas section.

Join the students in writing for 5–10 minutes; then confer with individual students.

CLASS ASSESSMENT NOTE

Observe the students and ask yourself:

- Do the students write readily? Does the writing make sense?

- Do the students who initially have difficulty eventually start writing, or do they continue to struggle?

- Does their difficulty seem to be in coming up with ideas for writing, or getting the ideas onto paper, or both?

Help struggling students by having them tell you what they want to write about.

Record your observations in the *Assessment Resource Book*.

Signal to let the students know when writing time is over.

SHARING AND REFLECTING

4 ▶ Introduce Pair Conferences

Teacher Note ▶

In Unit 1, pairs begin conferring by informally sharing their writing with each other during Sharing and Reflecting time. They learn procedures for conferring and think about how to interact productively and respectfully. In subsequent units, the students will learn more about how to give and receive specific feedback about their writing.

If your students are already familiar with pair conferring from prior grades, simply review your expectations with them.

Explain that the students will meet in pairs this year to *confer*, or to share and help each other with their writing. These meetings will be called *pair conferences*. They will learn a lot this year about how to work with partners to give and receive helpful feedback about their writing.

Explain that you would like the students to confer with their assigned partner about the writing they did today. Point out that conferring means not just reading their writing to each other, but talking about the writing as well. Encourage partners to express their interest in and appreciation for each other's writing today.

Ask and briefly discuss:

Q *What can you say or do after your partner reads his writing to you to show that you are interested in it and appreciate hearing it?*

Students might say:

"I could tell her what part I liked in her story."

"I can ask him questions about what he wrote."

"I can say, 'Thanks. I enjoyed hearing your writing.'"

Give partners several minutes to share and discuss their writing.

5 ▶ Reflect on Pair Conferences

Signal for the students' attention and then ask:

Q *What went well in your pair conference today?*

Q *What problems did you have? How will you avoid those problems the next time you confer?*

Q *How did your partner express interest in or appreciation for your writing? How did that feel?*

Students might say:

"It was fun hearing my partner's writing and reading him mine."

"There wasn't enough time for my partner to finish reading his story. Next time I'll stop sooner."

"My partner told me he thought my poem was funny. That made me feel good."

Explain that the students will have many opportunities this year to confer about their writing.

◀ **Teacher Note**

Consider having pairs spread out so partners can better hear each other.

UNIT 1: THE WRITING COMMUNITY

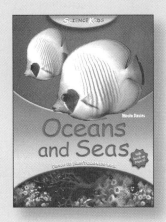

Oceans and Seas
by Nicola Davies
(Kingfisher, 2007)

Photographs, text, and other features give information about the ocean.

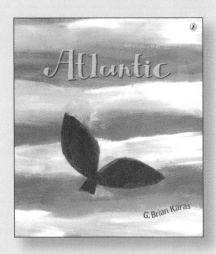

Atlantic
by G. Brian Karas
(Puffin, 2002)

"I am the Atlantic Ocean" begins the narrator of this story of the sea.

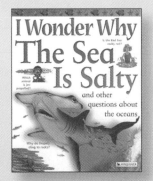

I Wonder Why the Sea Is Salty
by Anita Ganeri
(Kingfisher, 2003)

Interesting questions about the ocean are answered.

Writing Focus

- Students hear and discuss factual and nonfiction writing.

- Students explore prewriting techniques.

- Students write freely about things that interest them.

- Partners confer with each other.

- Teacher confers with students.

Social Focus

- Students build the writing community.

- Students build on one another's thinking during class discussion.

- Students use writing and pair conference time responsibly.

- Students express interest in and appreciation for one another's writing.

DO AHEAD

- Prior to Day 1, write these three prompts on a sheet of chart paper:

  "I agree with _____ because…"

  "I disagree with _____ because…"

  "In addition to what _____ said, I think…"

- Prior to Day 4, collect a variety of examples of nonbook writing, such as flyers, brochures, recipes, signs, instructions, advertisements, letters, newspapers, catalogs, magazines, and e-mail messages.

TEACHER AS WRITER

"We do not write what we know; we write what we want to find out."
         — Wallace Stegner

In your writing notebook, write five questions that you have wondered about. For example:

- Why does a year seem to pass more quickly the older I get?

- What is dust made of?

- What was life like for my grandparents at my age?

- How does one ant let the rest of them know when I leave the sugar out?

- When socks go missing, where do they go?

Choose one question and write a possible answer.

Day 1

Materials

- *Oceans and Seas*
- Charted discussion prompts (see "Do Ahead" on page 79)
- "Writing Ideas" chart
- *Assessment Resource Book*

Getting Ideas from Nonfiction

In this lesson, the students:

- Hear and discuss a narrative text based on factual information
- Learn discussion prompts to build on one another's thinking
- Write freely about things that interest them
- Use writing and pair conference time responsibly

GETTING READY TO WRITE

▶1 Teach Discussion Prompts

Gather the class with partners sitting together, facing you. Have them bring their writing notebooks and pencils with them. Remind the students that you have been reading and discussing various texts to help them get ideas for their own writing.

Teacher Note

The discussion prompts are:

- "I agree with _____ because…"
- "I disagree with _____ because…"
- "In addition to what _____ said, I think…"

Point out that in class discussions it is important to listen carefully and contribute their ideas. Direct the students' attention to the charted discussion prompts, and read them aloud. Explain that you would like them to use the prompts when they add to the discussion today and that doing so will help them listen and build on one another's thinking.

▶2 Read Aloud from *Oceans and Seas*

Show the cover of *Oceans and Seas* and read the title and the author's name aloud. Read pages 6–13 aloud slowly and clearly, showing the illustrations and clarifying vocabulary as you read.

Suggested Vocabulary

molten rock: rock that is so hot that it is a liquid (p. 9)

stimulated: made more active (p. 12)

ELL Vocabulary

English Language Learners may benefit from discussing additional vocabulary, including:

sunlit surface: the top of the water with the sun shining through it (p. 7)

landscape: view of natural scenery (p. 10)

gushes: pours out quickly (p. 11)

Ask:

Q *How is this book different from a story like* Fortunately *or* Oliver Button Is a Sissy?

Students might say:

"It's about real things. Stories are made up."

"It's just telling information about the ocean. In a story, something happens."

"There are no characters."

"It has real pictures."'

Point out that in a nonfiction book like *Oceans and Seas* the author writes true information about a specific topic. Direct the students' attention to the "Writing Ideas" chart and add *nonfiction books* to it.

 Quick-Write: Brainstorm Nonfiction Topics

Ask the students to consider the following question individually for a moment:

Q *What nonfiction topic would you like to know more about?*

Have the students do a 5-minute quick-write in which they jot their ideas on a page labeled "Nonfiction Ideas" in the writing ideas section of their writing notebooks. After the quick-write, have partners share their ideas with each other and then have several volunteers share their ideas with the class. Encourage the students to continue to add to their nonfiction ideas during writing time, if they wish.

WRITING TIME

▶4 Write Independently

Ask the students to return to their seats. Write the following choices
on the board and have the students write silently for 20–30 minutes.

- Add to your list of interesting nonfiction topics.

- Work on a piece you started earlier.

- Start a new piece of writing.

Join the students in writing for 5–10 minutes; then confer with
individual students.

TEACHER CONFERENCE NOTE

Continue to call individual students to a back table and
quietly confer with them for 5–10 minutes each. Have
the students read their writing aloud to you, and discuss
questions such as:

Q *Where did you get this idea?*

Q *What do you like about writing so far this year?*

Q *What kinds of things do you want to write, or write about,
in the coming year?*

Q *How do you want to improve as a writer this year?*

Document your observations for each student using the
"Conference Notes" record sheets (BLM1).

Signal to let the students know when writing time is over.

SHARING AND REFLECTING

▶ 5 Confer in Pairs

Explain that partners will meet to confer about their writing. Remind them that during pair conferences both partners will read and discuss their writing with each other. Ask:

Q *What will you and your partner do to act responsibly during pair conference time today?*

Q *What are some things you can say to your partner to show that you are interested in his or her writing?*

> **Students might say:**
>
> "I can say, 'I like the part where this or that happened.'"
>
> "My partner and I can be responsible by focusing on our writing and not talking about other things."

Give the students several minutes to confer in pairs.

CLASS ASSESSMENT NOTE

Observe the students, without interacting with them, as they confer in pairs. Ask yourself:

- Do partners seem able to hear each other?

- Are they reading their writing to each other?

- Are they taking time to talk about the writing?

- What problems are pairs having that I want to bring up during the reflection discussion?

Record your observations in the *Assessment Resource Book.*

When you notice the pair conferences winding down, signal for attention and bring the class back together.

Reflect on Pair Conferences

Ask and briefly discuss the questions that follow. Remind the students to use the prompts when they contribute to the discussion.

Q *What went well in your pair conference today?*

Q *What problems did you have? How will you avoid those problems the next time you confer?*

Q *I noticed that some pairs had trouble [hearing each other because the room was so loud]. How can we avoid that problem next time?*

Day 2

Getting Ideas from a Story Based on Facts

In this lesson, the students:

- Hear and discuss a narrative text based on facts
- Use discussion prompts to build on one another's thinking
- Write freely about things that interest them
- Use writing and pair conference time responsibly

Materials

- *Atlantic*
- Charted discussion prompts from Day 1
- *Assessment Resource Book*

GETTING READY TO WRITE

▶1 Gather and Briefly Review

Gather the class with partners sitting together, facing you. Remind the students that yesterday they heard part of *Oceans and Seas,* a nonfiction book about Earth's oceans. Explain that today they will hear how an author writes about the same topic in a different way. Ask the students to think about whether they might like to try writing something like this themselves.

▶2 Read *Atlantic* Aloud

Show the cover of *Atlantic* and read the title and the author's name aloud. Read pages 5–11 aloud; then reread from the beginning, asking the students to listen carefully for anything they might have missed the first time. Continue reading slowly and clearly, showing the illustrations and clarifying vocabulary as you read.

Suggested Vocabulary

ebb and flood: water going away from the shore and coming back in (p. 19)

probed: investigated carefully (p. 20)

longlines: long fishing lines (p. 23)

cerulean, cobalt and ultramarine: different shades of blue (p. 24)

ELL Vocabulary

English Language Learners may benefit from discussing additional vocabulary, including:

conquered: took over (p. 20)

oyster beds: areas at the bottom of the ocean where a lot of oysters grow (p. 23)

3 ▶ Discuss *Atlantic* and Compare with *Oceans and Seas*

Ask and briefly discuss the question that follows. Remind the students to use the three prompts to add to the discussion.

Q *How is this book similar to* Oceans and Seas? *How is it different?*

> **Students might say:**
>
> "They are both about the ocean."
>
> "I agree with [Kevin] because both books told things about the ocean, like how there are tides and how the ocean changes shape."
>
> "In addition to what [Joanne] said, *Atlantic* is more like a story."
>
> "I agree with [Dierdre]. It doesn't have chapters or tell you what the words mean."

Point out that the author of *Atlantic* gives readers information about the Atlantic Ocean using "I," as if the ocean were telling the story.

Q *If you wanted to write a story in which "I" is a thing rather than a person, what could that thing be?*

As the students generate ideas, record the ideas where everyone can see them.

Teacher Note

The discussion prompts are:

- "I agree with _____ because…"
- "I disagree with _____ because…"
- "In addition to what _____ said, I think…"

Teacher Note

If you notice that the students are not using the prompts, pause during the discussion to ask, "How can you say that using one of the discussion prompts?"

> "I" could be:
>
> lava
>
> a shark
>
> a tree
>
> a fire truck

◀ **Teacher Note**

If the students have difficulty generating ideas for "I," suggest some like those in the diagram to stimulate their thinking.

4 ▶ **Quick-Write: Using "I" for an Inanimate Thing**

Ask partners to choose one of the recorded ideas and together come up with a couple of "I" sentences they could write from that thing's point of view. Give partners a few moments to talk; then have a few pairs share their sentences with the class.

Have each student pick another of the recorded ideas and do an individual 5-minute quick-write, writing several "I" sentences from that thing's point of view. Have the students write on the next blank page of their writing notebooks.

After 5 minutes, signal for the students' attention and have several volunteers read their sentences aloud. Encourage the students to continue to add to this piece of writing during writing time, if they wish.

WRITING TIME

5 ▶ **Write Independently**

Ask the students to return to their seats. Write the following choices on the board. Have the students write silently for 20–30 minutes.

- Continue the "I" piece you started during today's quick-write.

- Work on a piece you started earlier.

- Start a new piece of writing.

Join them in writing for 5–10 minutes; then confer with individual students.

TEACHER CONFERENCE NOTE

Continue to confer with individual students for 5–10 minutes each. Have them read their writing aloud to you. Discuss questions such as:

Q *Where did you get this idea?*

Q *What do you like about writing so far this year?*

Q *What kinds of things do you want to write, or write about, in the coming year?*

Q *How do you want to improve as a writer this year?*

Document your observations for each student using the "Conference Notes" record sheets (BLM1).

Signal to let the students know when writing time is over.

SHARING AND REFLECTING

 Confer in Pairs

Explain that partners will meet to confer about their writing. Remind them that during pair conferences each partner will read his writing aloud to the other, and they'll talk about their writing.

Give the students several minutes to confer in pairs.

CLASS ASSESSMENT NOTE

Observe the students, without interacting with them, as they confer in pairs. Ask yourself:

* Do partners seem able to hear each other?

* Are they reading their writing to each other?

continues

CLASS ASSESSMENT NOTE *continued*

- Are they taking time to talk about the writing?

- What problems are pairs having that I want to bring up during the reflection discussion?

Record your observations in the *Assessment Resource Book*.

When you notice the pair conferences winding down, signal for attention and bring the class back together.

 Reflect on Pair Conferences

Ask and briefly discuss:

Q *What went well in your pair conference today?*

Q *What problems did you have? How will you avoid those problems the next time you have a pair conference?*

Day 3

Materials

- *I Wonder Why the Sea Is Salty*
- Charted discussion prompts

Getting Ideas from Nonfiction

In this lesson, the students:

- List questions about a nonfiction topic
- Write freely about things that interest them
- Use discussion prompts to build on one another's thinking
- Use writing and pair conference time responsibly
- Express interest in and appreciation for one another's writing

GETTING READY TO WRITE

▶1 Gather and Briefly Review

Gather the class with partners sitting together, facing you. Remind the students that they heard *Atlantic* and parts of *Oceans and Seas*. Ask the question that follows, and remind the students to use the discussion prompts as they respond.

Q *What do you remember about the ways the authors communicated information about the ocean in these two books?*

Explain that you will read from another nonfiction book on the topic of oceans and seas. Point out that this one is organized differently from the other two, and invite the students to think about whether they might like to try writing a book like this today.

▶2 Read from *I Wonder Why the Sea Is Salty* Aloud

Show the cover of *I Wonder Why the Sea Is Salty* and read the title aloud. Show the table of contents on pages 2–3 and read some of the questions aloud. Read pages 4–9 aloud slowly and clearly, showing the illustrations and clarifying vocabulary.

FACILITATION TIP

Continue to reinforce the students' responsibility during class discussions by reminding them to **turn and look** at the person who will speak, having speakers wait until they have the class's attention before starting to speak, and asking one another to speak up if they can't hear. Also remind the students to use the discussion prompts to address their comments directly to one another. Notice the effect of using these facilitation techniques on the students' engagement in class discussions over time.

Suggested Vocabulary

merchant ships: ships loaded with things to sell (p. 8)

ELL Vocabulary

English Language Learners may benefit from discussing additional vocabulary, including:

enormous: very big (p. 4)

Ask and discuss the question that follows. Be ready to reread from the text to help the students recall what they heard. Remind them to use the charted prompts to add to the discussion.

Q *How does the author give us information about the ocean in this book?*

Students might say:

"The author writes a question and then gives an answer."

"In addition to what [Tania] said, there's information about the ocean in the captions that go with the pictures."

Read several more questions in the table of contents aloud. Select a few as a class and read the answers aloud.

▶3 ## Quick-Write: Generate Questions About a Nonfiction Topic

Ask the students to review the nonfiction topics they listed earlier in the week in the writing ideas section of their notebooks and pick one they are especially curious about. Have them open their notebooks to the next blank page and write that topic at the top of the page. Ask them to think quietly for a moment about:

Q *If you were going to write a question-and-answer book about the topic you chose, what questions might you ask in your book?*

Have the students take 5 minutes to jot down their own questions; then have them discuss their topics and questions in pairs. Signal for their attention and give them a few minutes to write down any additional questions that came up while they were talking. Have a few volunteers share their topic and some of their questions with the class.

Teacher Note

The discussion prompts are:

- "I agree with _____ because…"
- "I disagree with _____ because…"
- "In addition to what _____ said, I think…"

Encourage the students to add to their list of questions during writing time today, if they wish.

WRITING TIME

4▶ Write Independently

Ask the students to return to their seats. Write the following choices on the board and have the students write silently for 20–30 minutes.

- Write more questions about a nonfiction topic.

- Work on a piece you started earlier.

- Start a new piece of writing.

Join the students in writing for 5–10 minutes; then confer with individual students.

TEACHER CONFERENCE NOTE

Continue to confer with individual students for 5–10 minutes each. Have them read their writing aloud to you. Discuss questions such as:

Q *Where did you get this idea?*

Q *What do you like about writing so far this year?*

Q *What kinds of things do you want to write, or write about, in the coming year?*

Q *How do you want to improve as a writer this year?*

Document your observations for each student using the "Conference Notes" record sheets (BLM1).

Signal to let the students know when writing time is over.

SHARING AND REFLECTING

5▶ Confer in Pairs

Have partners meet for pair conferences. Encourage them to listen again today for at least one thing they like about their partner's writing to share with the class.

6▶ Reflect on Pair Conferences

After partners have conferred, signal for their attention. Ask and briefly discuss:

Q *What is one thing you liked about your partner's writing? Why did you like that part?*

Q *What is one thing your partner liked about your piece of writing? You may read that part aloud, if you wish.*

EXTENSION

Technology Tip: Further Explore Oceans and Seas

If the students are interested, encourage them to research oceans and seas further by doing an online search using the keywords "oceans and seas." They might also be interested in researching particular bodies of water (e.g., the Indian Ocean, the Gulf of Mexico) or particular animals that live in the ocean (e.g., sharks, whales, dolphins).

Day 4

Materials

- Collected nonbook writing (see "Do Ahead" on page 79)
- "Writing Ideas" chart
- Charted discussion prompts
- Chart paper and a marker
- *Assessment Resource Book*

Getting Ideas from Nonfiction

In this lesson, the students:

- Discuss examples of nonbook writing
- Write freely about things that interest them
- Use discussion prompts to build on one another's thinking
- Ask one another questions about their writing
- Use pair conference time responsibly

GETTING READY TO WRITE

1 Gather and Discuss Using Prompts

Gather the class with partners sitting together, facing you. Remind them that they learned three prompts to help them build on one another's thinking during class discussions. Ask and briefly discuss:

Q *How does using the prompts help you listen carefully during class discussions?*

Encourage the students to continue to use the prompts today and tell them that you will check in with them periodically.

Teacher Note ▶

Encourage the students to continue to use the prompts during whole-class discussions throughout the year to help them listen and connect their ideas. Regularly remind them to use the prompts until it becomes natural for them to do so.

2 Discuss Examples of Nonbook Writing

Briefly review that the students have heard different kinds of writing in the past few weeks. Point out that there are many kinds of writing besides books. Show and briefly describe the flyers, brochures, instructions, advertisements, and/or other writing examples you have collected.

Explain that all of these pieces of writing are examples of the kinds of things the students can try writing on their own. Take just a few minutes to discuss questions such as:

Q *If you were going to write an advertisement for your favorite thing, what might you write about?*

Q *If you were going to write a brochure for your fantasy vacation, what might you include in it?*

Q *If you were going to write instructions for something you know how to do, what might it be?*

WRITING TIME

3 **Write Independently**

Ask the students to return to their seats. Write the following choices on the board and have the students write silently for 20–30 minutes.

- Write advertisements, flyers, signs, recipes, brochures, or other kinds of nonbook writing.

- Work on a piece you started earlier.

- Start a new piece of writing.

Join the students in writing for 5–10 minutes; then confer with individual students.

TEACHER CONFERENCE NOTE

Continue to confer with individual students for 5–10 minutes each. Have them read their writing aloud to you. Discuss questions such as:

Q *Where did you get this idea?*

Q *What do you like about writing so far this year?*

continues

> **TEACHER CONFERENCE NOTE** *continued*
>
> **Q**   *What kinds of things do you want to write, or write about, in the coming year?*
>
> **Q**   *How do you want to improve as a writer this year?*
>
> Document your observations for each student using the "Conference Notes" record sheets (BLM1).

Signal to let the students know when writing time is over.

SHARING AND REFLECTING

4 ▶ **Discuss Asking a Question During Pair Conferences**

Explain that today partners will ask questions about each other's writing during pair conferences. Ask each student to take a moment to reread the writing he will share with his partner today. Then ask:

Teacher Note ▶

Q   *What is one question you'd like to ask your partner about your own piece of writing?*

Students might say:

"I can ask my partner what part he liked best."

"I can ask my partner to tell me if anything was confusing."

"I want to ask my partner how she felt when I read her my piece."

Briefly discuss:

Q   *What will you and your partner do to act responsibly during pair conference time today?*

Tell the students you will check in with them afterward to see how they did. Give them time to confer in pairs.

Teacher Note

If the students have difficulty generating questions, offer some suggestions like those in the "Students might say" note.

CLASS ASSESSMENT NOTE

Observe the students, without interacting with them, as they confer in pairs. Ask yourself:

- Do partners seem able to hear each other?

- Are they reading their writing to each other?

- Are they asking each other questions about their own writing?

- What problems are pairs having that I want to bring up during the reflection discussion?

Record your observations in the *Assessment Resource Book*.

When you notice the pair conferences winding down, signal for attention and bring the class back together.

5 ▶ Reflect on Pair Conferences and Community

Ask and briefly discuss:

Q *What question did you ask your partner about your writing today? How did your partner respond?*

Q *How did you act responsibly during your pair conference?*

Q *I noticed that in some pairs, students [forgot to talk about the writing after reading it aloud]. How can we avoid that problem next time? Why is that important?*

Q *How do you think we're doing building our writing community? What else can we do?*

Overview

UNIT 1: THE WRITING COMMUNITY

Hello Ocean
by Pam Muñoz Ryan, illustrated by Mark Astrella
(Charlesbridge, 2001)

A young girl experiences the ocean with all of her senses.

In November
by Cynthia Rylant, illustrated by Jill Kastner
(Harcourt, 2000)

Sensory words describe this cold winter month.

Writing Focus

- Students hear and discuss good writing.

- Students use sensory details in their writing.

- Students write about things that interest them.

- Partners confer with each other.

- Teacher confers with students.

Social Focus

- Students build the writing community.

- Students express interest in and appreciation for one another's writing.

"For me, a good page of prose is where one hears the rain."
        — John Cheever

Close your eyes and imagine being in one of your favorite (or least favorite) places. Ask yourself:

- What do you see around you? What is the light like?

- What sounds do you hear?

- What do you smell? Taste?

- Is it cold? Warm? Hot? What other sensations do you feel?

Describe this place in writing. Include sensory details that a reader could use to "hear the rain."

Day 1

Materials

- *Hello Ocean*
- Chart paper and a marker

Getting Ideas for Sensory Details

In this lesson, the students:

- Hear and discuss a narrative text
- Use sensory details in their writing
- Write freely about things that interest them
- Give their full attention to the person who is speaking
- Express interest in and appreciation for one another's writing

GETTING READY TO WRITE

1▶ Build the Writing Community

Gather the class with partners sitting together, facing you. Have the students bring their writing notebooks and pencils with them.

Remind the students that they are working on creating a safe, caring writing community in which everyone feels comfortable expressing their creativity through writing. Ask:

 Q *If a new student were to join our class, what would you tell him or her about our writing community? Turn to your partner.*

Have several volunteers share with the class. Ask follow-up questions such as:

Q *What would you want to tell the new student about our independent writing time? Pair conferring? Sharing our writing as a class?*

Q *What more can we do to make our writing community caring and respectful for everyone?*

Encourage the students to keep their ideas in mind and to continue to build a community that feels good for everyone.

2 ▶ Read *Hello Ocean* Aloud

Explain that this week the students will hear two more books and think about how to tell more in their writing using sensory details. Explain that sensory details are details that help a reader imagine using the five senses: sight, hearing, smell, taste, or touch.

Show the cover of *Hello Ocean* and read the title and the author's and illustrator's names aloud. Ask the students to listen for words that help them imagine using their senses.

Read the book slowly and clearly, showing the illustrations and clarifying vocabulary as you read.

Suggested Vocabulary

chameleon: a lizard that changes color (p. 4)

disclose: tell (p. 22)

fragrant ore: rocks that have a nice smell (p. 23)

kelp: seaweed (p. 24)

ELL Vocabulary

English Language Learners may benefit from discussing additional vocabulary, including:

embrace: hug (p. 14)

aromas: smells (p. 22)

inhale: breath in (p. 22)

3 ▶ Discuss the Story

Discuss the questions that follow. Be ready to reread from the text to help the students recall what they heard.

Q *What is this place like?*

Q (Show page 3.) *What do you think is meant by "I'm here with the five of me, again?"*

Point out that in *Hello Ocean* the child experiences the ocean using all five senses, "five of me," and sensory details help us as readers imagine using those senses, too.

Ask:

Q (Reread pages 14–19.) *What sensory details did you hear that help you imagine what this place feels like?*

Students might say:

"I heard the words 'wet embrace.' I imagined the ocean giving her a hug."

"In addition to what [Kieran] said, the words 'sudden breezes' made me imagine the wind blowing on the beach."

"When I heard the words 'tide that tickles' I imagined feeling the water tickling me."

▶ 4 Quick-Write: Sensory Details for a Favorite Place

Ask the students to think of a place that they really like to be. After a moment, have them close their eyes and get a mental picture as they listen to the questions that follow. Pause between the questions to give the students time to visualize. Ask:

Q *What do you see around you?*

Q *What sounds do you hear?*

Q *What do you smell and/or taste?*

Q *What other things do you feel in this place?*

Have the students open their eyes. Call on four or five volunteers to share some of the sights, sounds, smells, tastes, and sensations they imagined. As they share, record their ideas as brief notes on a sheet of chart paper entitled "Sensory Details."

Sensory Details

sand and water

noises from electronic games

the smell of pizza

sweet chocolate flavor

cold water in the pool

Have the students turn to the next blank page of their writing notebooks and write some other sensory details to describe the place they imagined. After 5 minutes, signal for the students' attention and have several volunteers read what they wrote to the class. Encourage the students to continue to include sensory details in the writing they do today.

WRITING TIME

 5 Write Independently

Ask the students to return to their seats. Write the following choices on the board and have students write silently for 20–30 minutes.

- Work on a piece you started earlier.

- Start a new piece of writing.

- Include sensory details like those you wrote during the quick-write.

Join the students in writing for 5–10 minutes; then confer with individual students.

TEACHER CONFERENCE NOTE

Continue to confer with individual students for 5–10 minutes each. Have them read their writing aloud to you. Discuss questions such as:

Q *Where did you get this idea?*

Q *What do you like about writing so far this year?*

Q *What kinds of things do you want to write, or write about, in the coming year?*

Q *How do you want to improve as a writer this year?*

Document your observations for each student using the "Conference Notes" record sheets (BLM1).

Signal to let the students know when writing time is over.

SHARING AND REFLECTING

6▶ Confer in Pairs

Explain that partners will meet to confer about their writing. Remind them that during pair conferences each partner will read his writing aloud to the other and they'll talk about their writing. Give the students several minutes to confer in pairs.

7▶ Reflect on Writing and Pair Conferences

Signal for the students' attention. Facilitate a discussion using the questions that follow and encourage the students to give their full attention to the person who is speaking.

Q　*What did your partner write about today?*

Q　*What sensory details did you hear in your partner's writing?*

 Q　*What did you enjoy or appreciate about your partner's writing today? Turn and tell your partner.*

Q　*Were you able to give your full attention to the person who was speaking? If not, what will help you do that next time?*

Teacher Note

Save the "Sensory Details" chart to use on Day 2 and throughout the coming weeks.

Day 2

Getting Ideas for Sensory Details

In this lesson, the students:

- Hear and discuss a narrative text
- Use sensory details in their writing
- Write freely about things that interest them
- Give their full attention to the person who is speaking
- Express interest in and appreciation for one another's writing

Materials

- *In November*
- "Writing Ideas" chart
- "Sensory Details" chart from Day 1

GETTING READY TO WRITE

▶1 Gather and Briefly Review

Gather the class with partners sitting together, facing you. Remind the students that they heard *Hello Ocean* and thought about sensory details in their writing. Direct the students' attention to the "Writing Ideas" chart and review the items on it. Add *using sensory details to help the reader imagine using the senses (sight, hearing, smell, taste, touch)*. Remind the students to use the chart to help them get ideas for their own writing.

Explain that the students will hear another book in which the author uses many sensory details. Ask the students to listen for these as you read.

▶2 Read *In November* Aloud

Show the cover of *In November* and read the title and the author's and illustrator's names aloud. Read the story slowly and clearly, showing the illustrations.

Discuss the Story and Generate Ideas About Other Months

Briefly discuss the questions that follow. Be ready to reread from the text to help the students recall what they heard.

Q *What is the month of November like in this book?*

Q *What kinds of things do we smell in November? Hear? Taste? Feel?*

As the students respond, record their ideas on the "Sensory Details" chart. Use "Think, Pair, Share" to have the students first think about and then discuss:

 Q *If you wanted to write a story like this about a different month, what month would you choose and what would you say?* [pause] *Turn to your partner.*

Have several volunteers share with the class. Record their ideas on the chart.

Teacher Note ▶

If the students have difficulty generating ideas, suggest some like those in the "Students might say" note and ask, "What else could you write about?"

> ***Students might say:***
>
> "I would write about October. In October you carve pumpkins and put on costumes."
>
> "I would write about June. That's the beginning of summer vacation!"
>
> "In August we go swimming and wear shorts and eat popsicles."

Encourage the students to write about a month they like during writing time, if they wish, and to use sensory details in their writing.

WRITING TIME

 Write Independently

Ask the students to return to their seats. Write the following choices on the board and have students write silently for 20–30 minutes.

- Write about a month you like.

- Work on a piece you started earlier.

- Start a new piece of writing.

Join students in writing for 5–10 minutes; then confer with individual students.

Signal to let the students know when writing time is over.

SHARING AND REFLECTING

5▶ Confer in Pairs

Have partners meet for pair conferences. Remind them that partners will read and discuss their writing with each other. Encourage them to listen for at least one thing they like about their partner's writing to share with her.

6▶ Reflect on Pair Conferences

Signal for the students' attention. Facilitate a discussion using the questions that follow and encourage the students to give their full attention to the person who is speaking. Ask:

Q *Did you or your partner write a book like* In November *today? Tell us about it.*

Q *What sensory details did you or your partner include?*

Q *What did you enjoy or appreciate about your partner's writing today? Turn and tell your partner.*

Day 3

Materials

- *In November* from Day 1
- *Student Writing Handbook* for each student

Getting Ideas for Sensory Details

In this lesson, the students:

- Hear and discuss a narrative text
- Use sensory details in their writing
- Write freely about things that interest them
- Give their full attention to the person who is sharing
- Express interest in and appreciation for one another's writing

GETTING READY TO WRITE

▶ 1 Gather and Explore Sensory Details in *In November*

Gather the class with partners sitting together, facing you. Remind the students that yesterday they heard *In November* by Cynthia Rylant. Ask:

Q *What do you remember from this book about the month of November?*

Ask the students to close their eyes and imagine as you read a passage aloud from the book. Ask them to listen for words and phrases that help them get a mental picture. Read the following passage aloud twice.

p. 4 "In November, the earth is growing quiet. It is making its bed, a winter bed for flowers and small creatures. The bed is white and silent, and much life can hide beneath its blankets."

Ask:

Q *What words or phrases did you hear that helped you imagine?*

Distribute the *Student Writing Handbooks,* one to each student. Explain that the *Student Writing Handbook* contains copies of passages from the read-alouds, as well as spelling lists and other kinds of pages to help the students with their writing this year.

Have the students open their *Student Writing Handbook* to page 2, and explain that this passage and several others from *In November* are reproduced on the page. Ask partners to work together to read the four passages and to underline words and phrases that help them get mental images.

After a few minutes, call for the students' attention and have several pairs share words that they underlined. Encourage them to give their full attention to the people who are speaking.

Before writing time today, ask the students to circle a word or phrase they particularly like on *Student Writing Handbook* page 2. Challenge them to try to include that word or phrase somewhere in their own writing today.

WRITING TIME

 2 Write Independently

Ask the students to return to their seats. Write the following choices on the board and have the students write silently for 20–30 minutes.

- Work on a piece you started earlier.

- Start a new piece of writing.

- Try to include the circled word or phrase in your own writing.

- Include other sensory details.

Join the students in writing for 5–10 minutes; then confer with individual students.

Signal to let the students know when writing time is over.

SHARING AND REFLECTING

 Confer in Pairs

Have partners meet for pair conferences. Remind them that partners will read and discuss their writing with each other. Encourage them to listen for at least one thing they like about their partner's writing to share.

4 ▶ **Reflect on Pair Conferences**

Signal for the students' attention. Facilitate a discussion using the questions that follow. Encourage the students to give their full attention to the person who is speaking.

Q   *Were you able to use the word or phrase from* In November *you circled in your own writing today? Read us what you wrote.*

Q   *What other sensory details did you or your partner write today?*

Q   *What did you enjoy or appreciate about your partner's writing today?*

Day 4

Getting Ideas and Sharing

Materials

• *Assessment Resource Book*

In this lesson, the students:

• Select and share a favorite sentence

• Write freely about things that interest them

• Give their full attention to the person who is speaking

• Express interest in and appreciation for one another's writing

• Ask one another questions about their writing

GETTING READY TO WRITE

▶ 1 Gather and Share Favorite Sentences

Gather the class with partners sitting together, facing you. Remind them to bring their writing notebooks and pencils with them.

Ask the students to take a moment to look over this week's writing and to underline a favorite sentence they wrote to share with the class. Explain that it can be a sentence with good sensory details, interesting action, or anything else that makes it a special sentence.

After allowing sufficient time for students to underline their sentences, go around the room and have each student read his sentence aloud, without discussion. Encourage the students to give their full attention to the person who is speaking.

When everyone has shared, ask and briefly discuss:

Q *What sentence did you hear that got you interested in someone else's writing?*

Q *What questions do you want to ask a classmate about his or her writing?*

Tell the students that they will share favorite sentences after independent writing time today, and encourage them to write interesting sentences that they can share with the class.

WRITING TIME

 Write Independently

Ask the students to return to their seats. Write the following choices on the board and have the students write silently for 20–30 minutes.

- Work on a piece you started earlier.

- Start a new piece of writing.

Join the students in writing for 5–10 minutes; then walk around and observe.

CLASS ASSESSMENT NOTE

Observe the students and ask yourself:

- Do the students write readily?

- Do the students who initially have difficulty eventually start writing, or do they continue to struggle?

- Are they focused and engaged in their own writing? Do they stay engaged for the full writing time?

Note students who still struggle to start writing or have difficulty sustaining their writing focus. Continue to try to tap into their intrinsic motivation by encouraging them to write about things that genuinely interest them. Plan to closely monitor these students as you proceed with the next unit.

Record your observations in the *Assessment Resource Book*.

Signal to let the students know when writing time is over.

SHARING AND REFLECTING

3 ▶ **Share Favorite Sentences**

Ask the students to look over today's writing and underline a favorite sentence that they wrote to share with the class. After allowing sufficient time for students to select their sentences, go around the room and have each student read her sentence aloud, without discussion. Encourage the students to give their full attention to the person who is sharing his writing.

When everyone has shared, ask and briefly discuss:

Q *What did you hear that got you interested in someone else's writing?*

Q *Did knowing that you were going to share a sentence help you to write more interesting sentences today? Tell us about it.*

4 ▶ **Reflect on Sharing and Giving Full Attention to the Person Speaking**

Ask and briefly discuss:

Q *How does it feel to have everyone's full attention when you share your writing? How does it feel when you don't have everyone's full attention?*

Students might say:

"I feel like people are really interested in what I've written. That feels good."

"I agree with [Henry]. When everyone listens, I feel like my writing is interesting to other kids."

"In addition to what [Maria] said, if I know that people are really going to listen to my writing, it makes me try harder to be a good writer."

Encourage the students to continue to build the writing community by giving their full, respectful attention whenever a classmate is sharing her thinking or writing.

◀ **Teacher Note**

Students will keep the same partner in Unit 2.

Unit 2

The Writing Process

Unit 2

The Writing Process

Unit 2

The Writing Process

During this three-week unit, the students learn about the writing process by working with a piece of writing from the first draft through publication. They select a draft to develop, reread their work critically, ask themselves questions about their writing, and revise, proofread, and publish their writing. They learn about a professional author's writing process, and they continue to confer about their writing in a caring and responsible way.

UNIT OVERVIEW

WEEK	DAY 1	DAY 2	DAY 3	DAY 4
1	**Selecting Drafts** **Focus:** Author Judy Blume	**Completing First Drafts** **Focus:** Finishing pieces in preparation for revision	**Analyzing and Revising Drafts** **Focus:** Guided rereading to add details	**Pair Conferring** **Focus:** Asking questions
2	**Analyzing and Revising Drafts** **Focus:** Guided revision to add interesting words	**Analyzing and Revising Drafts** **Focus:** Guided revision of opening sentences	**Analyzing and Revising Drafts** **Focus:** Good titles	**Pair Conferring** **Focus:** Initiating pair conferences
3	**Proofreading** **Focus:** Spelling	**Proofreading and Publishing** **Focus:** Punctuation	**Publishing** **Focus:** Making books	**Publishing** **Focus:** Sharing from the Author's Chair

UNIT 2: THE WRITING PROCESS

"More About Judy Blume"
excerpted from Author Talk, compiled and edited by
Leonard S. Marcus (Simon & Schuster, 2000) and from
www.judyblume.com (see page 136)

Judy Blume shares about her writing process.

Writing Focus

- Students review their recent drafts and select one to develop and publish.

- Students reread their writing critically.

- Students add sensory details to their writing.

- Students revise their writing with input from others.

- Students confer with one another and the teacher.

Social Focus

- Students work in a responsible way.

- Students listen respectfully to the thinking of others and share their own.

- Students help one another improve their writing.

DO AHEAD

- (Optional) Prior to Day 3, review the pieces you have written so far this year and select a short passage to use to model adding details to a draft. Make a transparency of the passage. Alternatively, you can use the "Sample First Draft" (BLM2–BLM3).

TEACHER AS WRITER

"One of the secrets of literature that every writer knows is that any life will do. It's not necessary to go bathe one's feet in the Ganges and travel around the world and work on a steamer to be a poet.… Meaning is in small things."

— *Marvin Bell*

Choose a list from those you wrote in Unit 1, Week 3. Write a short passage using some ideas from that list. For example:

Quiet Things

Sleeping dog	Sunday morning
Laundry drying	Cup of tea
Midnight	Wet grass
Breeze	Mute button
Stars	Whispers

At dawn on Sunday, I step outside with a steaming cup of tea. The last stars fade as I cross the lawn, my bare feet whispering on wet grass. A breeze stirs the laundry, left overnight on the line. I feel the shirts and pants with my hands. I ask myself, are they still damp or just cold?

Day 1

Materials

- "More About Judy Blume" (see page 136)
- *The Pain and The Great One* from Unit 1

Selecting Drafts

In this lesson, the students:

- Learn about an author's writing process
- Review their recent drafts and select one to develop and publish
- Reread their writing critically
- Ask one another questions about their writing
- Share their partner's thinking with the class

About Teaching the Writing Process

In Unit 2, the students are introduced to the writing process. They select a draft to develop, analyze and revise the draft, proofread their work, and publish it. They confer about their drafts and consider various ways to improve their writing. The process they learn in this unit will be repeated in each of the genre units, so the students will have multiple opportunities to hone their revision, proofreading, and publishing skills.

If your students are familiar with the writing process from prior years, acknowledge this prior learning. Explain that during this unit they will review and learn more about the writing process.

GETTING READY TO WRITE

Teacher Note

In this unit, students will work with the same partner they had in Unit 1.

1 ▶ **Gather and Briefly Review**

Gather the class with partners sitting together, facing you. Remind the students that over the past weeks they have been hearing various kinds of books and getting many different ideas for writing. Explain that in the coming weeks each student will develop one piece of writing into a book for the classroom library. Point out that because other people will read their books, they will want to make the books as interesting, inviting, and free of errors as any other book in the library. Today they will review all the drafts they have written so far this year and select one to finish and develop into a book.

Before the students select their drafts, explain that they will learn a little about how Judy Blume, a professional author they met in Unit 1, develops a piece of writing into a book.

2 ▶ Learn More About Judy Blume

Remind the students that they heard *The Pain and The Great One* earlier in the year. Briefly review the story by asking:

Q *What do you remember about this story?*

Have a few volunteers share. Reread a few passages, if necessary, to help the students recall the story.

Explain that you will read a little more about Judy Blume. Point out that in these passages Judy Blume talks about her typical day and how she drafts and writes her books.

Read "More About Judy Blume" aloud slowly and clearly. Ask:

Q *What did you learn about Judy Blume's writing process?*

Q *Why do you think she feels the most creative when she's rewriting?*

> **Students might say:**
>
> "I learned that Judy Blume thinks revising is what she likes best about writing."
>
> "I think she means that she has her story together and now she can have some fun with it and jazz it up."

3 ▶ Prepare to Review Drafts

Point out that a professional author usually works a long time on a piece of writing to get it ready to be *published*, or made into a book to be read by others. An author starts with an idea or a first draft. After that, she rewrites, does research, adds and takes out words and information, and makes the piece more interesting. This process is called *revision*. Explain that in the coming three weeks the students will revise a piece of writing to get it ready to publish.

ELL Note

You might provide the prompt "I remember that…" to your English Language Learners to help them verbalize their answers to this question.

Explain that during writing time today you would like the students to carefully reread all the drafts they have written in their writing notebooks and select one draft to revise and publish. Encourage the students to select a draft they are interested in, that they can imagine making changes to, and that will be fun to develop into a book for their classmates to read.

WRITING TIME

▶4 Reread Drafts and Select One to Develop

Have the students return to their seats, reread their drafts, and select one that they want to develop into a book. Once they have chosen a draft, they should start thinking about what they can add or change to make it more interesting and complete.

As the students review their drafts, circulate around the room. Support students by asking them questions such as:

Q *Why did you choose this piece to revise?*

Q *What can you imagine adding to or changing in this piece to make it more interesting?*

SHARING AND REFLECTING

▶5 Share About Selected Drafts in Pairs

Gather the class with partners sitting together. Explain that partners will talk about the drafts that they selected and why they chose those drafts. Ask:

Q *What questions can you ask your partner about the draft he or she chose?*

Students might say:

"I could ask my partner why she chose that draft to publish."

"I could ask my partner how he's thinking of changing his draft to make it interesting for someone to read."

Teacher Note ▶

Encourage the students to select pieces that offer revision possibilities. These include narratives of most kinds. If you notice them selecting pieces with limited potential for revision (for example, one word per page alphabet books), gently guide them toward a more appropriate choice. Also, guide them away from drafts that are not double-spaced.

Alert the students to listen carefully to each other, and tell them that they will share what their partner said in the whole-class discussion. Ask partners to start talking.

After several minutes of pair sharing, signal for the students' attention. Have several students share what their partners said about the drafts they chose. Follow up with questions such as:

Q *Why did your partner select that draft?*

Q *What is intriguing to you about your partner's draft?*

Q *What else did your partner tell you about the draft she or he is going to work on to publish?*

6 ▶ Reflect on Partner Work

Help the students reflect on their partner work by briefly discussing:

Q *What did you do today to make sure you could accurately share what your partner said with the class?*

Explain that in future lessons you will ask the students to share their partner's thinking with the class, and encourage them to listen responsibly to each other.

EXTENSION

Technology Tip: Learn More About Judy Blume

If the students are interested in finding out more about Judy Blume, encourage them to do an online search using the keywords "Judy Blume."

Note

You might provide the prompt "My partner said…" to your English Language Learners to help them verbalize their answers to this question.

Day 2

Materials

*   *Assessment Resource Book*

Completing Drafts

In this lesson, the students:

*   Complete the first draft of the piece they will publish
*   Use writing time responsibly
*   Work independently during writing time

GETTING READY TO WRITE

1 Discuss Working Independently

Have partners sit together at desks today. Remind them that they each selected a draft to develop and publish as a book. Explain that you will refer to this draft as the "first draft" of their book. Tell them that in the coming days you will take them through the steps of finishing their first draft, revising it, checking it for correctness, and writing a final version to make the book. They will then read their completed book aloud to the class and place it in the class library.

Point out that during the coming days the students may not always be working on the same step of the writing process at the same time. For example, some students may be revising their first draft while others are illustrating their final version.

Q *What might be challenging about working independently when people are working on different things?*

Q *Why is it important for you to take responsibility for working on and completing your own book?*

Q *If you're not sure what to do next, what can you do?*

Students might say:

"If everyone's working on their own thing, it might be easy to get distracted. We'll have to concentrate."

"I agree with [Felicia]. If I don't take responsibility for my own book, I won't have one to share at the end."

"If we're not sure what to do, we can ask you."

"In addition to what [Lawrence] said, if you're busy, we can ask our partner or someone who's gone on to the next step."

Encourage the students to be aware of how they are taking responsibility for their own work today and over the next several days. Tell them that you will check in with them to see how they are doing.

2 ▶ Discuss Completing First Drafts

Have the students open their writing notebooks to their first draft and quietly reread it. When they have finished, ask them to think quietly to themselves about the following questions. Ask the questions one at a time, pausing after each to give the students time to think. (Don't stop to discuss the questions at this point.)

Q *Does your writing make sense? What parts might you want to check again to make sure that they make sense?*

Q *What still needs to be added to your first draft for it to be finished?*

Q *What else might a reader want to know about when he or she is reading your piece?*

Q *Read the last sentence of your piece. Does it feel like an ending? What more can you write to make it feel like an ending?*

Have partners turn to each other to discuss their thinking. After both partners have had a chance to share their writing and thinking, signal for the students' attention and have a few volunteers share with the class.

Teacher Note

If necessary, remind the students to use the discussion prompts that they learned in Unit 1 as they respond. They are:

- "I agree with _____ because…"
- "I disagree with _____ because…"
- "In addition to what _____ said, I think…"

Explain that the students will finish their drafts today, making sure they've included everything they want to say at this point. If they finish with the draft, they may set it aside until tomorrow and work on another piece of writing. Encourage them to work responsibly and independently during writing time.

WRITING TIME

 Complete First Drafts of Selected Pieces

Have the students work silently for 20–30 minutes to finish their first drafts. Join them in writing for 5–10 minutes and then circulate around the room and observe.

CLASS ASSESSMENT NOTE

Observe the students as they work on their drafts. Ask yourself:

* Have the students selected drafts that lend themselves to revision?

* Will most of them have a finished draft that they can start revising tomorrow?

* If not, how much additional time might they need to finish their drafts?

If you notice that many students need more time to finish their first drafts, have them continue to work on the drafts for an additional day before going on to the Day 3 lesson. Students who have finished may work on another piece of writing.

Record your observations in the *Assessment Resource Book*.

Signal to let the students know when writing time is over. Explain that they will begin to revise their drafts tomorrow.

SHARING AND REFLECTING

4 ▶ **Reflect on Writing and Taking Responsibility**

Help the students reflect on their work today by asking:

Q *What did you do to take responsibility for your own work during writing time today?*

Q *How does it help to build our community when you do that?*

Day 3

Materials

- Pad of small (1½" x 2") self-stick notes for each student
- Transparency of your own writing (see "Do Ahead" on page 119) OR transparency of "Sample First Draft" (BLM2–BLM3)
- Overhead pen

Analyzing and Revising Drafts

In this lesson, the students:

- Reread their drafts critically
- Mark places where they might want to revise
- Think about sensory details they can add
- Begin revising the drafts
- Work responsibly and independently during writing time

About Teaching Revision

The lessons in this unit are designed to give the students guided practice with rereading and critically analyzing their drafts before they put pen to paper to revise. In the initial step of the process, you will ask the students specific questions about their drafts, and they will use self-stick notes to mark places where they could possibly revise. They will then watch you model making some revisions to your piece before starting to revise their own drafts.

GETTING READY TO WRITE

Teacher Note

The purpose of the guided rereading is to give the students experience thinking about their drafts and reading them critically *before* they begin to revise.

▶ 1 Facilitate Guided Rereading of Drafts

Have the students stay at their desks today. Explain that they will think about how they might revise and improve their draft to make it a more interesting book. Have them open their writing notebooks to their draft and quietly reread it. Ask them to look up when they are finished.

Distribute a pad of self-stick notes to each student. Explain that you will ask the students to look for and think about several specific things in their draft.

Say the following prompts one at a time, giving the students several quiet minutes between each prompt to review their drafts and mark passages with the self-stick notes.

- *Find one place in your draft that you really like. This might be a place where you used words you like or one where you wrote a sentence that you like. Put a self-stick note in the margin next to that place and write "I like" on it.*

- *Find a place in your draft where you describe, or could describe, what something looks like. Put a self-stick note in the margin next to that place and write "looks" on it.*

- *Find a place in your draft where you describe, or could describe, sounds. Mark the margin with a self-stick note and write "sounds" on it.*

- *Find a place in your draft where you describe, or could describe, how things smell or taste. Mark the margin with a self-stick note and write "smells" or "tastes" on it.*

When most students have finished, signal for their attention and ask several volunteers to read what they marked. Stimulate their thinking by asking questions such as:

Q *What sensory details might you add there to help the reader imagine what's happening?*

2 Model Revising a Marked Section of the Draft

Explain that during writing time today the students will look at the places that they marked with self-stick notes and add details to help their readers imagine what's happening. Ask the students to watch as you model adding details to a draft.

Show the transparency of your own writing (or the "Sample First Draft," see diagram on page 130) and read it aloud, if you have not yet done so. Wonder aloud about sensory details you could add. Have volunteers share ideas for sensory details and write these on the spaces between the lines.

◀ **Teacher Note**

If necessary, model attaching a self-stick note to the outer margin of a notebook page so it marks the text without covering it up. (See diagram on page 130 for example.)

Teacher Note

If the students have difficulty identifying places in their drafts, call for their attention and show the transparency of your own writing (or the "Sample First Draft," see diagram on the next page) on the overhead projector. Read the passage aloud and model marking a passage. (You might say, "I like the words, 'I wanted to be home riding my shiny red bike' here; they help the reader get a good mental picture.")

You might say, "'Four small puppies came running up to us!' I wonder what I could add here to give the reader a physical description of the puppies. Maybe I'll describe the puppies by writing *The puppies had fluffy black fur and little pink tongues*."

Sample First Draft

One Saturday last year, my parents drove my brother

and me to the home of their friends George and Patty. I

didn't want to go. I wanted to be home riding my shiny

red bike.

George and Patty met us at the door with beaming

smiles. We followed them through their house and out to

the backyard. I heard some tiny barks and some loud barks.

The puppies had fluffy black fur and little pink tongues.
Four small puppies came running up to us! There also was

a big dog that turned out to be the puppies' mother.

looks, smells

Using the same procedure, model a few more examples of adding sensory details to your draft. Explain that the students will follow the same procedure to add sensory details to their own drafts today.

WRITING TIME

Teacher Note ▶

Students may not need a full 20–30 minutes of writing time to make their revisions. Shorten the time, if appropriate.

▶ **3 Revise First Drafts**

Write the following tasks on the board and have the students work silently on them for 15–20 minutes.

* Review the places you marked with self-stick notes.

* Add sensory details to help the reader imagine what's happening.

* Remove the self-stick notes when you finish adding the details.

* If you finish, look for other places to add sensory details, or work on another piece of writing.

As the students work, circulate around the room. Support students who are having difficulty adding to their draft by having them join you at a back table and quietly discussing questions such as:

Q *What were you thinking about when you marked this place on your draft?*

Q *What words could you add here to help your reader [see/hear/ smell/taste/feel] [the apples you picked]?*

Signal to let the students know when writing time is over. Explain that they will continue to revise their drafts in the coming days.

SHARING AND REFLECTING

4▶ Reflect on Writing and Taking Responsibility

Have the students put their pencils away and gather with their notebooks to share their writing. Discuss the questions that follow, and invite the students to read from their drafts as they share.

Q *What details did you add to your draft? Read us that part.*

Q *What do you imagine when you hear [Mindy's] passage?*

Q *What did you do to take responsibility for your own work during writing time today? What might we need to work on as a class?*

Day 4

Materials

- Chart paper and a marker
- *Assessment Resource Book*

Pair Conferring

In this lesson, the students:

- Ask for and receive feedback about their writing
- Give feedback in a helpful way
- Use pair conference time responsibly

GETTING READY TO WRITE

Prepare for Pair Conferences

Explain that today partners will meet to confer about their drafts. This is an opportunity to get feedback from a reader about the strengths of a piece and how it might be improved.

Explain that in the writing community the goal of giving feedback is to help the other person create the best possible piece of writing. It's important that the student both share what she likes about a piece and offer suggestions and questions to help her partner improve the piece. Ask:

Q *What kind of feedback do you think would be helpful to improve a piece of writing? Why?*

Q *If you have questions or suggestions for improving a piece, how would you want to communicate that so it helps your partner?*

Encourage partners to use a helpful tone when giving each other feedback about their writing.

2 ▶ Think About What to Ask Partners During Pair Conferences

Before beginning the pair conferences, ask the students to reread their own draft and think about what they want to ask their partner about the draft. After the students have had a chance to read, ask:

Q *What would you like to ask your partner today about your own draft?*

Have volunteers share their thoughts and record these as questions on a sheet of chart paper labeled "Questions About My Draft."

> **Students might say:**
>
> "I want to ask my partner what part she likes the best."
>
> "I want to ask my partner if he can imagine what's happening."
>
> "I want to find out if anything is confusing to my partner."
>
> "Maybe my partner will have some ideas that I can put into my story."

Explain that each partner will read her draft, including revisions, aloud. Remind the students to use questions on the chart to get specific feedback before going on to the other partner's draft.

3 ▶ Confer in Pairs

Give the students ample time to confer in pairs.

◀ **Teacher Note**

If the students have difficulty answering this question, suggest some ideas like those in the "Students might say" note and ask, "What else can you ask your partner?"

◀ **Teacher Note**

You may want to let pairs spread out in the classroom during the conferences so partners can hear each other.

CLASS ASSESSMENT NOTE

Observe conferring pairs without interacting with them.
Ask yourself:

* Are pairs staying on task, reading and discussing their writing?

* Are they discussing questions from the "Questions About My Draft" chart?

* Are they giving each other specific feedback?

* Are they giving feedback in a helpful way?

Note any difficulties you observe to discuss with the students in Step 4. Record your observations in the *Assessment Resource Book*.

When most pairs have had time to discuss their drafts, signal for the class's attention.

 4 ▶ Reflect on Pair Conferences and Feedback Received

Gather the class and briefly discuss:

Q *What was helpful about the way your partner talked to you today?*

Q *What problems, if any, did you have during pair conferences? What will you do to avoid those problems next time?*

Share any problems you noticed and discuss what the students will do to avoid those problems next time. Ask:

Q *What is one thing your partner told you about your piece?*

Explain that authors take feedback very seriously, although they may not always agree with the feedback. Authors need to decide for themselves what will result in the best possible piece of writing.

WRITING TIME

 Work on Drafts Based on Conference Feedback

Write the following tasks on the board and have the students work silently on them for 15–20 minutes.

- Add or change things in your draft based on partner feedback.

- Add more sensory details to help the reader imagine what's happening.

- If finished, work on another piece of writing.

As the students work, circulate around the room. Support students who are having difficulty incorporating feedback into their draft by having them join you at a back table and quietly discussing questions such as:

Q *What feedback did your partner give you about your draft? Do you agree or disagree with it? Why?*

Q *Your partner said that she [got confused at the end of your story]. What did she say was [confusing] to her? How can you rewrite it [so it's clear]?*

Signal to let the students know when writing time is over.

> ◀ **Teacher Note**
>
> Students may not need a full 20–30 minutes of writing time to make their revisions. Shorten the time, if appropriate.

SHARING AND REFLECTING

 Share Revisions

Have a few volunteers share a revision that they made today by reading the original passage aloud and then reading the revised passage. Have them tell the class why they made the revision and how they think it improves their piece.

> ◀ **Teacher Note**
>
> Save the "Questions About My Draft" chart to use in Week 2.

More About Judy Blume

Excerpted from *Author Talk*, compiled and edited by
Leonard S. Marcus (pp. 7–8) and www.judyblume.com

What is a typical workday like for you?

When I'm working on a book, I eat my breakfast, get dressed, and
go to work, pretending that I'm leaving the house and going to
an office. I work until lunchtime. I force myself to sit at my desk.
I might doodle a lot while I'm writing a first draft. Doodling is
very important to me. I'll write down a word and decorate it. By
the time I get to the end of a first draft, I have a good sense of
the characters. During the next two rewrites I work longer hours
and with more enthusiasm. By the third draft, I'm so into my
characters, I have to be dragged away from my desk.

How do you go about writing a book?

I started by filling out a notebook with notes on characters—
anything and everything that may never go into the book. This
becomes my security blanket. Over the years I've learned to worry
less that the words and ideas won't come. I trust they will.

Do you know from the start how a book will end?

I know the beginning—about the day when something different
happens—and generally where the story's going. But how it will
get there is what I worry about every time I begin a new book. I ask
myself, How am I going to fill up two hundred or three hundred
pages? But if I think of it as a whole book too soon, I'm going to
scare myself. So I try to focus on one scene at a time. It may be just
a page, it may be five or ten pages.

continues

More About Judy Blume

continued

Judy Blume's advice to young writers:

Whenever I talk to kids about writing and tell them it's the rewriting I enjoy most, they groan. I guess if you're in school, rewriting means copying your papers over. But to me, rewriting is the most exciting part of the process. When I'm rewriting, I feel most creative. I've got all the pieces to the puzzle and now I get to put them together. I go through four or five drafts of each book.

Read your work aloud! This is the best advice I can give. When you read aloud you find out how much can be cut, how much is unnecessary. You hear how the story flows. And nothing teaches you as much about writing dialogue as listening to it.

Week 2 Overview

UNIT 2: THE WRITING PROCESS

Writing Focus

- Students analyze and revise their drafts.

- Students generate alternatives for overused words.

- Students look for confusing or extraneous information in their drafts.

- Students explore strong opening sentences.

- Students confer with one another and the teacher.

Social Focus

- Students work in a responsible way.

- Students listen respectfully to the thinking of others and share their own.

- Students help one another improve their writing.

- Students express interest in and appreciation for one another's writing.

DO AHEAD

- (Optional) If computers are available, you might have some students type and print their pieces for publication beginning on Day 4 of this week. You can also recruit parent volunteers to help with this task.

TEACHER AS WRITER

"The beautiful part of writing is that you don't have to get it right the first time, unlike, say, a brain surgeon. You can always do it better, find the exact word, the apt phrase, the leaping simile."

— Robert Cormier

Select a short draft that you've written to revise and develop. Ask yourself the questions that follow and use self-stick notes to mark places you might revise.

- What places in your draft do you really like? Why do you like them?

- Where could you add sensory details to create a mental picture?

- Where could you tell more?

- What could you delete?

- What words could you replace with more interesting ones?

Revise your draft, either by marking up your first draft or by writing a second draft.

Day 1

Materials

- Transparency of your own revised writing OR revised transparency of "Sample First Draft" from Week 1
- Overhead pen
- Chart paper and a marker

Analyzing and Revising Drafts

In this lesson, the students:

- Reread their drafts critically
- Generate alternatives for overused words
- Revise their drafts
- Work independently during writing time
- Give their full attention to the person who is speaking

GETTING READY TO WRITE

1 ▶ Gather and Briefly Review

Have partners sit together at desks today. Review that they began to revise their drafts last week. Remind the students that the purpose of revision is to make their piece of writing as interesting and readable as possible before publishing it. Explain that today you will ask them to think about several more specific ways that they might improve their drafts.

2 ▶ Generate Interesting Words

Explain that a fun part of writing is using new and interesting words to communicate. Authors often try to avoid overused words and instead use other, more interesting words to communicate exactly what they mean.

Write the word *good* at the top of a sheet of chart paper and point out that it can be an overused word. Ask:

Q *What other words could we use to mean "good"?*

Record the words as students report them.

> ***Students might say:***
>
> "spectacular"
>
> "ideal"
>
> "first-class"
>
> "superior"
>
> "excellent"
>
> "delicious"

Follow the same procedure to have partners brainstorm alternative words for *big* and *small*.

Point out that in addition to *adjectives* (or descriptive words) like *good*, *big*, and *small*, there are many common *verbs* (or action words), such as *run*, *walk*, *sit*, and *said*, that can be replaced with more interesting words. Ask:

 Q *What interesting words can you think of to replace* said? *Turn to your partner.*

Have partners discuss for a few moments. Then signal for attention and ask volunteers to report their ideas as you record them on chart paper.

3 ▶ Facilitate Guided Rereading of Drafts

Have the students get out their writing notebooks and pads of self-stick notes. Using the same procedure you used on Week 1, Day 3 (see pages 128–129), take the students through the prompts that follow, saying them one at a time and giving the students several quiet minutes between each prompt to mark passages with self-stick notes.

- *Look for the word* good *in your draft. Mark the margins next to them with self-stick notes that say "replace."*

- *Look for other overused words that you might be able to replace with more interesting ones. Mark the margins with self-stick notes that say "replace."*

◀ **Teacher Note**

Alternatives for *big* include *large*, *huge*, *humongous*, and *enormous*. Alternatives for *small* include *tiny*, *little*, *short*, *miniscule*, and *microscopic*.

◀ **Teacher Note**

Alternatives for *said* include: *asked*, *shouted*, *replied*, *exclaimed*, *mumbled*, *whined*, and *cried*.

Have a couple of volunteers share words they marked with the class, and probe their thinking by asking questions such as:

Q   *Why did you decide to mark that word?*

Q   *What word could you substitute for the one you marked?*

4 ▶ Model Revising

Explain that during writing time today the students will look at the words they marked with self-stick notes and replace them with more interesting words. Ask the students to watch as you model making revisions.

Show the transparency of your own revised writing from Week 1 (or the revised "Sample First Draft") and read it aloud. Model replacing words like *good*, *big*, and *small* by crossing them out and writing alternative words above or below them.

Sample First Draft

One Saturday last year, my parents drove my brother

and me to the home of their friends George and Patty. I

didn't want to go. I wanted to be home riding my shiny

red bike.

George and Patty met us at the door with beaming

smiles. We followed them through their house and out to

the backyard. I heard some tiny barks and some loud barks.

    little   The puppies had fluffy black fur and little pink tongues.
Four ~~small~~ puppies came running up to us! There also was

  an older
~~a big~~ dog that turned out to be the puppies' mother.

replace

replace

continues

Sample First Draft *continued*

My brother and I played with the puppies for a while.

friendly

They were all ~~good~~ dogs. Then my father said something I

still can't believe.

"Which puppy do you want, kids?" he said. "That is, if

you even want one."

Did we ever! It only took us a minute to agree on the

smallest puppy of the group. And that's how we got Beck,

the best dog in the world. ●

replace

WRITING TIME

5 ▶ Revise Drafts

Write the following tasks on the board and have the students work silently on them for 15–20 minutes.

- Review the places you marked with self-stick notes.

- Replace overused words with more interesting ones.

- Remove the self-stick notes when you finish the revision.

- If you finish, look for other places to make the words more interesting, or work on another piece of writing.

Explain that you will confer with students after the first 5–10 minutes of writing time so you expect the students to work independently. Join the students in writing for a few minutes; then confer with individual students.

ELL Note

English Language Learners may benefit from talking with a partner as they mark and write revisions. Provide a place for them to confer quietly during writing time.

TEACHER CONFERENCE NOTE

Over the next couple of weeks, confer for 5–10 minutes with each student about the piece he is developing for publication. Ask the student to tell you about the part he is working on now and to read his draft aloud. As you listen, ask yourself:

- Does this student's writing communicate clearly? If not, what's unclear?

- Do the ideas connect in a way that makes sense?

- Do the revisions make sense and improve the piece?

Help the student revise unclear writing by rereading confusing passages back to him and explaining what is confusing you. Ask questions such as:

Q *What do you want your reader to be thinking at this part? How can you write that?*

Q *What is another way you can say this? Write that down.*

Q *What sentence could you add to give your reader more information?*

Document your observations for each student on the "Conference Notes" record sheet (BLM1). Use the "Conference Notes" record sheets during conferences throughout the unit.

Signal to let the students know when writing time is over. Explain that they will continue to revise their drafts tomorrow.

SHARING AND REFLECTING

 Share Revisions and Reflect on Participation

Have a few volunteers share a revision they made today by reading the original passage aloud and then reading the revised passage. Encourage the rest of the students to give their full attention to the person who is sharing. Facilitate discussion about each volunteer's revised passage by asking the questions that follow. Have volunteers reread their passages aloud, if necessary.

Q *[Robin], why did you choose to revise that passage?*

Q *How do you think [Robin's] revision improves the piece?*

Q *What questions can we ask [Robin] about her revision?*

Help the students reflect on their participation in this discussion by asking:

Q *How did you do today giving your full attention to the person who was sharing her writing?*

Q *If you weren't giving your full attention today, what will help you give your full attention the next time we have a class discussion?*

Teacher Note

If the students have difficulty answering this question, offer some suggestions like those in the "Students might say" note.

Students might say:

"I was distracted today. I think it would help for me to sit closer to the person who's sharing."

"It might help if we don't have our hands on our papers or pencils when people are sharing."

"I want to remember to turn and face the person who's sharing."

EXTENSION

Generate Alternatives for Other Overused Words

Following the procedure described in Step 2 of this lesson, brainstorm and chart words that can replace other overused words, such as *bad* and *sad*. (Examples of words you might substitute for *bad* are *awful*, *terrible*, *appalling*, *ghastly*, and *horrific*; for *sad*, examples include *depressing*, *gloomy*, *miserable*, *pitiful*, and *tragic*.)

Day 2

Materials

- *The Pain and The Great One* from Unit 1
- *Grandpa's Face* from Unit 1
- *In November* from Unit 1
- *Atlantic* from Unit 1

Analyzing and Revising Drafts

In this lesson, the students:

- Explore strong opening sentences
- Reread their writing critically
- Finish revising their drafts
- Ask one another questions about their writing

GETTING READY TO WRITE

 Read and Discuss Strong Opening Sentences

Have partners sit together at desks today. Explain that authors often pay close attention to the first few sentences of their pieces. The opening sentences need to get readers interested and make them want to keep reading. Today the students will look at opening sentences from several read-aloud books from earlier in the year. They will think about how each author tries to "hook us" at the very beginning of the book.

Show the first page of *The Pain and The Great One* and read it aloud twice. First in pairs and then as a class, discuss:

Q *Do these sentences grab your attention and make you want to keep reading? Why or why not?*

Students might say:

"When it says he powders the whole bathroom and doesn't get his face clean, it makes you imagine what's happening."

"In addition to what [Edward] said, it makes you want to keep reading to find out why she calls her brother a pain."

"In addition to what [Charlotte] said, the opening sentences make it seem like the book is going to be funny."

Making Meaning® Teacher

You might want to include opening sentences from books In *Making Meaning* Units 1 and 2 In this discussion. These are: *Miss Nelson Is Missing! Officer Buckle and Gloria; Have You Seen Bugs? Cherries and Cherry Pits; The Spooky Tail of Prewitt Peacock*; and *Aunt Flossie's Hats (and Crab Cakes Later)*.

Repeat this procedure using the opening sentences from *Grandpa's Face*, *Atlantic*, and *In November*.

Point out that strong opening sentences often intrigue the reader with interesting details ("In November, the earth is growing quiet. It is making its bed, a winter bed for flowers and small creatures") or hint at what is coming in the piece ("I am the Atlantic Ocean").

2 Review Opening Sentences in Drafts

Ask the students to reread the first few sentences of their own drafts. Use "Think, Pair, Share" to have partners first think about and then discuss:

 Q *How might you revise your opening sentences to "hook" your reader and make him want to keep reading?* [pause] *Turn to your partner.*

Students might say:

"I think my opening sentence will grab the reader's attention because it says 'I thought it was going to be a regular old Saturday, but it wasn't.'"

"Maybe the readers will want to find out what happens."

"I think I'm going to revise my opening sentences because right now it just starts with 'Once upon a time.' It's not very interesting."

Encourage the students to revise their opening sentences during writing time today.

WRITING TIME

3 Revise Drafts

Tell the students that tomorrow they will start writing a final version of their piece to go into their books. Write today's tasks on the board and have the students work silently on them for 15–20 minutes.

- Revise your opening sentences so that they "hook" your reader.

- Make any other revisions you think are needed to make your piece as interesting as it can be.

◀ **Teacher Note**

Today's lesson is just an introduction to thinking about opening sentences. The students will learn more about the characteristics of strong opening sentences in the genre units this year.

Join the students in writing for 5–10 minutes; then confer with individual students.

TEACHER CONFERENCE NOTE

Continue to confer for 5–10 minutes with each student about the piece she is developing for publication. Ask the student to tell you about the part she is working on now and to read her draft aloud. As you listen, ask yourself:

- Does this student's writing communicate clearly? If not, what's unclear?

- Do the ideas connect in a way that makes sense?

- Do the revisions make sense and improve the piece?

Help the student revise unclear writing by rereading those passages back to her and explaining what is confusing you. Ask questions such as:

Q *What do you want your reader to be thinking at this part?*

Q *What is another way you can say this? Write that down.*

Q *What sentence could you add to give your reader more information?*

Document your observations for each student on the "Conference Notes" record sheet (BLM1).

Signal to let the students know when writing time is over.

SHARING AND REFLECTING

 Share Revised Opening Sentences as a Class

Have several volunteers share opening sentences they revised by reading the original and the revised sentences. As the students share, encourage discussion by asking the class the questions that follow. Be ready to ask the volunteers to reread what they shared, if necessary.

Q *How is [Emilia's] revised opening different from the original?*

Q *What do you think about when you hear the revised opening?*

Q *What questions can we ask [Emilia] about her revised opening sentences?*

Q *What are you learning about revising to make writing better?*

Day 3

Materials

- Read-aloud books from Unit 1
- Supply of lined paper for final drafts

Making Meaning® Teacher

You might want to include opening sentences from books In *Making Meaning* Units 1 and 2 In this discussion. These are: *Miss Nelson Is Missing! Officer Buckle and Gloria; Have You Seen Bugs? Cherries and Cherry Pits; The Spooky Tail of Prewitt Peacock*; and *Aunt Flossie's Hats (and Crab Cakes Later)*.

Teacher Note ▶

If the students have difficulty answering these questions, offer some ideas like those in the "Students might say" note.

Analyzing and Revising Drafts

In this lesson, the students:

- Explore effective titles
- Reread their writing critically
- Finish revising their drafts
- Ask one another questions about their writing

GETTING READY TO WRITE

1 ▶ **Review and Discuss Effective Titles**

Remind the students that yesterday they heard examples of strong opening sentences and thought about whether they wanted to revise their own opening sentences to make them stronger. Explain that, just as authors pay attention to their opening sentences, they think carefully about what title to give their piece of writing. Display the read-aloud books from earlier in the year along a chalk rail and read the titles aloud. Ask:

Q *What do you notice about these titles?*

Q *How does the title* [The Pain and the Great One] *make you want to read the book?*

Q *What are some things that you might want to keep in mind when you are deciding on a title?*

Students might say:

"The title *The Pain and the Great One* makes me curious. I want to know who is the pain and who is the great one."

"Good titles sometimes make readers get a question in their head, like 'Why is Oliver Button a sissy?'"

"A good title gives a clue about what the book is about."

Think About Their Own Titles

Ask the students to think about the title of the piece they are developing for publication. Use "Think, Pair, Share" to have partners first think about and then discuss:

 Q *What might you call your piece to intrigue a reader and get him or her to open your book?* [pause] *Turn to your partner.*

Have a few volunteers share their thinking with the class.

Encourage the students to think about an effective title for their piece as they revise their drafts today.

WRITING TIME

 ## Revise Drafts

Write the following tasks on the board and have the students write silently for 20–30 minutes.

* Come up with an effective title for your piece.

* Make other changes until you are satisfied that your piece is as interesting and readable as possible.

Join the students in writing for 5–10 minutes; then confer with individual students.

Signal to let the students know when writing time is over. Explain that pairs will confer about their drafts tomorrow.

SHARING AND REFLECTING

 ## Share Revisions as a Class

Have several volunteers share their titles with the class. As the students share, encourage discussion by asking the class the questions that follow.

Q *What do you think about when you hear [Joshua's] title?*

Q *What questions can we ask [Joshua] about this title?*

Day 4

Materials

- "Questions About My Draft" chart from Week 1
- Supply of lined paper for final versions
- *Assessment Resource Book*

Pair Conferring

In this lesson, the students:

- Begin writing the final versions of their pieces
- Initiate pair conferences
- Use pair conference and writing time responsibly
- Ask for and receive feedback about their writing
- Give feedback in a helpful way

GETTING READY TO WRITE

1 ▶ Discuss Initiating Pair Conferences

Explain that in the coming days partners will confer about their revised drafts. In earlier lessons, everyone conferred at the same time. On some days, however, the students may initiate their own conference with another person whenever they want feedback about their writing.

Explain that today you will signal about halfway through the writing time that the students may confer in pairs about their writing, if they wish. If possible, designate a place in the room for pair conferences a little apart from where other students are writing. Tell the students that they should ask their assigned partner first. If their own partner is busy writing and would rather not stop to confer, they may ask another student. Ask:

Q *How can you respectfully ask someone to confer with you?*

FACILITATION TIP

After **asking open-ended questions**, remember to use **wait-time** 5–10 seconds or more to give everyone a chance to think before talking. If you often hear from the same few students during class discussions, extend the wait time to encourage broader participation in the discussion.

Q *If someone asks you to confer with them and you would rather keep writing, how can you respond to that person respectfully?*

Q *What else will you do to be responsible if you confer with a partner today?*

Direct the students' attention to the "Questions About My Draft" chart from Week 1 and review the chart. Ask:

Q *What other questions might you want to ask your partner about your draft?*

Add any new questions to the chart and encourage the students to use the questions, if they choose to confer with a partner today.

WRITING TIME

2 ▶ Write Independently and Confer

Write the following tasks on the board and have the students work silently on them for 20–30 minutes.

- Reread your draft.

- Make any other revisions you think are needed to make your piece the most interesting it can be.

- When you are satisfied with it, start copying it neatly, in pencil, on lined paper.

Join the students in writing for 5–10 minutes; then walk around and observe. About halfway through the writing period, signal that the students may confer in pairs, if they wish.

◀ **Teacher Note**

If computers are available, you might have some students type their final versions (see "Do Ahead" on page 139).

CLASS ASSESSMENT NOTE

Observe the students as they initiate and participate in pair conferences. Ask yourself:

- Are the students able to find partners and begin conferring with minimal disruption to the class?

- What problems are students having initiating pair conferences?

- Do conferring pairs seem to stay on task, reading and discussing their writing?

- Do they return promptly to writing at the end of their conference?

- Is the noise level such that students can continue to write if they wish?

Note any problems that you observe and be ready to bring them up during the reflection. Record your observations in the *Assessment Resource Book*.

Signal to let the students know when writing time is over.

SHARING AND REFLECTING

 Reflect on Pair Conferences

Gather the students to discuss how they did during writing and pair conference time today. Remind them that in the writing community the goal of giving feedback is to help the other person create the best possible piece of writing. Ask:

Q *If you participated in a pair conference today, what questions did you ask your partner about your writing?*

Q *What did your partner do or say that helped you?*

Q *If you continued to write while pair conferences were going on, were you able to concentrate? Why or why not?*

Q *I noticed that [the room got very noisy when people were walking around looking for a partner to confer with]. What can we do next time to avoid this problem?*

Teacher Note

Save the "Questions About My Draft" chart to use in the personal narrative genre unit.

Week 3 Overview

UNIT 2: THE WRITING PROCESS

Writing Focus

• Students learn procedures for proofreading their writing.

• Students write their final versions and publish them as books.

• Students present their books to the class from the Author's Chair.

• Students confer with one another and the teacher.

Social Focus

• Students work in a responsible way.

• Students act in fair and caring ways.

• Students make decisions and solve problems respectfully.

• Students express interest in and appreciation for one another's writing.

DO AHEAD

• Prior to Day 1, collect enough folders (manila, pocket, or any other kind) for each student in the class.

• Prior to Day 3, create a sample handmade book by stapling together several blank pages with a construction-paper cover.

• Prior to Day 4, establish a procedure for the students to follow when they are ready to present their completed book from the Author's Chair. You might have them place finished work in a basket; then, during the sharing time, you can call authors in the order that they completed their books to read them aloud to the class. Designate a place in the class library for the students' published works after they have been shared from the Author's Chair.

TEACHER AS WRITER

"I believe more in the scissors than I do in the pencil."
— *Truman Capote*

Carefully reread the draft you revised in Week 2. Ask yourself:

• Are there words or sentences in this draft that seem extraneous—like they don't really belong?

• Are there ideas I can express in fewer words?

Think about what you can delete from your draft or rewrite for conciseness. Make these revisions, either by marking on your current draft or writing a new one.

Day 1

Materials

- *Student Writing Handbook*
- Writing folder for each student (see "Do Ahead" on page 155)
- Supply of lined paper for final versions

Proofreading

In this lesson, the students:

- Proofread their drafts for spelling
- Become familiar with their word bank and learn how to add words to it
- Use writing and pair conference time responsibly
- Act considerately toward others

More About Revision and Proofreading Early in the Year

Remember that the students are just being introduced to the writing process in this unit. They will repeat the process in every genre unit, giving them multiple opportunities to practice their revision and proofreading skills and to learn new skills (see the "Skill Development" chart in the back matter of volume 2). Do not worry at this point if you notice that students are publishing pieces that could have undergone more revision. The students will improve with repeated practice over time.

GETTING READY TO WRITE

1▶ Discuss Proofreading for Spelling

Have the students stay at their seats today. Explain that this week the students will work on their final versions and make them into books for the class library. Point out that published pieces of writing need to be spelled correctly and have as few errors as possible. Today and tomorrow the students will proofread their drafts, checking them for spelling and punctuation errors.

2▶ Introduce the Word Bank in the *Student Writing Handbook*

Ask the students to reread their revised draft (even if they have already begun copying it as a final version) and circle any words for which they are unsure of the spelling. Stop the students after a couple of minutes and ask:

Q *What words have you circled so far?*

Have several volunteers report the words that they circled. Ask the students to open their *Student Writing Handbook* to the section titled "Word Bank." Explain that this section contains an alphabetical list of correctly spelled words that students their age often use in writing.

Ask the students to look up the first word that they circled in their word bank, check the spelling, and correct it in the draft, if necessary.

Ask:

Q *If the word does not appear in the word bank, what else might you do to check the spelling?*

> **Students might say**
>
> "I could ask someone at my table if they know how to spell it."
>
> "I could ask my partner about it during a conference."
>
> "I could ask you."
>
> "If I know where I read that word in a book, I can go look it up there."
>
> "I could look it up in a dictionary."

Point out that each page of the word bank has blank lines where the students can add the new words that they learn. After finding the correct spelling of a new word, they will add it to the appropriate page in the word bank (see diagram). The word will be there for them in the future, if they need it.

◀ **Teacher Note**

If the students have difficulty looking up words, take time to review dictionary skills. Write a word on the board and then look it up together as a class. Repeat with other words, if necessary.

◀ **Teacher Note**

If the students have difficulty answering this question, suggest some ideas like those in the "Students might say" note.

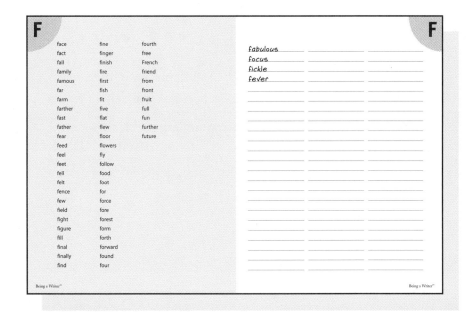

F				F
face	fine	fourth	*fabulous*	
fact	finger	free	*focus*	
fall	finish	French	*fickle*	
family	fire	friend	*fever*	
famous	first	from		
far	fish	front		
farm	fit	fruit		
farther	five	full		
fast	flat	fun		
father	flew	further		
fear	floor	future		
feed	flowers			
feel	fly			
feet	follow			
fell	food			
felt	foot			
fence	for			
few	force			
field	fore			
fight	forest			
figure	form			
fill	forth			
final	forward			
finally	found			
find	four			

Being a Writer™

Being a Writer™

Explain that the word bank is the first place the students should go to check the spelling of a word. Tell them that they will check and correct their spelling before starting or continuing to work on their final versions today.

WRITING TIME

▶ 3 Write Independently and Confer in Pairs

Write the following tasks on the board and have the students work silently on them for 20–30 minutes.

- Check and correct your draft for spelling.

- Start or continue to write your final version neatly in pencil.

Remind the students that you will signal after 10–15 minutes of quiet writing to indicate that they may confer in pairs, if they wish. Briefly discuss:

Q *If you choose to confer with a partner today, how will you go about it in a way that is considerate of your classmates?*

Encourage the students to act responsibly and considerately during the writing time.

Join the students in writing for a few minutes; then confer with individual students.

Teacher Note ▶

If necessary, remind the students who have already begun writing their final versions to correct any misspellings they may have copied into them.

TEACHER CONFERENCE NOTE

Continue to confer with individual students about the piece that each is developing for publication. Ask yourself:

- Does this student's writing communicate clearly? If not, what's unclear?

- Do the ideas connect in a way that makes sense?

continues

> **TEACHER CONFERENCE NOTE** *continued*
>
> - Do the revisions make sense and improve the piece?
>
> - Does this student recognize misspelled words and correct them?
>
> Continue to help the students revise unclear writing using the suggestions in the Teacher Conference Notes on Week 2, Day 2 (page 148). Document your observations for each student on the "Conference Notes" record sheet (BLM1).

After 10–15 minutes, signal that the students may confer in pairs.

Signal to let the students know when writing time is over. Distribute a writing folder to each student and explain that they will keep any loose pages they are working on in their folder. Ask the students to write their name on the front of their folder.

SHARING AND REFLECTING

 Reflect as a Class

Ask and briefly discuss:

Q *What words did you check the spelling for today? What words did you find in your word bank? How did you check on words that were not in the word bank?*

Q *If you participated in a pair conference, what did you do to be considerate of your classmates? How do you think that helped your classmates today?*

Explain that the students will continue to work on their final versions tomorrow.

Day 2

Materials

- *Student Writing Handbook,* proofreading notes section
- Supply of lined paper for final versions
- Transparency of "Proofreading Notes" (BLM19)

Proofreading and Publishing

In this lesson, the students:

- Proofread for punctuation
- Become familiar with their proofreading notes section and start using it
- Use writing and pair conference time responsibly
- Discuss problems that arise in pair conferences

GETTING READY TO WRITE

▶1 Discuss and Model Proofreading for Punctuation

Have the students stay at their seats today. Review that yesterday the students learned how to proofread their draft for spelling. Remind them that published pieces of writing need to be as free from errors as possible. Today they will learn how to proofread their draft for punctuation.

Teacher Note ▶ ### 2 Introduce Proofreading Notes Section in the *Student Writing Handbook*

Beginning and ending punctuation and capitalizing the first letters of proper nouns will be review for many of your students. However, if you have students who still struggle with these skills, take time to review them using the related activities in the *Skill Practice Teaching Guide.*

Explain that the students will reread their revised draft and check that each sentence begins with a capital letter and ends with a period, question mark, or exclamation point. Also ask them to check whether they have capitalized the first letter of any *proper nouns* (or names).

Have the students take several minutes to proofread their draft for punctuation (even if they have already begun copying the final version).

Ask the students to open their *Student Writing Handbook* to the "Proofreading Notes" section. Explain that the students will use this section to keep track of the rules (or conventions) of writing that they will learn this year. Over time, this section will become a checklist of things to pay attention to when they get ready to publish their drafts.

Write the notes in the diagram below on the transparency, and ask the students to copy these notes onto the first page of their proofreading notes section.

Rule	Example	Notes
Capitalize the first letter of sentences.	Once upon a time...	
Punctuate at the end of sentences.	He ran. Did he run? Boy, can he run!	
Capitalize names.	John. United States. Saturday. Boston. November.	Includes names of people, countries, cities, days, months.

Explain that the students will check and correct their punctuation before they work on their final versions today.

◀ **Teacher Note**

Additional conventions are taught in the genre units of this program (see "Skill Development" chart in the appendix in volume 2). The students will record the conventions that they learn in their proofreading notes section as they learn them.

WRITING TIME

3 ▶ Write Independently and Confer in Pairs

Write the following tasks on the board and have the students work silently on them for 20–30 minutes.

- Check and correct your draft for punctuation.

- Finish checking and correcting your draft for spelling.

- Continue to write your final version neatly in pencil.

Remind the students that you will signal after 10–15 minutes of silent writing to indicate that they may confer in pairs. As the students write, confer with individual students.

◀ **Teacher Note**

Remind the students who have already begun writing their final versions to correct any punctuation errors they may have copied into them.

TEACHER CONFERENCE NOTE

Continue to confer with individual students about the piece that each is developing for publication. Ask yourself:

- Does this student's writing communicate clearly? If not, what's unclear?

- Do the ideas connect in a way that makes sense?

- Do the revisions make sense and improve the piece?

- Does this student recognize misspelled words and correct them?

- Does he proofread his writing using his proofreading notes?

Continue to help the students revise unclear writing using the suggestions in the Teacher Conference Note on Week 2, Day 2 (page 148). Document your observations for each student on the "Conference Notes" record sheet (BLM1).

After 10–15 minutes, signal that the students may confer in pairs.

Signal to let the students know when writing time is over. Have them put their loose pages in their writing folders until tomorrow.

SHARING AND REFLECTING

 Reflect on Pair Conferences

Remind the students that the goal of conferring is to help one another create the best possible piece of writing. By helping one another, they build the writing community. However, sometimes problems can arise during pair conferences. Ask:

Q *What kinds of problems have you experienced when finding a partner to confer with? How can we avoid those problems?*

Q *What kinds of problems have you experienced [during/at the end of] conferences? How can we avoid those problems?*

Q *I've noticed that [some students get asked to confer often, while other students don't get asked very much]. Why do we want to make sure that doesn't happen in our writing community? What can we do to make sure everyone is invited to confer sometimes?*

Students might say:

"Sometimes I have to ask five different people before anyone will confer with me. It's frustrating."

"It seems like people don't know what to do after they finish a conference. They hang around and start bothering people."

"We want to make sure everyone gets invited to confer so no one feels left out of our community. Maybe we can try to ask someone we haven't asked before."

At the end of this discussion, summarize the students' ideas for avoiding or solving problems during pair conferences. Encourage the students to keep these things in mind the next time that they confer. Tell them that you will check in with them to see how they are doing.

Day 3

Materials

- Read-aloud books from Unit 1
- Sample handmade book (see "Do Ahead" on page 155)
- Supply of lined paper for final versions
- Supply of unlined paper for illustrations
- Construction paper for book covers
- Markers, crayons, and other supplies for making illustrations
- Stapler

Publishing

In this lesson, the students:

- Explore features of published books
- Make their final versions into books
- Handle materials responsibly
- Share materials fairly

About Publishing for the Class Library

In this lesson, the students learn a simple procedure for turning their final version into a book. They will staple the pages of the final version, along with any illustrations they have created, using construction-paper covers. The goal at this point is to give the students a way to publish their writing quickly, without investing a great deal of time in a bookmaking project. However, there are a number of methods for creating beautiful handmade books that you might want to teach your students this year. Search for ideas online using the keywords "making books with children."

GETTING READY TO WRITE

1 Explore Features of Published Books

Gather the class with partners sitting together, facing you. Explain that the students who have finished writing their final versions may create their books today.

Show the sample book that you made and pass it around for the students to see. Explain that they may add illustrations on unlined paper, if they wish. They will assemble the completed pages in the proper order with a construction-paper cover and then write the book title and their name on the cover.

Explain that the students may wish to include additional features that professional authors sometimes include in their books. Use the read-aloud books from Unit 1 to review some of the features they could include—such as a title page, dedication, author note, and back-cover blurb. Tell the students that these books will be available during writing time so they can look at these features more closely.

2 Discuss Handling Materials Responsibly and Sharing Them Fairly

Make sure all of the necessary bookmaking materials are in a central location and explain the procedure you would like the students to follow to get and return the materials. Ask and briefly discuss:

Q *How will you handle the bookmaking materials responsibly?*

Q *You may need to share supplies, like markers or the stapler. If someone is using something you need, what can you do?*

Q *If you're using something that someone else needs, what can you do to share it fairly?*

Encourage the students to keep these things in mind as they work today. Tell them that you will check in with them later to see how they did.

WRITING TIME

3 Write Independently and Confer in Pairs

Write the following tasks on the board and have the students work silently on them for 20–30 minutes.

- Finish your final version.

- Include illustrations and other features, if you wish.

- Assemble your book and staple it together with a cover.

- Write the title and your name on the cover and decorate it.

Making Meaning® Teacher
You might include books from *Making Meaning* Units 1 and 2 in this discussion. These are: *Miss Nelson Is Missing! Officer Buckle and Gloria; Have You Seen Bugs? Cherries and Cherry Pits; The Spooky Tail of Prewitt Peacock;* and *Aunt Flossie's Hats (and Crab Cakes Later).*

Remind the students that you will signal after 10–15 minutes of silent writing to indicate that they may confer in pairs. As the students write, confer with individual students.

TEACHER CONFERENCE NOTE

Continue to confer with individual students about the piece that each is developing for publication. Ask yourself:

* Does this student's writing communicate clearly? If not, what's unclear?

* Do the ideas connect in a way that makes sense?

* Do the revisions make sense and improve the piece?

* Does this student recognize misspelled words and correct them?

* Does he proofread his writing using his proofreading notes?

Continue to help the students revise unclear writing using the suggestions in the Teacher Conference Note on Week 2, Day 2 (page 148). Document your observations for each student on the "Conference Notes" record sheet (BLM1).

After 10–15 minutes, call for the students' attention and say that in a moment you will signal that they may confer in pairs. Remind them that yesterday they talked about some possible problems that could arise during pair conferences and how they might avoid those problems. Ask and briefly discuss:

Q *What do you want to remember today to help avoid problems during pair conference time?*

Signal that the students may confer in pairs.

Signal to let the students know when writing time is over. Have the students return classroom materials to their proper places.

SHARING AND REFLECTING

 Reflect on Writing and Pair Conference Time

Ask and briefly discuss:

Q *How did you handle our class materials responsibly today?*

Q *What problems did we have with sharing the materials today? How can we avoid those problems tomorrow?*

Q *What problems were you able to avoid or solve during pair conference time today?*

Q *I noticed today that [people returned to their seats when they finished their conference]. How did that help our writing time go smoothly?*

Encourage the students to continue to think of ways to be responsible during writing and pair conference time.

FACILITATION TIP

Reflect on your experience over the past three weeks with **asking open-ended questions** and **using wait-time**. Do these techniques feel comfortable and natural for you? Do you find yourself using them throughout the school day? What effect has repeated use of them had on your students' thinking and participation in discussions? We encourage you to continue to use and reflect on these techniques.

Day 4

Materials

- Chart paper and a marker
- A chair to use for the Author's Chair

Publishing

In this lesson, the students:

- Review and reflect on the writing process
- Finish making their books
- Present their books to the class from the Author's Chair
- Express interest in and appreciation for one another's writing
- Ask one another questions about their writing

GETTING READY TO WRITE

1▶ Reflect on Writing Process and Community

Gather the class with partners sitting together, facing you. Explain that over the past several weeks they have learned about how to take a piece of writing through the writing process, from the very first idea to a published book. Ask:

Q *What have you learned about how to take a piece of writing from a first draft to a published book?*

Write the steps on a sheet of chart paper entitled "Writing Process" as you remind the students what they did (see diagram on next page).

> ### Writing Process
>
> 1. Generate ideas.
>
> 2. Write drafts.
>
> 3. Select one to develop.
>
> 4. Analyze and revise it.
>
> 5. Proofread it.
>
> 6. Write a final version and publish it.

Explain that the students will go through this writing process numerous times this year as they explore different kinds of writing, including fiction, nonfiction, and poetry.

Remind the students that they have been building a writing community in which everyone feels safe, cared for, and supported. Use "Think, Pair, Share" to have partners first think about and then discuss:

 Q *How will being part of a writing community help us as we go though the writing process?* [pause] *Turn to your partner.*

 Q *What part(s) of the writing process do you want to get better at this year?* [pause] *Turn to your partner.*

WRITING TIME

2 **Write Independently and Confer in Pairs**

Write the following tasks on the board and have the students work silently on them for 20–30 minutes.

- Finish your final version.

- Include illustrations and other features, if you wish.

- Assemble your book and staple it together with a cover.

- Write the title and your name on the cover and decorate it.

- If you finish, work on another piece of writing.

◀ **Teacher Note**

You might want to shorten the writing time today to leave sufficient time to introduce Author's Chair sharing.

If necessary, review the procedures for getting materials. As the students write, confer with individual students.

TEACHER CONFERENCE NOTE

Continue to confer with individual students about the piece that each is developing for publication. Ask yourself:

- Does this student's writing communicate clearly? If not, what's unclear?

- Do the ideas connect in a way that makes sense?

- Do the revisions make sense and improve the piece?

- Does this student recognize misspelled words and correct them?

- Does he proofread his writing using his proofreading notes?

Continue to help the students revise unclear writing using the suggestions in the Teacher Conference Note on Week 2, Day 2 (page 148). Document your observations for each student on the "Conference Notes" record sheet (BLM1).

After 10–15 minutes, signal that the students may confer in pairs.

Signal to let the students know when writing time is over. As the students return classroom materials to their proper places, place the chair that you have designated as the Author's Chair at the front of the area where you gather the class.

SHARING AND REFLECTING

 Introduce Author's Chair Sharing

Gather the class with partners sitting together, facing you. Explain that when they publish a piece of writing this year, they will present it to the class from the Author's Chair.

Explain the procedure you would like the students to follow when they are ready to present their book from the Author's Chair (see "Do Ahead" on page 155).

4 ▶ Discuss Speaking Clearly and Expressing Interest in Other People's Writing

Before asking a volunteer to share from the Author's Chair today, have a discussion about how the students will act, both as presenting authors and as members of the audience. Ask and discuss:

Q *Why is it important to speak in a loud, clear voice when you're sharing your book with the class?*

Q *If you're in the audience and you can't hear the author, how can you politely let him or her know?*

Q *How will you let the author know that you're interested in his or her writing? Why is it important to express interest in other people's writing?*

Encourage the students to be attentive and considerate audience members. Tell them that you will check in with them later to see how they did.

5 ▶ Conduct the Author's Chair Sharing

Ask for a volunteer who has finished publishing her book to read it aloud from the Author's Chair. Encourage the author to show any illustrations and any additional features she included. At the end of the reading, facilitate a discussion using questions like those that follow. Give the author an opportunity to respond to the class's comments and questions.

Q *What was interesting to you about [Jana's] book?*

Q *What part did you really like? Why?*

Q *What parts were [funny/scary/suspenseful/surprising]? Why?*

Q *What questions can we ask [Jana] about her book?*

Teacher Note ▶

Repeat today's lesson for a few more days, or even another week, to allow all of the students to finish publishing their books (see "Open Weeks" in the front matter on page xvi). Students who finish may begin a new piece of writing or continue working on a piece they started earlier.

Teacher Note

Post the "Writing Process" chart where everyone can see it.

Teacher Note

This is the end of Unit 2. The next unit you teach will be a genre unit. While the genre units may be taught in any order, we recommend that you teach the Expository Nonfiction unit later in the year. Personal Narrative or Fiction are good choices at this point.

You will need to assign new partners before starting the next unit.

Follow this procedure and have a few more students share from the Author's Chair. Assure the students that they will all have a chance to share their book from the Author's Chair in the next few days.

6 ▶ Reflect on Audience Behavior During Author's Chair Sharing

Ask and briefly discuss:

Q *How did we do today as an audience? What might we want to work on during the next Author's Chair sharing time?*

Q *If you shared a book today, how did you feel? What did the audience do that made you feel [relaxed/nervous/proud]?*

Show the students the place in the class library that you've designated for the students' published books. Explain that these books will be available for them to read during independent reading time. Emphasize that the students must handle their classmates' handmade books carefully and return them to the class library when they are done.

EXTENSION

Technology Tip: Publishing Student Writing Online

There are a number of websites where students can publish their writing online. Publishing online allows family members and friends to easily access and enjoy students' writing. You might make this an option for interested students. Search for websites online using the keywords "publishing children's writing."

Personal Narrative

Personal Narrative

Genre

Personal Narrative

During this four-week unit, the students explore the genre of personal narrative and write about significant topics and events from their lives. They explore what goes into a good personal narrative, including sensory details to make stories come alive. They hear, discuss, and write personal narratives. Socially, they ask one another questions about their writing and give feedback in helpful and respectful ways. They also practice giving their full attention to the person who is speaking and expressing interest in other people's writing.

Development Across the Grades

Grade	Elements of Personal Narrative	Language and Craft	Skills and Conventions
3	• Writing about interesting events or topics from own lives	• Using sensory details • Writing engaging openings	• Identifying and correcting commonly misused words (*then/than, your/you're*)
4	• Writing about single events from own lives	• Using sensory details • Writing engaging openings	• Identifying and correcting commonly misused words (*its/its', to/too/two*) • Recognizing and rewriting very long sentences
5	• Writing about significant experiences from own lives • Exploring how those experiences resulted in learning or change	• Using sensory details • Writing engaging openings • Adding information about learning or change	• Identifying and correcting commonly misused words (*there/their/they're*) • Recognizing and rewriting very long sentences
6	• Writing about experiences that resulted in learning or change	• Using sensory details • Integrating information about learning or change • Cultivating an individual voice	• Identifying and correcting commonly misused words (*accept/except; lose/loose; who's/whose*) • Recognizing and rewriting very long sentences

UNIT OVERVIEW

WEEK	DAY 1	DAY 2	DAY 3	DAY 4
	Immersion and Drafting			
1	**Exploring Personal Narrative:** *Grandma's Records* **Quick-Write:** Experiences with loved ones	**Exploring Personal Narrative:** "Our House" **Focus:** Writing about home	**Exploring and Drafting Personal Narrative:** "Chores" **Quick-Write:** Sensory details	**Exploring and Drafting Personal Narrative:** "Candy" **Focus:** Sensory details
2	**Exploring and Drafting Personal Narrative:** "John and the Snake" **Focus:** Writing about single incidents	**Exploring and Drafting Personal Narrative:** "First Day of School" **Focus:** Remembering the first day of school	**Exploring and Drafting Personal Narrative:** "Believing in Myself" **Quick-Write:** Perseverance through challenges	**Exploring Personal Narrative and Pair Conferring:** "How I Saved a Dog's Life" **Focus:** Learning situations
	Revision, Proofreading, and Publication			
3	**Selecting Drafts** **Focus:** What to look for when selecting drafts	**Analyzing, Completing, and Revising Drafts** **Focus:** Sensory details	**Analyzing and Revising Drafts** **Focus:** Sensory details	**Analyzing and Revising Drafts** **Focus:** Strong opening sentences
4	**Self-Assessing and Pair Conferring** **Focus:** Giving and receiving feedback	**Proofreading** **Focus:** Commonly misused words	**Publishing** **Focus:** Class book features	**Publishing** **Focus:** Author's Chair sharing

Overview

GENRE: PERSONAL NARRATIVE

Grandma's Records
by Eric Velasquez (Walker & Company, 2004)

Eric's grandmother plays the music of her childhood in Puerto Rico.

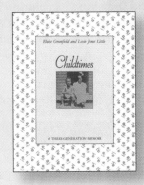

Childtimes: A Three-Generation Memoir
by Eloise Greenfield and Lessie Jones Little (HarperTrophy, 1993)

Three generations of women remember their "childtimes."

Writing Focus

- Students hear and discuss personal narrative.

- Students generate writing ideas from their own lives.

- Students visualize sensory details.

- Students draft personal narratives, focusing on interesting events or topics from their own lives.

Social Focus

- Students build the writing community.

- Students listen respectfully to the thinking of others and share their own.

- Students express interest in and appreciation for one another's writing.

DO AHEAD

- Prior to Day 1, decide how you will randomly assign partners to work together during this unit. See the front matter for suggestions about assigning partners randomly (page xiii) and for possible considerations for pairing English Language Learners (page xxviii).

- Consider prereading this week's read-aloud selections with your English Language Learners. Stop during the reading to discuss vocabulary and to check for understanding. Because the readings from *Childtimes* do not have illustrations, consider bringing in visual aids (such as photographs of houses and gardens) to support the students' comprehension.

TEACHER AS WRITER

"No surprise for the writer, no surprise for the reader. For me the initial delight is in the surprise of remembering something I didn't know I knew."
— *Robert Frost*

Think about memorable events from your life that you could write about. List these in your notebook; then select one or two of the most vivid memories to describe in short drafts. Write about what happened, when it happened, who was involved, and what was memorable about each event.

Day 1

Materials

- *Grandma's Records*
- *Assessment Resource Book*

Exploring Personal Narrative

In this lesson, the students:

- Work with a new partner
- Hear and discuss a personal narrative
- Quick-write about special objects
- Write freely about things that interest them

About Personal Narrative

Personal narratives offer writers the opportunity to think about and write true stories about the meaningful experiences of their lives. Personal narratives describe significant events and explain how those events led to learning or a change of some kind. Character change in a narrative, whether of a fictional character or a real person, often results from learning an important lesson or gaining a new realization about oneself or the world. Personal narratives also include sensory details to make them come alive for the reader.

In the study of personal narrative at grade 3, the students identify interesting events or topics from their lives and write about them in detail. They use sensory details and learn to concentrate their writing on just the salient points of a narrative.

GETTING READY TO WRITE

1 ▶ Pair Students and Discuss Working Together

Randomly assign partners and make sure they know each other's names (see "Do Ahead" on page 177). Ask the students to gather for a read-aloud with partners sitting together, facing you. Remind them to bring their writing notebooks and pencils.

Explain that today's lesson is the beginning of a four-week unit in which the students will explore a kind of writing called *personal narrative*. In personal narratives, authors tell stories about true

Making Meaning® Teacher

You can either have the students work with their current *Making Meaning* partner or assign new partners for this unit.

Teacher Note ▶

The partners you assign today will stay together for the unit. If necessary, take a few minutes at the beginning of today's lesson to let them get to know each other better by talking informally in a relaxed atmosphere.

things that have happened to them. Explain that partners will stay together for the unit. Ask:

Q   *What have you learned about working with a partner that can help your new partnership go well?*

Students might say:

"We can ask each other questions and help each other."

"I agree with [Felicia], you can work better together if you get to know someone."

"In addition to what [Zach] said, you don't have to be best friends—you just have to work together."

Encourage the students to keep these ideas in mind as they begin working with their new partner today.

2 Introduce and Read *Grandma's Records* Aloud

Show the cover of *Grandma's Records* and read the title and author's name. Explain that the author, Eric Velasquez, has written a personal narrative about growing up in Spanish Harlem in the 1960s. Read aloud the dedication on page 3, in both Spanish and English. Ask:

Q   *What does the dedication tell us about the author?*

Students might say:

"The book is dedicated to the author's grandmother, so he must like her a lot."

"In addition to what [Mele] said, the dedication is in Spanish and English, so I bet the author's grandmother spoke Spanish."

Explain that in this book the author describes memories of summers he spent with his grandmother. Ask the students to think as they listen about what it might be like to write about their own memories.

Read *Grandma's Records* aloud slowly and clearly, clarifying vocabulary as you read.

◀ **Teacher Note**

Regularly remind the students to use the discussion prompts they learned when they participate in class discussions. The prompts are:

● "I agree with _____ because…"

● "I disagree with _____ because…"

● "In addition to what _____ said, I think…"

◀ **Teacher Note**

To review the procedure for defining vocabulary during the read-aloud, see page 45.

Suggested Vocabulary

El Barrio: (Spanish) the neighborhood (p. 4)

percussion: instruments played by striking or shaking them
(for example, drums and maracas) (p. 15)

ELL Vocabulary

English Language Learners may benefit from discussing additional
vocabulary, including:

concert: music performance (p. 17)

subway: underground train (p. 21)

3 ▶ Briefly Discuss the Reading

Ask and briefly discuss the question that follows. Be ready to reread
from the text to help the students recall what they heard.

Q　*In this story, Eric writes about special things he did with someone
he loved. What special things does he write about?*

4 ▶ Quick-Write: Special Things Done with a Loved One

Ask:

 Q　*If you wanted to write about special things you've done
with someone you love, what could you write about? Turn to
your partner.*

Signal for the students' attention and have several volunteers share
their ideas.

Have the students open their writing notebooks to the next blank
page in the writing ideas section, label it "Special Things I've Done,"
and spend a few minutes listing some special things they have done
with a loved one. After a few minutes, have a few volunteers share
their lists with the class.

Explain that during writing time today the students may write about
one of the ideas they listed or about anything that interests them.

Teacher Note ▶

To review the procedure for "Turn
to Your Partner," see page xiv.

Teacher Note

Note that on Days 1 and 2 of this
week, the students may write
personal narratives or anything
else they wish. On Day 3, after
exposure to a couple examples
of personal narrative, they will all
begin writing in this genre.

WRITING TIME

5 ▸ **Write Independently**

Ask the students to return to their seats. Write the following choices on the board and have the students write silently for 20–30 minutes.

- Write about something special you've done with someone you love.

- Write about anything else that interests you.

Remind the students to double-space their writing. If necessary, review that during the writing period there should be no talking, whispering, or walking around.

Join the students in writing for a few minutes; then walk around the room and observe.

CLASS ASSESSMENT NOTE

Observe the students and ask yourself:

- Are the students staying in their seats and writing silently?

- Do they write readily about themselves?

- Are they double-spacing their writing?

- Do the students who have difficulty getting started eventually do so, or do they continue to struggle?

If you notice many students having difficulty starting to write, call for the class's attention and have partners talk to each other about what they might write. Have a few volunteers share their ideas with the class and then have them resume silent writing. If necessary, remind students to double-space their writing.

Record your observations in the *Assessment Resource Book*.

Signal to let the students know when writing time is over.

ELL Note

English Language Learners may benefit from drawing their ideas before they write. Encourage them to draw what they want to write about and then talk quietly with you or a partner about their drawing. If necessary, write out key words and phrases they want to use so that they can copy the words into their writing.

SHARING AND REFLECTING

 Briefly Share Writing and Reflect

Have partners share with each other what they wrote today. Then ask and briefly discuss the following questions. Invite students to read passages of their writing aloud as they share.

Q *Did you write about something special you did with a loved one? Tell us about it.*

Q *What other topics did you write about? Tell us about them.*

Q *What did you find out about your partner today?*

Day 2

Exploring Personal Narrative

In this lesson, the students:

- Hear and discuss a personal narrative
- Informally explore features of personal narratives
- Write freely about things that interest them

GETTING READY TO WRITE

1 Start "Notes About Personal Narratives" Chart

Gather the class with partners sitting together, facing you. Have them bring their writing notebooks and pencils with them. Remind the students that yesterday they heard *Grandma's Records*, a personal narrative by Eric Velasquez.

On a sheet of chart paper, write "Notes About Personal Narratives." Remind the students that a *personal narrative tells a true story from the author's own life*. Add this to the chart. Explain that you will continue to add to the chart as they learn more about what makes personal narratives different from other kinds of writing.

2 Introduce *Childtimes*

Show the cover of *Childtimes* and read the title and authors' names aloud. Explain that the subtitle, *A Three-Generation Memoir*, means that this book of personal narratives contains true stories of the memories of three generations of women from a single family: Eloise Greenfield; her mother, Lessie Jones Little; and her grandmother, Pattie Ridley Jones. Remind the students that they heard the fiction stories *Grandpa's Face* and *She Come Bringing Me That Little Baby Girl* by Eloise Greenfield earlier this year.

Materials

- "Our House" (pages 19–23 in *Childtimes*)
- Chart paper and a marker
- *Grandpa's Face* from Unit 1
- *She Come Bringing Me That Little Baby Girl* from Unit 1

Show the photographs of the women on pages 1, 49, and 119, and explain that each section contains stories told by one of the women about what it was like to grow up during her time.

Explain that you will read some of the personal narratives from *Childtimes* in the coming days. Encourage the students to think about what it might be like to write narratives like these themselves.

3 ▶ Read "Our House" Aloud

Explain that the personal narrative you will read today is by Pattie Ridley Jones, the oldest of the three women. Read page 7 aloud slowly and clearly; then read "Our House" (pages 19–23) aloud, clarifying vocabulary as you read.

> **Suggested Vocabulary**
>
> **plank:** flat piece of wood (p. 22)
> **mill:** factory where tree trunks are made into boards for building (p. 22)

4 ▶ Discuss the Reading

Ask and briefly discuss the questions that follow. Be ready to reread from the text to help the students recall what they heard.

Q   *What do we find out about Pattie Ridley Jones's childhood from this piece?*

Q   *What are some special things she remembers about her house?*

Point out that in this piece, Pattie Ridley Jones does not try to describe her whole childhood; she just describes her house and what she remembers about it. Use "Think, Pair, Share" to have partners first think about and then discuss:

 Q   *If you were going to write about your house, what might you say?* [pause] *Turn to your partner.*

Teacher Note

To review the procedure for "Think, Pair, Share," see page xiv. Remember to pause for 10–15 seconds for students to think before you say "Turn to your partner."

After partners have talked, signal for their attention and have a few volunteers share their thinking with the class. Today invite the students to write about their house, their memories, or about anything else they wish.

WRITING TIME

 Write Independently

Ask the students to return to their seats. Write the following choices on the board and have the students write silently for 20–30 minutes.

- Write about your house.

- Write about your memories.

- Write about anything else that interests you.

Remind the students to double-space their writing. Join them writing for a few minutes; then walk around the room and observe.

Signal to let the students know when writing time is over.

SHARING AND REFLECTING

 Reflect on Writing

Ask and briefly discuss the questions that follow. Invite the students to read passages of their writing aloud as they share.

Q *Did you write about your house today? Tell us about it.*

Q *Did you write about a memory today? Tell us about it.*

Q *What other topics did you write about? Tell us about them.*

Teacher Note

Save the "Notes About Personal Narratives" chart to use later this week and throughout the unit.

Day 3

Materials

- "Chores" (pages 31–33 in *Childtimes*)
- "Notes About Personal Narratives" chart from Day 2
- "Conference Notes" record sheet for each student (BLM1)

Exploring and Drafting Personal Narrative

In this lesson, the students:

- Hear, discuss, and draft personal narratives
- Visualize sensory details
- Share their partner's thinking with the class
- Quick-write sensory details
- Express interest in one another's writing

GETTING READY TO WRITE

1 ▶ Add to "Notes About Personal Narratives" Chart

Gather the class with partners sitting together, facing you. Review that the students heard *Grandma's Records* and "Our House," both personal narratives. Remind the students that in each of these narratives, the author writes about things he or she remembers from childhood. Direct the students' attention to the "Notes About Personal Narrative" chart and add *writing about memories* to it.

Explain that today you will read another personal narrative by Pattie Ridley Jones. Remind the students that she is the oldest of the three women who tell about their lives in *Childtimes: A Three Generation Memoir*. Explain that in this personal narrative she uses words to help the reader imagine what's happening. Invite the students to listen for these words as you read.

2 ▶ Read "Chores" Aloud

Read "Chores" (pages 31–33) aloud slowly and clearly, clarifying vocabulary as you read.

> **Suggested Vocabulary**
>
> **mattress:** part of the bed you sleep on (p. 32)
>
> **bedstead:** bed frame (p. 32)

 Discuss the Reading

Ask:

 **Q** *What did you see in your mind as you listened to this personal narrative? Turn to your partner.*

Have a few volunteers share with the class.

> **Students might say:**
>
> "I imagined designs on the ground from the broom."
>
> "In my mind, I saw a really hot stove with irons sitting on top of it."
>
> "I imagined the bed with the puffed up mattresses and lacy pillows."

4 ▶ **Quick-Write: Sensory Details**

Ask the students to think quietly as they listen to the questions that follow. Say the questions one at a time, pausing between each question (without discussing it) to give the students time to think.

Q *What kinds of chores do you do at home?*

Q *Imagine yourself doing one of those chores. What do you see? Hear? Smell?*

Q *What do you touch with your hands when you do the chore? What does that feel like?*

Ask the students to open their writing notebook to the next blank page and do a quick-write about what they imagined. Stop them after 3–4 minutes of silent writing and have partners talk about their thinking; then have them resume silent writing for a few more minutes.

Signal for the students' attention and have several volunteers share their ideas with the class.

Explain that you would like all of the students to try writing about their own lives during writing time today. Encourage them to include *sensory details*, or words that help a reader see, hear, smell, taste, and feel what's happening. They may continue a piece they started earlier or write any true story about their lives.

WRITING TIME

5 ▶ Draft Personal Narratives

Have the students return to their seats and work silently on personal narratives for 20–30 minutes. Remind them to double-space their writing. Join them in writing for a few minutes; then begin conferring with individual students.

Teacher Note

The students are just beginning to explore personal narrative. They are not expected to know or incorporate specific features of the genre into their writing at this point. They will build on their understanding as they explore the genre in the coming weeks.

TEACHER CONFERENCE NOTE

Over the next two weeks, confer with individual students about their personal narratives. Ask each student to show you his writing and read some of it aloud to you. Help the student extend his thinking about personal narrative by asking questions such as:

Q *Why did you choose to write about this [event/ memory/thing]?*

Q *What else do you remember about it that you can add to the narrative?*

Q *What words are you using to describe what you [saw/ heard/smelled/tasted/felt]?*

Q *What other experiences from your own life might you want to write about?*

Document your observations for each student using the "Conference Notes" record sheet (BLM1). Use the "Conference Notes" record sheets during conferences throughout the unit.

Signal to let the students know when writing time is over.

SHARING AND REFLECTING

6 ▶ Share One Sentence and Reflect

Ask the students to review the writing they did today and underline one sentence they like to share with the class. Give the students a moment to select their sentences; then go around the room and have each student read his sentence aloud, without comment.

Facilitate a brief discussion using the following questions:

Q *What sentence did you hear that got you interested in someone else's writing?*

Q *What questions do you want to ask a classmate about his or her writing?*

Explain that the students will continue to write drafts of personal narratives during the coming week. At the end of next week, they will select one of their drafts to develop, revise, and publish for the class library.

◀ **Teacher Note**

The intention in this activity is to hear one sentence from every student in the class. This lets the students hear what their classmates are writing and builds their accountability. After they underline their sentences, have them put their pencils away. Have them read their sentences promptly, one after another, without stopping to comment. In the discussion afterward, they are not expected to remember every sentence they heard.

Day 4

Exploring and Drafting Personal Narrative

In this lesson, the students:

* Hear and discuss a personal narrative
* Explore sensory details in a passage
* Draft personal narratives
* Express interest in one another's writing
* Ask one another questions about their writing

GETTING READY TO WRITE

1 **Briefly Review Personal Narrative**

Gather the class with partners sitting together, facing you. Review that yesterday they began writing drafts of personal narratives. Ask and briefly discuss:

Q *What makes personal narrative writing different from other kinds of writing?*

If necessary, review the "Notes About Personal Narratives" chart to help the students remember what they learned. Add any new ideas they mention.

2 **Read and Discuss "Candy"**

Show the cover of *Childtimes* and remind the students that they heard "Our House" and "Chores" by Pattie Ridley Jones. Ask and briefly discuss:

Q *What have we already found out about Pattie Ridley Jones's life as a child?*

Materials column

* Transparency or excerpt from *Childtimes* (BLM4)
* *Student Writing Handbook* page 3

 Note

You might provide the prompt "I learned that she…" to your English Language Learners to help them verbalize their answers to this question.

Explain that you will read about another of Pattie Ridley Jones's memories, and encourage the students to listen for words that help them imagine what's happening.

Read "Candy" on pages 41–42 aloud, slowly and clearly.

3 ▶ Explore Sensory Details

Ask and briefly discuss:

Q *What did you imagine seeing as you listened to this passage? What did you imagine hearing?*

Q *What other senses did you imagine using?*

Ask the students to open to *Student Writing Handbook* page 3, where the passage is reproduced. Ask partners to reread the passage and together underline words that help them imagine using their senses.

After a few moments, place the transparency of the excerpt on the overhead projector and signal for the students' attention. Ask a few pairs to share words they underlined. As they share, underline those words on the transparency and ask:

Q *What sense do those words make you imagine using?*

Point out that in many personal narratives, including this one, the author includes sensory details that help us imagine what happens using our senses. Direct the students' attention to the "Notes About Personal Narratives" chart, and add *sensory details help the reader see, hear, smell, taste, or feel what's happening*.

Explain that the students will continue to write personal narratives today, and encourage them to look for places they can include sensory details. They may continue a personal narrative they started earlier or begin a new one.

◀ **Teacher Note**

If helpful, write the five senses on the board for students to refer to; they are sight, hearing, smell, taste, and touch.

Some sensory details in this narrative include: "sugar got hot," "when the candy cooled enough," "put butter on our hands," "it would be brown," "it looked right silvery," and "lay it all around the platter and break it into sticks."

WRITING TIME

4 Draft Personal Narratives

Have the students return to their seats and work silently on personal narratives for 20–30 minutes. Join them in writing for a few minutes; then confer with individual students.

> ## TEACHER CONFERENCE NOTE
>
> Continue to confer with individual students, having them show and read their writing to you. Help them extend their thinking about personal narrative by asking questions such as:
>
> **Q** *Why did you choose this [event/memory/thing] to write about?*
>
> **Q** *What else do you remember about it that you can add to the narrative?*
>
> **Q** *What words are you using to describe what you [saw/ heard/smelled/tasted/felt]?*
>
> **Q** *What other experiences from your own life might you want to write about?*
>
> Document your observations for each student using the "Conference Notes" record sheet (BLM1).

Signal to let the students know when writing time is over.

SHARING AND REFLECTING

5 Share One Sentence and Reflect

As you did yesterday, ask the students to review the writing they did today and underline one sentence to share with the class. Give the students a moment to select their sentence; then go around the room and have each student read her sentence aloud, without comment.

After all the students have read their sentences, facilitate a brief discussion by asking:

Q   *What sentence did you hear that got you interested in someone else's writing?*

Q   *What questions do you want to ask a classmate about his or her writing?*

Explain that the students will continue to draft personal narratives next week.

GENRE: PERSONAL NARRATIVE

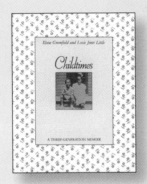

Childtimes: A Three-Generation Memoir
by Eloise Greenfield
and Lessie Jones Little (HarperTrophy, 1993)

Three generations of women remember their "childtimes."

Essays

"First Day of School,""Believing in Myself,"
and**"How I Saved a Dog's Life"**
excerpted from *Kids Write Through It: Essays from Kids Who Have Triumphed over Trouble* compiled by the editors at Fairview Press (Fairview Press, 1998) (see pages 212–216)

Young people write about how they have triumphed over trouble.

Writing Focus

- Students hear, discuss, and draft personal narratives.

- Students explore sensory details.

- Students generate writing ideas from their own lives.

- Students learn about a professional author's writing practice.

Social Focus

- Students listen respectfully to the thinking of others and share their own.

- Students make decisions and solve problems respectfully.

- Students express interest in and appreciation for one another's writing.

DO AHEAD

- Prior to Days 2, 3, and 4, consider prereading the essays with your English Language Learners. Stop during the reading to discuss vocabulary and to check for understanding. You might also invite the students to share experiences they have had that are similar to those described in the essays.

TEACHER AS WRITER

"Try to be one of the people on whom nothing is lost."
— *Henry James*

Select one of the pieces you wrote last week about a memorable event and reread it. Where could you include words and phrases that would help a reader imagine using her senses? See how many senses you can appeal to with the sensory details you add to your piece.

Day 1

Materials

- "John and the Snake"
  (pages 35–38 in *Childtimes*)

Exploring and Drafting Personal Narrative

In this lesson, the students:

- Hear, discuss, and draft personal narratives
- Explore writing about interesting incidents from their own lives
- Explore sensory details in text

GETTING READY TO WRITE

▶1 Gather and Briefly Review Week 1

Gather the class with partners sitting together, facing you. Review that they have been exploring personal narratives. This week they will hear personal narratives by some other writers, and they will continue to write their own drafts. Next week they will select one of their drafts to work on and publish for the class library.

▶2 Read "John and the Snake" Aloud

Show the cover of *Childtimes* and remind the students that they heard "Our House," "Chores," and "Candy" last week. Explain that today you will read "John and the Snake." In it, Pattie Ridley Jones describes one incident from her childhood. Invite the students to imagine what's happening as they listen.

Read "John and the Snake" on pages 35–38 aloud.

3▸ Briefly Discuss the Reading

Ask and briefly discuss:

Q *What incident does Pattie Ridley Jones describe in this personal narrative?*

Q *What did you see in your mind? What other senses did you imagine using?*

Point out that many personal narratives, like this one, tell about just one interesting incident from the author's life. Have partners use "Think, Pair, Share" to first think about and then discuss:

 Q *What is one interesting incident from your life that you could write about?* [pause] *Turn to your partner.*

After partners have discussed the question, signal for their attention and have a few volunteers share their ideas. Explain that the students will continue to write personal narratives today. Encourage them to think of interesting incidents from their own lives to write about and to use sensory details.

WRITING TIME

4▸ Write Independently

Ask the students to return to their seats. Write the following choices on the board and have the students write silently for 20–30 minutes.

- Write about an interesting incident from your own life.

- Work on a personal narrative you started earlier.

- Start a new personal narrative about anything from your own life.

Join the students in writing for a few minutes, then confer with individual students.

TEACHER CONFERENCE NOTE

As you did in Week 1, continue to confer with individual students, having them show and read their writing aloud to you. Help them extend their thinking about personal narrative by asking questions such as:

Q *Why did you choose to write about this [event/memory/ thing] ?*

Q *What else do you remember about it that you can add to the narrative?*

Q *What words are you using to describe what you [saw/ heard/smelled/tasted/felt]?*

Q *What other experiences from your own life might you want to write about?*

Document your observations for each student using the "Conference Notes" record sheet (BLM1).

Signal to let the students know when writing time is over.

SHARING AND REFLECTING

▶ 5 Briefly Share Writing and Reflect

Ask and briefly discuss the questions that follow. Invite the students to read passages of their writing aloud as they share.

Q *Did you write about an interesting incident from your own life? Tell us about it.*

Q *What other topics did you write about? Tell us about it.*

EXTENSION

Read More from *Childtimes*

If your students are interested, read and discuss other narratives from *Childtimes*. Take time to discuss how the narrators describe memories about specific incidents, using sensory details to help the reader imagine what happened. Encourage the students to continue to think about interesting events in their own lives they can write about.

Day 2

Materials

- "First Day of School" (see page 212)
- "Notes About Personal Narratives" chart

Exploring and Drafting Personal Narrative

In this lesson, the students:

- Hear, discuss, and draft personal narratives
- Explore writing about interesting incidents from their own lives
- Share their partner's thinking with the class
- Discuss and solve problems that arise in their work together

GETTING READY TO WRITE

▶1 Add to "Notes About Personal Narratives" Chart

Gather the class with partners sitting together, facing you. Review that the students heard "John and the Snake" yesterday and talked about how a personal narrative can be about just one interesting incident, such as when your brother was bitten by a snake. Direct the students' attention to the "Notes About Personal Narratives" chart, and add *writing about single, interesting incidents* to it.

▶2 Read "First Day of School" Aloud

Explain that today you will read a personal narrative written by a ten-year-old named Jennifer. In it, she writes about a single incident in her life that was important to her. Encourage the students to think as they listen about the important incident she writes about.

Read "First Day of School" aloud slowly and clearly.

Discuss the Reading

Ask and briefly discuss:

Q *What incident does Jennifer describe in this personal narrative?*

Q *What did she learn on the first day of school?*

 Q *What do you remember about your own first day of school? Turn to your partner.*

Explain that everyone will work on personal narratives during writing time today. Invite the students to write about what they remember about their first day of school, if they wish.

WRITING TIME

Write Independently

Ask the students to return to their seats. Write the following choices on the board and have the students write silently for 20–30 minutes.

- Write what you remember about your first day of school.

- Work on a personal narrative you started earlier.

- Start a new personal narrative about anything from your own life.

Join the students in writing for a few minutes. Then confer with individual students.

TEACHER CONFERENCE NOTE

Continue to confer with individual students, having them read their writing aloud to you. Help them extend their thinking about personal narrative by asking questions such as:

Q   *Why did you choose to write about this [event/memory/thing]?*

Q   *What else do you remember about it that you can add to the narrative?*

Q   *What words are you using to describe what you [saw/heard/smelled/tasted/felt]?*

Q   *What other experiences from your own life might you want to write about?*

Document your observations on the "Conference Notes" record sheet (BLM1).

Signal to let the students know when writing time is over.

SHARING AND REFLECTING

5 **Share Writing in Pairs**

Explain that partners will share with each other what they wrote today. Alert them to be ready to share something their partner wrote about during the whole-class discussion.

Have partners share, then signal for their attention and ask:

Q   *What did your partner write about today?*

Q   *Did your partner include any sensory details in his or her writing? Tell us about one.*

Q   *What problems, if any, did you and your partner have working together today? What can you do to avoid those problems next time?*

Day 3

Exploring and Drafting Personal Narrative

In this lesson, the students:

- Hear, discuss, and draft personal narratives
- Quick-write about perseverance
- Use sensory details in their writing
- Express interest in one another's writing
- Ask one another questions about their writing

GETTING READY TO WRITE

1 Read "Believing in Myself" Aloud

Gather the class with partners sitting together, facing you. Have them bring their writing notebooks and pencils with them. Review that the students have been writing drafts of personal narratives and that next week they will select one to develop, revise, and publish for the class.

Explain that today you will read another personal narrative by a ten-year-old. In it, the writer describes a challenge he faces and how he overcomes it. Encourage the students to think as they listen about how they might write about their own challenges.

Read "Believing in Myself" slowly and clearly, clarifying vocabulary as you read.

Suggested Vocabulary

corrective reading and math classes: classes to help students improve at reading and math

psychologist: person who studies human behavior

learning disabilities: difficulties with learning

Materials

- "Believing in Myself" (see pages 213–214)

ELL Vocabulary

English Language Learners may benefit from discussing additional vocabulary, including:

pronouncing: saying

had trouble grasping: had trouble understanding

▶2 Discuss the Reading

Ask and briefly discuss:

Q *What challenges does Joshua describe in his personal narrative?*

Q *In what ways do you think Joshua has persevered to overcome his challenges?*

Teacher Note ▶

If necessary, explain that *persevere* means "to keep trying without giving up."

▶3 Quick-Write: Perseverance Through Challenges

Use "Think, Pair, Share" to have partners first think about and then discuss the following questions:

 Q *What challenge have you faced that you might be able to write about?* [pause] *Turn to your partner.*

 Q *What did you do to persevere when you faced that challenge?* [pause] *Turn to your partner.*

Without discussing the questions as a class, ask the students to open their writing notebooks to the next blank page and spend a few minutes writing about a time they persevered in the face of challenge. After about 5 minutes, signal for attention and have a few volunteers share what they wrote with the class.

> *Students might say:*
>
> "I wrote about learning to ride a bike. I fell lots of times and I had to keep getting back up."
>
> "I sometimes have asthma at night. That's challenging for me because sometimes we have to go to the hospital. I have to persevere until I feel better."
>
> "It's challenging to have a baby brother. I wrote that he needs lots of attention!"

Explain that the students will continue to write personal narratives today. They may continue the piece they started during the quick-write or work on any personal narrative.

WRITING TIME

4 ▶ Draft Personal Narratives

Ask the students to return to their seats. Write the following choices on the board and have the students write silently for 20–30 minutes.

- Work on the piece you started during the quick-write.

- Continue a personal narrative you started earlier.

- Start a new personal narrative.

- Include sensory details in your writing.

Join the students in writing for a few minutes, then confer with individual students.

TEACHER CONFERENCE NOTE

Continue to confer with individual students, having them read their writing aloud to you. Help them extend their thinking about personal narrative by asking questions such as:

Q *Why did you choose to write about this [event/memory/thing]?*

Q *What else do you remember about it that you can add to the narrative?*

Q *What words are you using to describe what you [saw/heard/smelled/tasted/felt]?*

Q *What other experiences from your own life might you want to write about?*

Document your observations on the "Conference Notes" record sheet (BLM1).

Signal to let the students know when writing time is over.

SHARING AND REFLECTING

 Share One Sentence and Reflect

Ask the students to review the writing they did today and to underline one sentence to share with the class. Give the students a moment to select their sentences; then go around the room and have each student read his sentence aloud, without comment.

After all the students have read their sentences, facilitate a brief discussion by asking:

Q *What sentence did you hear that got you interested in someone else's writing?*

Q *What questions do you want to ask a classmate about his or her writing?*

Day 4

Exploring Personal Narrative and Pair Conferring

In this lesson, the students:

* Hear, discuss, and draft personal narratives
* Informally explore the idea of learning in personal narratives
* Practice procedures for pair conferences
* Express interest in and appreciation for one another's writing

GETTING READY TO WRITE

1 ▶ Add to "Notes About Personal Narratives" Chart

Gather the class with partners sitting together, facing you. Remind the students that they heard "First Day of School" and "Believing in Myself," two personal narratives written by young people. Ask:

Q *What do you remember about "First Day of School"?*

Point out that in "First Day of School" Jennifer learns that even new and uncomfortable situations can turn out all right if you focus on looking for kind faces and being yourself. Explain that good personal narratives usually include something about what the writer learns as a result of what happens.

Ask:

Q *What do you remember about "Believing in Myself"? What did the author learn as a result of his learning disabilities?*

Materials

* "How I Saved a Dog's Life"(see pages 215–216)
* "Notes About Personal Narratives" chart
* *Assessment Resource Book*

 Note

You might provide the prompt "I remember that…" to your English Language Learners to help them verbalize their answers to these questions.

Students might say:

"I think he learned that if he keeps working hard, he can do well in school."

"I agree with [Nancy]. He named the story 'Believing in Myself' because that's what he learned to do."

Direct the students' attention to the "Notes About Personal Narratives" chart and add *the writer learns something*. Explain that you will read another narrative by a young person today. Invite the students to listen for what the writer learns.

▶2 Read "How I Saved a Dog's Life" Aloud

Explain that today's personal narrative is written by a seven-year-old named Kate. Read "How I Saved a Dog's Life" aloud slowly and clearly.

▶3 Discuss the Reading

Ask and briefly discuss the questions that follow. Be ready to reread from the text to help the students recall what they heard.

Q *What experience does Kate write about in this personal narrative?*

Q *What does she learn from adopting Shelly?*

Use "Think, Pair, Share" to have partners first think about then discuss:

Q *When did you learn something, and how did you learn it?* [pause] *Turn to your partner.*

After partners have discussed the question, signal for their attention and have a few volunteers share with the class.

Students might say:

"When I was in kindergarten, I learned how to read."

"I learned how to play my favorite video game when my brother taught me."

"I learned how to play soccer last year."

FACILITATION TIP

Continue to cultivate students' listening skills and sense of responsibility by **asking questions once** without repeating or rewording them. Remember to use wait-time before calling on anyone so that the students have a chance to think before talking. Encourage them to ask you a question if they are confused or if they didn't hear your question.

Teacher Note

The concept of learning in personal narratives can be challenging for young students. In this unit, the students explore the idea very informally. If they have difficulty thinking of times that they learned something, suggest some ideas like those in the "Students might say" note, then ask, "What else have you learned?"

Explain that the students will continue to write personal narratives today. Encourage them to write about situations in which they have learned something, if they wish.

WRITING TIME

4▶ **Draft Personal Narratives**

Ask the students to return to their seats. Write the following choices on the board and have the students write silently for 20–30 minutes.

- Continue a personal narrative you started earlier.

- Start a new personal narrative.

- Try to include information about what you learned.

Join the students in writing for a few minutes; then walk around and observe.

◀ **Teacher Note**

You may want to shorten today's writing time slightly to leave more time for the pair conferences in Step 5.

CLASS ASSESSMENT NOTE

Observe the students and ask yourself:

- Do the students write with engagement about their own lives?

- Do they include sensory details in their writing?

- Will all the students have a personal narrative draft that they can start to develop for publication next week?

If necessary, work with individual students to ensure that all students will have a draft that they can develop for publication, beginning on Day 1 of next week.

Record your observations in the *Assessment Resource Book*.

Signal to let the students know when writing time is over.

SHARING AND REFLECTING

 ## Confer in Pairs About Personal Narrative Drafts

Explain that today the students will read one of their personal narrative drafts to their partner and confer about it. Briefly review the procedure you established for pair conferring (see Unit 1, Week 4, Day 4, pages 76–77) and remind the students that conferring means not only reading their writing to each other but talking about it as well. Explain that today partners will tell each other one thing they like about the other's draft. Ask and briefly discuss:

Q *What will you do during the conference to show that you are interested in your partner's draft?*

> **Students might say:**
>
> "I'll show I'm interested by asking my partner questions about her draft."
>
> "I'll listen to my partner's whole story without interrupting."
>
> "I will tell him things I liked in his story."

Teacher Note ▶

Consider having pairs spread out so partners can better hear each other. If necessary, signal about halfway through sharing time so partners can switch roles if they have not yet done so.

Have partners share their writing. Scan the class without intervening, providing sufficient time for both partners to share their writing before signaling for their attention.

 ## Reflect on Pair Conferences

Help partners reflect on their work together by asking:

Q *What did your partner do or say to show interest in your draft? How did that feel?*

Q *Why is it important that we all get to feel that our partner is interested in our writing?*

EXTENSION

Write in Response to Literature

Remind the students that in "How I Saved a Dog's Life," Kate writes about a puppy that she adopts and takes care of. Ask and briefly discuss:

Q *Who or what do you take care of in your daily life?*

Have the students choose a person, pet, or thing and write about how they take care of it in their notebooks.

First Day of School

by Jennifer, age 10

from *Kids Write Through It: Essays from Kids Who Have Triumphed Over Trouble*

When I first started going to school, I was scared that the other kids might laugh at me. I had never been to school before, and I didn't really know what to think. I remember when I first saw my classroom I felt bad and started to cry. I instantly knew I wanted my mom, but when I looked back, my mom was gone. Being in a strange place, I wasn't sure everyone was friendly, and now that my mom was gone, I started to cry even more. My teacher came to me and kindly told me that everything was going to be fine. That didn't help right away, but after a while I felt better about being there.

Having a kind teacher and friends who were nice to me on my first day of school makes this memory a good one. If you ask me what I learned on my first day of school, I'd tell you that even though you're in a new place doing something you never did before, and it's uncomfortable, if you look for kind faces and be yourself, it'll be all right. Kind faces and loving acts can make everything around you seem a little better.

Essay

Believing in Myself

by Joshua Jay L., age 10

from *Kids Write Through It: Essays from Kids Who Have Triumphed Over Trouble*

Hi. My name is Joshua and I'm ten years old. I'm in the fourth grade. I seemed to have problems in school pronouncing words, understanding what I read, talking loud enough, and even doing some math problems. This led to me being put in corrective reading and math classes. There seemed to be a slight improvement, but I still needed more help.

The next step was to be tested by the school psychologist. I was diagnosed with learning disabilities. The school psychologist told my mom and dad that I had trouble grasping every word the teacher said. I needed help with my vowel sounds, speaking out in class, and other skills. The psychologist did say that I had potential and, with some hard work, could improve. They decided to keep me in corrective classes but added speech classes to the list.

I was upset. It was bad enough that I was in two of those classes, now they had added another one. I was angry at myself. I felt different from the other kids. I had no confidence in myself. I was afraid to speak in front of others because I felt they would laugh at me if I pronounced a word wrong. So I began writing my thoughts and feelings on paper. Then one day my mom saw an article in one of her magazines about a club for kids who like to write.

I joined the club, called The Write News. Every month or so, they have a contest in their newsletter. I decided to enter one of my essays and, to my surprise, I won! After that, I won about three or four other times. I also won a contest in school for a poem I wrote.

This made me believe in myself. I'm working harder at school and starting to read a lot better in class. I'm no longer afraid to speak in front of my classmates.

continues

Believing in Myself
continued

    I'm still in corrective classes, but my teachers have seen a great improvement in me. They are great. With their help and the help of my family, I found the strength to overcome my disabilities.

    I hope my story will help other children with learning disabilities to overcome their fears and to believe in themselves. I hope each of them will become the confident person that I have become.

Essay

How I Saved a Dog's Life

by Kate, age 7

from *Kids Write Through It: Essays from Kids Who Have Triumphed Over Trouble*

When my old dog, Winston, died, it was sad for all of us. So one day we went to the SPCA to look for a new dog. Of course, I knew we could never, ever, replace Winston, but if I didn't have a dog I would be sad forever. When I went in, I wanted every puppy in sight. Then I saw Shelly. I wanted her so badly, I thought my heart was going to hop right out of my chest. I had to get her.

Sometimes, the dogs at the SPCA are put to sleep if people don't buy them. Not this dog. I saved her.

Shelly is a very lucky puppy. She got a good owner, and she didn't have to be killed. I am glad she wasn't killed, and so is my whole family. Shelly is very cute and funny, but not always. Sometimes she gets into trouble. She is always cute, though.

To get her, we had to sign a sheet of paper, tell them what her name would be, and promise that we would take care of her. We had to promise to feed her the right food and to take her to the vet to get her shots.

I don't like to watch them give her shots, but I do any way. I taught her some tricks, too. I taught her to catch the treat when I throw it in the air. And I taught her to fetch. I'm going to teach her more stuff, but I try to remember she is just a dog. Shelly is the best puppy in the world. I know that.

Sometimes I cry when I think of Winston. And sometimes Shelly makes me mad because she bites me. I don't like that. But I'm not the only one who gets bitten. My sister Katie, my mommy, and my step-dad also get bitten. She even bites herself sometimes. Other than that, she is a good puppy.

When I am grown up I'm going to be a veterinarian. I will help the sick puppies, especially Shelly. I really want to be a

continues

How I Saved a Dog's Life

continued

veterinarian. I hope I get the job because I like animals. And so does my friend. And I like God, too. And animals.

What I learned from my experience of getting a dog from the SPCA is that you need to give a dog a chance. You need to give them a good home to live in. And you need to treat them like any other person. You also need to give your love, and a lot of it.

You may cry sometimes when you remember your old dog. I do that a lot. I remember how I used to play with him. I bet other children will cry sooner or later if their dog dies, or maybe they already did. I'm glad to give them my experience for fair warning.

Week 3 Overview

GENRE: PERSONAL NARRATIVE

Writing Focus

- Students review their drafts and select one to develop, revise, proofread, and publish.

- Students add sensory details to their writing.

- Students explore strong opening sentences.

- Students confer with one another and the teacher.

Social Focus

- Students work in a responsible way.

- Students listen respectfully to the thinking of others and share their own.

DO AHEAD

- Prior to Day 2, review the pieces you have written so far this year and select a page of personal narrative to use to model how to develop and revise a draft. Make a transparency of the page. Alternatively, you can use the "Sample Personal Narrative" (BLM5–BLM6).

- (Optional) If computers are available, you might have some students type and print their drafts or recruit parent volunteers to help the students do so.

Day 1

Selecting Drafts

In this lesson, the students:

- Review their drafts and select one to develop and publish
- Reread their writing critically
- Use writing and pair conference time responsibly
- Ask one another questions about their writing
- Share their partner's thinking with the class

GETTING READY TO WRITE

1▶ Review Personal Narrative

Gather the class with partners sitting together, facing you. Review that over the past two weeks the students have been writing drafts of personal narratives. Ask:

Q *What have you learned about personal narrative, compared to other kinds of writing?*

Direct the students' attention to the "Notes About Personal Narratives" chart and review the items on it.

Explain that this week the students will select one of their drafts and begin to develop it for publication. They will revise it to make it clearer and more interesting, proofread it for correctness, and publish it by contributing it to a class book.

2▶ Prepare to Review Drafts

Explain that today the students will reread all the personal narrative drafts they have written so far and select one to develop for the class book. Explain that the draft they select does not have to be complete, and it should be one that they can imagine making changes to. Ask:

Q *As you're looking through your drafts, what might you want to look for to help you decide on one to develop?*

> **Students might say:**
>
> "I want to look for a draft that I'm really interested in or have some strong feelings about."
>
> "I will look for drafts that describe situations where I learned something."
>
> "I want my story to be different from everyone else's, so I'm going to look for a draft that is unique."

◀ **Teacher Note**

If the students have difficulty answering this question, offer some ideas like those in the "Students might say" note and ask, "What else might you look for?"

WRITING TIME

▶3 Reread Drafts and Select One to Develop

Have the students return to their seats, reread their drafts, and select one to develop and publish. Students who select their draft before the time is up can start thinking about how they can change, add to, or improve the draft.

As the students review their drafts, circulate around the room and support students by asking them questions such as:

Q *Why did you choose this piece to revise?*

Q *What can you imagine adding or changing in this piece to make it more interesting?*

If you notice the students selecting pieces with limited potential for revision (for example, pieces they feel are already "perfect," very long or very short pieces, pieces not double-spaced), gently guide them toward a more workable choice.

SHARING AND REFLECTING

 ## Confer in Pairs About Selected Drafts

Explain that pairs will confer about the drafts they selected and why they chose those drafts. Ask:

Q *What questions can you ask your partner about the draft he or she chose?*

> **Students might say:**
>
> "I could ask my partner why she chose that draft to publish."
>
> "I could ask my partner how he's thinking of revising his draft."

Alert the students to listen carefully to each other because you will ask them to share what their partner said in the whole-class discussion. Ask partners to start talking.

After several minutes of pair sharing, signal for the students' attention. Have several students share what their partner said. Follow up with questions such as:

Q *Why did your partner select that draft?*

Q *What is interesting to you about your partner's draft?*

Q *What else did your partner tell you about the draft he is going to work on to publish?*

Reflect on Pair Conferences

Help the students reflect on their partner work by briefly discussing:

Q *What did you do today to make sure you could accurately share what your partner said with the class?*

Q *Why is it important that each of us take responsibility for listening carefully to our partner?*

Explain that the students will begin revising their drafts tomorrow.

FACILITATION TIP

Continue to practice **asking questions once** without repeating or rewording them. Notice the effect this has on the students' attentiveness during class discussions.

Day 2

Analyzing, Completing, and Revising Drafts

In this lesson, the students:

- Reread their writing critically
- Mark places in their drafts where they might add sensory details
- Complete and begin revising their drafts
- Use writing time responsibly

GETTING READY TO WRITE

1 ▶ **Facilitate Guided Rereading of Drafts**

Have the students stay at their desks today. Ask them to open their writing notebooks to the personal narrative draft they selected yesterday. Explain that the students will carefully reread their drafts and that you will help them think about ways they can add to, revise, and improve them. They will also have time to complete their drafts today, if necessary. Have them quietly reread their drafts and look up when they are finished.

Distribute a pad of self-stick notes to each student. Explain that you will ask the students to look for and think about several specific things in their draft.

Say the following prompts one at a time, giving the students several quiet minutes between each prompt to review their draft and mark passages with self-stick notes.

- *Find one place in your draft that you really like. This might be a place where you used words that you like or where you like a sentence you wrote. Put a self-stick note in the margin next to that place and write "I like" on it.*

Materials

- Pad of small (1½" x 2") self-stick notes for each student
- Transparency of your own personal narrative (see "Do Ahead" on page 217) OR transparency of "Sample Personal Narrative" (BLM5–BLM6)
- Overhead pen
- *Assessment Resource Book*

◀ **Teacher Note**

The purpose of the guided rereading is to give the students experience reading their drafts critically *before* they begin to revise. They will not need pencils for this. Note that some students will not be finished with their piece and will need time this week to both complete and revise their drafts.

Teacher Note

◀ If necessary, model attaching a self-stick note to the outer margin of a notebook page so that it marks the text without covering it up.

If the students have difficulty identifying places they might revise, call for their attention and show the transparency of your own writing (or the "Sample Personal Narrative") on the overhead projector. Read the passage aloud, and model thinking aloud and marking it. (You might say, "I could add some detail about what the gas station looked like. I'll mark it to remind myself to add some details." Place the note in the margin next to the second paragraph.)

Teacher Note ▶

You might say, "I want to add words that tell what the gas station looks like. I'll add 'It was lit up brightly in the dark night.'"

- *Find a place in your draft where you describe, or could describe, what something looks like. Put a self-stick note in the margin next to it and write "looks" on it.*

When most students have finished, signal for their attention and ask several volunteers to read what they marked. Stimulate their thinking by asking questions such as:

Q *What sensory details might you add there to help the reader imagine what's happening?*

2 ▶ **Model Developing a Marked Section of the Draft**

Explain that during writing time today the students will look at the places they marked with self-stick notes and add details to help their readers imagine what's happening. Ask the students to watch as you model adding details to a draft.

Show the transparency of your own writing (or the "Sample Personal Narrative") on the overhead projector and read it aloud. Wonder aloud about sensory details you could add. Model using an arrow (caret) to insert new text.

Sample Personal Narrative

One summer, my mom packed up the car with suitcases,

sandwiches, and my brother Mike and me, and we drove

all night to visit my grandparents.

　　　　　　　　　　　　　It was lit up brightly in the dark night.
We pulled into a gas station. It was the middle of the

night when Mike and I were sound asleep, me in the front,

and him in back.

　　I didn't wake up until my mom slammed the door and

said, "That should do it. We won't need to stop again for

100 miles."

　　　　She drove out of the gas station and pulled up to a

Looks

Using the same procedure, model one or two more examples of adding visual details to your draft. Explain that the students will follow the same procedure to add details to their own drafts today.

WRITING TIME

▶ Revise First Drafts

Write the following tasks on the board and have the students work silently on them for 20–30 minutes.

- Complete your draft.

- Add sensory details to places you marked to help the reader imagine what's happening.

- Remove the self-stick notes when you finish adding details.

Join the students in writing for a few minutes; then walk around the classroom and observe.

CLASS ASSESSMENT NOTE

Observe the students and ask yourself:

- Are the students able to add sensory details to their drafts?

- Do they seem engaged in thinking of ways to develop their drafts?

Support students who are having difficulty by asking them questions such as:

Q *What were you thinking about when you marked this place on your draft?*

Q *What words could you add to help the reader imagine what's happening?*

Record your observations in the *Assessment Resource Book*.

Signal to let the students know when writing time is over.

SHARING AND REFLECTING

 Reflect on Writing and Taking Responsibility

Have the students put their pencils and self-stick notes away and gather with their notebooks to share their writing. Discuss the questions that follow, and invite the students to read from their drafts as they share.

Q *What sensory details did you add to your draft? Read us that part.*

Q *What do you imagine when you hear [Mindy's] passage?*

Q *What did you do to take responsibility for your own work during writing time today? How does that help to build our community?*

Explain that the students will continue to work on their drafts tomorrow.

Day 3

Analyzing and Revising Drafts

In this lesson, the students:

- Reread their writing critically
- Mark places in their drafts where they might add sensory details
- Revise their drafts
- Give their full attention to the person who is speaking
- Ask one another questions about their writing.

GETTING READY TO WRITE

1 ▶ Briefly Review Purpose of Revision

Have the students stay at their desks today. Ask them to open their writing notebooks to the personal narrative that they are developing. Review that they began to analyze and revise their drafts yesterday. Remind them that the purpose of revision is to make their piece as interesting and readable as possible before they publish it for their classmates.

Explain that today you will ask them to think about a couple more ways they might improve their drafts.

2 ▶ Facilitate Guided Rereading of Drafts

Have the students quietly reread their draft and look up when they are finished. Have them get out their self-stick notes and get ready to think about the following prompts. Say the prompts one at a time, giving the students several quiet minutes between each prompt to review their draft and mark passages with the self-stick notes.

- *Find a place where you describe, or could describe, what something sounds like. Put a self-stick note in the margin next to that place and write "sounds" on it.*

Materials

- Pad of small (1½" x 2") self-stick notes for each student
- Revised transparency of your own personal narrative OR of "Sample Personal Narrative" from Day 2
- Overhead pen

- *Find a place where you describe, or could describe, what something feels like. Put a self-stick note in the margin next to that place and write "feels" on it.*

- *Find a place where you describe, or could describe, how something smells or tastes. Put a self-stick note in the margin next to that place and write "smells" or "tastes" on it.*

3▶ Model Developing a Marked Section of the Draft

Explain that during writing time today, like yesterday, the students will look at the places they marked with self-stick notes and add sensory details to help their readers imagine what's happening. Use the same procedure you used yesterday to model adding sounds, smells, tastes, and/or sensations to your draft.

WRITING TIME

4▶ Revise First Drafts

Write the following tasks on the board and have the students work silently on them for 20–30 minutes.

- Add more sensory details to help the reader imagine what's happening.

- Remove the self-stick notes when you finish adding details.

- Add to your story until it is finished.

As the students work, circulate around the room. Support students who are having difficulty adding to their draft by having them join you at a back table and quietly discussing questions such as:

Q *What were you thinking about when you marked this place on your draft?*

Q *What were you thinking or feeling at this point in this situation? What sentence could you add to help your reader understand that?*

Q *What words could you add here to help your reader [see/hear/smell/taste/feel] what's happening?*

Signal to let the students know that writing time is over.

SHARING AND REFLECTING

5 ▶ **Reflect on Revisions and Participation**

Have several volunteers share by reading an original and a revised passage aloud to the class. Encourage discussion by asking the class the questions that follow. Be ready to have the volunteers reread aloud, if necessary.

Q *What did you imagine as you listened to [Robin's] revision?*

Q *How is [Robin's] revision different from her original passage?*

Q *What questions can we ask [Robin] about her revision?*

Help the students reflect on their participation in this discussion by asking:

Q *How did you do today giving your full attention to the people who were sharing their writing?*

Q *If you weren't giving your full attention today, what will help you give your full attention the next time we have a class discussion?*

Day 4

Materials

- Transparency of "Opening Sentences from Four Personal Narratives" (BLM7)
- *Student Writing Handbook* page 4

Analyzing and Revising Drafts

In this lesson, the students:

- Explore strong opening sentences
- Reread their writing critically
- Revise their drafts
- Give their full attention to the person who is speaking

GETTING READY TO WRITE

1 ### Read and Discuss Opening Sentences

Have partners get out their writing notebooks and *Student Writing Handbooks* and sit together at desks today. Explain that they will continue to work on their personal narrative drafts today. Before they start working, they will take some time to think about an important feature of all narratives: strong opening sentences.

Explain that the opening sentences of a piece of writing need to hook the reader, making him want to keep reading. Explain that you will read the opening sentences from several personal narratives they heard earlier in the unit. Ask them to think about how the authors get the reader interested with these openings.

Read the following passage aloud twice:

> "Every year, right after the last day of school, I'd pack a suitcase with my cool summer clothes, my favorite toys, and a sketchbook. Then my dog, Daisy, and I were off to Grandma's apartment in El Barrio." (from *Grandma's Records*)

Ask:

 Q *What do you think about or imagine when you hear this opening? Turn to your partner.*

Without stopping to discuss as a class, repeat this procedure with the following opening sentences:

> "We had right much work to do. In the house and out in the garden, too. We planted and weeded, and dug up sweet potatoes, and picked butter beans." (from "Chores")

> "A terrible thing happened to my brother John in the schoolyard one day." (from "John and the Snake")

> "When I first started going to school, I was afraid the other kids might laugh at me. I had never been to school before, and I didn't really know what to think. I remember when I first saw my classroom I felt bad and started to cry." (from "First Day of School")

▶2 Analyze Strong Opening Sentences

Have the students open their *Student Writing Handbook* to page 4, where the opening sentences are reproduced. At the same time, place the transparency of "Opening Sentences from Four Personal Narratives" on the overhead projector. Together, reread the first passage from *Grandma's Records*, and ask:

Q *What does the author do to get us interested in reading this piece?*

Q *What words or phrases help us imagine what's happening?*

Students might say:

"The author gets us interested by making us imagine the beginning of summer vacation."

"The words 'cool summer clothes' help me imagine shorts and T-shirts."

"The words 'my dog, Daisy' make me think it must be fun to take your dog to your grandmother's house with you."

"'El Barrio' tells me that his grandmother probably lives in an interesting neighborhood."

As volunteers respond, underline the words and phrases they mention on the transparency.

Ask the students to work in pairs to reread the remaining opening sentences and underline words and sentences that they feel are especially effective at making the reader want to keep reading the story.

Teacher Note

Words or phrases the students
might report include:

- "in the house," "out in the
  garden," "planted and weeded,"
  "dug up sweet potatoes,"
  "picked butter beans" (from
  "Chores")

- "a terrible thing happened,"
  "schoolyard" (from "John and
  the Snake")

- "I was afraid," "kids might laugh
  at me," "first saw my classroom,"
  "started to cry" (from "First Day
  of School")

After several minutes, signal for the students' attention. Ask
volunteers to report what they talked about for each of the
openings, and underline words and phrases they mention on
the transparency. As they report, ask:

Q *How does that [word/sentence] help you get interested in reading
the story?*

3 ▶ Review Opening Sentences in Drafts

Ask the students to reread the first few sentences of their own personal
narratives. Ask and have the students think to themselves about:

Q *How might you revise your opening sentences to "hook" the reader
and make him or her want to keep reading?*

Without discussion as a class, explain that the students will revise
their opening sentences, then work on completing the writing and
revision of their personal narrative today.

WRITING TIME

4 ▶ Revise and Complete Drafts

Write the following tasks on the board and have the students work
silently on them for 20–30 minutes.

- Revise your opening sentences so that they "hook" your reader.

- Make any other revisions or additions so that your piece is
  complete and as interesting as it can be.

During the writing time, begin conferring with individual students
about the piece that they are developing for publication.

TEACHER CONFERENCE NOTE

Over the coming week, confer with individual students about the pieces they are developing for publication. Ask each student to tell you about the part he is working on now and to read his draft aloud. As you listen, ask yourself:

- Does this student's writing communicate clearly? If not, what's unclear?

- Does this student's piece describe interesting personal experiences?

- Does the student use descriptive sensory details?

- Do the revisions make sense and improve the piece?

Help the student revise unclear writing by rereading those passages back to him and explaining what is confusing you. Ask questions such as:

Q *What do you want your reader to be thinking at this part? How can you write that?*

Document your observations for each student using the "Conference Notes" record sheets (BLM1).

Signal to let the students know when writing time is over.

SHARING AND REFLECTING

 Share Opening Sentences as a Class

Have several volunteers share the opening sentences of their personal narratives. As students share, encourage discussion by asking the class the questions that follow. Be ready to ask the volunteers to reread what they shared, if necessary.

Q *What words did you hear in [Emilio's] opening sentence(s) that make you want to keep reading?*

Q *What ideas, if any, does this give you for your own opening sentences?*

Week 4   Overview

GENRE: PERSONAL NARRATIVE

Writing Focus

- Students assess their own writing.

- Students proofread for spelling, grammar, and punctuation.

- Students write their final version and publish it in a class book.

- Students present their personal narrative to the class from the Author's Chair.

- Students confer with one another and the teacher

Social Focus

- Students work in a responsible way.

- Students help one another improve their writing.

- Students act in fair and caring ways.

- Students express interest in and appreciation for one another's writing.

DO AHEAD

- (Optional) If computers are available, you might have the students type and print their stories or recruit parent volunteers to help them do so.

- Prior to Day 1, create a chart labeled "Self-Assessment Questions" with the following questions written on it:

  Q *Does my piece describe an interesting personal experience?*

  Q *Is my meaning clear in every sentence?*

  Q *Are there sensory details in it?*

TEACHER AS WRITER

"For him no simple feeling exists. All that he sees, his joys, his pleasures, his suffering, his despair, all instantaneously become objects of observation."
— *Guy de Maupassant*

Look at the personal narrative draft you wrote in Week 3, in which you described an event and how it changed you. Close your eyes and try to remember what you felt before, during, and after the event. Look for places where you can insert information about your thoughts or feelings before, during, and after the event.

Day 1

Materials

- "Self-Assessment Questions" chart, prepared ahead (see "Do Ahead" on page 233)

- "Questions About My Draft" chart from Unit 2, Week 1

- Revised Transparency of your own personal narrative OR "Sample Personal Narrative" from Week 3

- *Assessment Resource Book*

Self-Assessing and Pair Conferring

In this lesson, the students:

- Assess their own writing

- Ask for and receive feedback about their writing

- Give feedback in a helpful way

- Ask one another questions about their writing

- Use pair conference time responsibly

GETTING READY TO WRITE

1 ▶ Prepare to Self-Assess

Explain that partners will meet to confer about their drafts today. Before conferring, the students will ask themselves some questions about their own drafts and decide what they want to ask their partner when they meet.

Direct the students' attention to the "Self-Assessment Questions" chart. Explain that you would like the students to ask themselves these questions as they reread their drafts. Read the questions aloud and then show the transparency of your revised writing from Week 3 (or the "Sample Personal Narrative"). Model rereading your draft, asking yourself the questions, and thinking aloud about the answers.

2 ▶ Self-Assess and Think About What to Ask Partners

Ask the students to reread their own draft and ask themselves the "Self-Assessment Questions." After most students have had time to finish, signal for their attention and ask:

Q *What questions do you want to ask your partner today about your draft?*

As the students report questions, record them on the "Questions About My Draft" chart. Remind the students that they started this chart earlier in the year, and review the questions on it. Ask:

Q *What other questions on this chart do you want to ask your partner today?*

Students might say:

"I want to ask my partner if she can imagine what's happening."

"I want to ask my partner if he can tell what I learned from what I wrote."

"I want to find out whether anything is confusing to my partner."

Explain that partners will read their drafts aloud to each other, including revisions, and then ask each other questions about their own drafts.

◀ **Teacher Note**

If the students have difficulty answering this question, suggest some ideas like those in the "Students might say" note.

▶3 Confer in Pairs

Give the students ample time to confer in pairs.

CLASS ASSESSMENT NOTE

Circulate among pairs and observe without intervening. Ask yourself:

* Are pairs staying on task, reading and discussing their writing?

* Are the students asking each other questions about their own drafts?

* Are they giving each other specific feedback?

* Are they giving feedback in a helpful way?

Note any difficulties you observe to discuss with the students in Step 4.

Record your observations in the *Assessment Resource Book*.

When most pairs have had time to discuss their drafts, call for the class's attention.

4 ▶ Reflect on Feedback

Gather the class and briefly discuss:

Q *What was helpful about the way your partner talked to you today?*

Q *What problems, if any, did you have during pair conferences? What will you do to avoid those problems next time?*

Share any problems you noticed and discuss what the students will do to avoid those problems next time. Ask:

Q *What is one thing your partner told you about your piece?*

Remind the students that authors take feedback very seriously, although they may not always agree with the feedback. Authors need to decide for themselves what will result in the best possible piece.

Explain that during writing time today each student will revise his draft based on his self-assessment and the feedback he received from his partner. Encourage the students to finalize their drafts today so that they can begin proofreading and publishing them tomorrow.

WRITING TIME

5 ▶ Revise and Complete Drafts

Write the following tasks on the board and have students work silently on them for 20–30 minutes.

- Revise your draft based on self-assessment and partner feedback.

- Finish writing and revising your draft.

- If you finish, work on another piece of writing.

During the writing time, confer with individual students about the pieces they are publishing.

TEACHER CONFERENCE NOTE

Continue to confer with individual students about the pieces they are developing for publication. Ask each student to tell you about the part she is working on now and to read her draft aloud. As you listen, ask yourself:

- Does this student's writing communicate clearly? If not, what's unclear?

- Does this student's piece describe an interesting personal experience?

- Does the student use sensory details?

- Do the revisions make sense and improve the piece?

Help the student revise unclear writing by rereading those passages back to her and explaining what is confusing you. Ask questions such as:

Q *What do you want your reader to be thinking at this part? How can you write that?*

Document your observations for each student using the "Conference Notes" record sheet (BLM1).

Signal to let the students know when writing time is over.

SHARING AND REFLECTING

▶6 **Reflect on Writing**

Help the students reflect on their work today by briefly discussing:

Q *What feedback from your partner did you incorporate into your revision today? Tell us about it.*

Explain that the students will start proofreading their final versions tomorrow.

EXTENSION

Technology Tip: Publishing Student Writing Online

This week the students will publish their personal narratives for the class library. Some students might also be interested in publishing their writing online. There are a number of websites where students can publish their writing online; search for them using the keywords "publishing children's writing." Publishing online allows family members and friends to easily access and enjoy students' writing.

Day 2

Proofreading

In this lesson, the students:

- Proofread for spelling, grammar and punctuation
- Check for correct use of *your/you're* and *then/than*
- Begin writing their final versions

GETTING READY TO WRITE

1 Prepare to Proofread First Drafts

Have the students stay at their desks today. Explain that the students will begin copying their first draft into a final version for the class book. Before this step, they will take time to proofread it to make sure that the writing is free from errors.

Remind the students that they learned to proofread their drafts for spelling and punctuation using the word bank and proofreading notes in the *Student Writing Handbook* (see Unit 2, Week 3 on pages 156–163). They will use these resources today to proofread their personal narratives.

2 Discuss Proofreading for Spelling and Punctuation

Ask the students to begin rereading their drafts (even if they are not finished with them) and circle any words that they're not sure how to spell. Stop the students after a couple of minutes and ask:

Q *What words have you circled so far?*

Have several volunteers report the words they circled. Have the students check their word bank to see if the words they circled are listed. If not, encourage them to check the spelling by another method during writing time today (see the Teacher Note) and to make sure to add the correctly spelled word to their word bank.

Materials

- Transparency of "Proofreading Notes" (BLM19)
- *Student Writing Handbook*
- Pad of small (1½" x 2") self-stick notes for each student
- Supply of lined paper for final versions
- (Optional) Computers for word processing

◀ **Teacher Note**

If you have students who have not yet finished writing and revising their first drafts, plan time for them to finish before they move on to proofreading. Ask all of the students to pay attention as you teach them about proofreading so that they will be able to do this step when they are ready.

Teacher Note

◀ The students can check the spelling of a word by asking another student, asking you, finding the word in a published book, or looking it up in a dictionary or online.

Discuss Proofreading for Grammar

Write the words *your* and *you're* where everyone can see them. Ask the students to go back and see whether they used these words anywhere in their personal narrative and to circle them if they did.

After a moment, signal for the students' attention. Point out that *your* and *you're* are both pronounced the same way but have different meanings. Ask and briefly discuss:

Q *How do you know whether you're using the right one in a sentence?*

If necessary, explain that *your* means *belonging to you*, while *you're* is short *for "you are."* Ask the students to open their *Student Writing Handbook* to the proofreading notes section as you show the transparency on the overhead projector. Write the notes in the diagram below on the transparency and ask the students to copy them into their proofreading notes.

Rule	Example	Notes
your	"Wipe your nose."	means belonging to you
you're	"You're funny."	short for "you are"

Teacher Note ▶

To provide your students with more practice identifying and correcting commonly misused words, do the related activity in the *Skill Practice Teaching* Guide with them.

Follow the same procedure to help the students distinguish between *than* (used when comparing two things; for example, *more than, less than*) and *then* (used when talking about time or order; for example, *now and then; first you, then me*).

Discuss Proofreading for Punctuation

Remind the students that their proofreading notes are a checklist of things to pay attention to when they proofread their drafts. Ask:

Q *What else is listed on your proofreading notes that you will check for in your draft today?*

Explain that the students will proofread their drafts and then begin copying them in their best handwriting on loose, lined paper (or preparing to print out a corrected version from the computer).

WRITING TIME

5 ▸ Proofread and Write Final Drafts

Write the following tasks on the board and have the students work silently on them for 20–30 minutes.

- Proofread your draft for spelling and punctuation.

- Check correct use of *your/you're* and *than/then*.

- Copy your final version on loose, lined paper.

During the writing time, confer with individual students.

TEACHER CONFERENCE NOTE

Continue to confer with individual students about the pieces that they are developing for publication. Ask each student to tell you about the part she is working on now and to read her draft aloud. As you listen, ask yourself:

- Does this student's writing communicate clearly? If not, what's unclear?

- Does this student's piece describe an interesting personal experience?

- Does the student use sensory details?

- Do the revisions make sense and improve the piece?

Help the student revise unclear writing by rereading those passages back to her and explaining what is confusing you. Ask questions such as:

Q *What do you want your reader to be thinking at this part? How can you write that?*

Document your observations for each student using the "Conference Notes" record sheet (BLM1).

Signal to let the students know when writing time is over.

SHARING AND REFLECTING

 Reflect on Proofreading

Briefly discuss questions such as:

Q *What corrections did you make when you proofread your draft?*

Q *What words did you find in your word bank? How did you check on words that were not in the word bank?*

Q *Did your proofreading notes help you find any errors? Tell us about them.*

Day 3

Publishing

In this lesson, the students:

- Discuss features for their class book
- Write their final versions
- Share their writing from the Author's Chair
- Give their full attention to the person who is speaking
- Express interest in and appreciation for one another's writing

Materials

- Supply of lined paper for final versions
- (Optional) Read-aloud books from Weeks 1 and 2
- Construction and/or drawing paper for class book cover and other features
- (Optional) Computers for word processing
- Chair to use for the Author's Chair

GETTING READY TO WRITE

▶1 Plan Features of the Class Book

Gather the class with partners sitting together, facing you. Explain that the students will have today and tomorrow to finish the final version of their personal narrative. Students who are finished will begin sharing their narratives from the Author's Chair today. Remind the students that the pages will be bound together as a class book.

As a class, brainstorm and decide on a title for the class book and decide whether any other features—such as a dedication page, back cover blurb, or illustrations—will be included. If helpful, review what these features look like by showing examples in read-aloud books from earlier in the unit. Assign volunteers to work on the cover and any other features when they finish their final versions.

WRITING TIME

▶2 Finish Final Versions

Ask the students to return to their seats and work on their final versions for 20–30 minutes. Provide the materials needed for creating a cover, illustrations, and any other features the students have agreed upon for the class book. As they work, confer with individual students.

> ### TEACHER CONFERENCE NOTE
>
> Continue to confer with individual students about the pieces they are developing for publication. Ask each student to tell you about the part he is working on now and to read his draft aloud. As you listen, ask yourself:
>
> * Does this student's writing communicate clearly? If not, what's unclear?
>
> * Does this student's piece describe an interesting personal experience?
>
> * Does the student use sensory details?
>
> * Do the revisions make sense and improve the piece?
>
> Help the student revise unclear writing by rereading those passages back to him and explaining what is confusing you. Ask questions such as:
>
> **Q** *What do you want your reader to be thinking at this part? How can you write that?*
>
> Document your observations for each student using the "Conference Notes" record sheet (BLM1).

Signal to let the students know when writing time is over.

SHARING AND REFLECTING

 Review Sharing Writing from the Author's Chair

Gather the class with partners sitting together, facing the Author's Chair. Explain that each student will read his personal narrative to the class from the Author's Chair before it is bound into the class book.

Remind the students of the procedure that you would like them to follow when they are ready to present their personal narratives from the Author's Chair.

Teacher Note

If necessary, review the procedures you established for Author's Chair sharing in Unit 2, Week 3, Day 4 (pages 170–171).

4 **Review Speaking Clearly and Expressing Interest in One Another's Writing**

Before asking anyone to share from the Author's Chair today, have a discussion about how the students will act, both as presenting authors and as members of the audience. Ask and discuss:

Q *Why is it important to speak in a loud, clear voice when you're sharing your narrative with the class?*

Q *If you're in the audience and you can't hear the author, how can you politely let her know?*

Q *How will you let the author know that you're interested in his writing? Why is it important to express interest in other people's writing?*

Encourage the students to be attentive audience members. Tell them that you will check in with them later to see how they did.

5 **Conduct Author's Chair Sharing**

Ask a student who has completed his personal narrative to read it aloud from the Author's Chair. At the end of the reading, facilitate a discussion using questions like those that follow, giving the author a chance to respond to the class's comments and questions.

 Q *What was interesting to you about [Jordan's] personal narrative? Turn to your partner.*

Q *What sensory details did you hear as you listened to his narrative? What did they make you imagine?*

Q (Have the student reread his opening sentences.) *How does [Jordan] "hook" the reader with his opening sentences?*

Q *What questions can we ask [Jordan] about his narrative?*

Collect the student's narrative to be bound later into the class book.

Follow this procedure to have a few more students share from the Author's Chair. Explain that they will continue to share tomorrow

FACILITATION TIP

Reflect on your experience over the past three weeks with **asking questions once** without repeating or rewording them. Does this technique feel comfortable and natural for you? Do you find yourself using it throughout the school day? What effect has using this technique had on your students' attentiveness and responsiveness in discussions? We encourage you to continue to use and reflect on this technique throughout the year.

and that everyone will have an opportunity to share their personal narrative from the Author's Chair.

6▶ Reflect on Audience Behavior During Author's Chair Sharing

Ask and briefly discuss:

Q *What did we do as an audience today to help Author's Chair sharing go well? What might we want to work on during the next Author's Chair sharing?*

Q *If you shared a narrative today, how did the audience make you feel? What did they do that made you feel [relaxed/nervous/proud]?*

Day 4

Publishing

In this lesson, the students:

- Reflect on personal narrative
- Write their final versions
- Share their writing from the Author's Chair
- Give their full attention to the person who is speaking
- Express interest in and appreciation for one another's writing

Materials

- (Optional) "Notes About Personal Narratives" chart
- Supply of lined paper for final versions
- (Optional) Computers for word processing

GETTING READY TO WRITE

▶ **Reflect on Personal Narrative**

Gather the class with partners sitting together, facing you. Review that over the past four weeks they learned about personal narrative and took their own personal narrative through the writing process, from a first draft to a published book. Ask:

Q *What have you learned about writing a good personal narrative?*

Students might say:

"I learned that personal narratives tell about something interesting that happened to the author."

"I learned that a good personal narrative has sensory details in it."

"I learned that a good personal narrative tells what the author learned."

Use "Think, Pair, Share" to have partners first think about and then discuss the following questions:

 Q *What is one way your final personal narrative has turned out better than your first draft?* [pause] *Turn to your partner.*

◀ **Teacher Note**

If necessary, refer the students' attention to the "Notes About Personal Narratives" chart.

Q *What is one thing you like about writing personal narrative?* [pause] *Turn to your partner.*

 Q *What did you find challenging about writing personal narrative?* [pause] *Turn to your partner.*

Remind the students that writers become better over time as they practice writing over and over. Encourage students who feel particularly drawn to personal narrative to continue to write it during their free time and during the open weeks of this program.

Explain that the students will work on finishing the final version of their personal narrative today. Those who have finished may write whatever they wish during writing time. After writing time, they will continue to share their narratives from the Author's Chair.

WRITING TIME

▶2 Finish Final Versions

Write the following tasks on the board and have the students work silently on them for 20–30 minutes.

- Finish your final version.

- If you finish, work on another piece of writing.

TEACHER CONFERENCE NOTE

Continue to confer with individual students about the pieces they are developing for publication. Ask each student to tell you about the part she is working on now and to read her draft aloud. As you listen, ask yourself:

- Does this student's writing communicate clearly? If not, what's unclear?

- Does this student's piece describe an interesting personal experience?

continues

- Does the student use sensory details?

- Do the revisions make sense and improve the piece?

Help the student revise unclear writing by rereading those passages back to her and explaining what is confusing you. Ask questions such as:

Q *What do you want your reader to be thinking at this part? How can you write that?*

Document your observations for each student using the "Conference Notes" record sheet (BLM1).

Signal to let the students know when writing time is over.

SHARING AND REFLECTING

▶3 Gather for Author's Chair Sharing

Gather the class with partners sitting together, facing the Author's Chair. Briefly discuss how they will act, both as presenting authors and as members of the audience. Ask and discuss:

Q *What will you do to be a respectful member of the audience today?*

Encourage the students to be attentive and considerate audience members, and tell them that you will check in with them to see how they did.

▶4 Conduct Author's Chair Sharing

Have some of the students read their personal narratives aloud from the Author's Chair. Facilitate brief discussions about each of the readings using questions like those that follow, giving the author a chance to respond to the class's comments and questions.

Q *What was interesting to you about [Bella's] personal narrative?*

Q *What did you [see/hear/smell/taste/feel] as you listened to her narrative and what words helped you imagine? Turn to your partner.*

Q (Have the student reread her opening sentences.) *How does [Bella] "hook" the reader with her opening sentences?*

Q *What questions can we ask [Bella] about her narrative?*

Teacher Note ▶

Repeat today's lesson for a few more days, or even another week, to allow all the students to finish publishing their personal narratives and presenting them from the Author's Chair (see "Open Weeks" in the front matter on page xvi). Students who have finished may begin a new piece of writing or work on any piece they started earlier.

Collect each personal narrative to be bound later into the class book.

If all the student have not had a chance to share, assure them that they will all have a chance to share their personal narrative from the Author's Chair in the next few days.

5 ▶ Reflect on Audience Behavior During Author's Chair Sharing

Ask and briefly discuss:

Q *What did we do as an audience today to help Author's Chair sharing go well? What might we want to work on during the next Author's Chair sharing?*

Q *If you shared a personal narrative today, how did the audience make you feel? What did they do that made you feel [relaxed/ nervous/proud]?*

Teacher Note ▶

When all the students have shared their personal narratives, compile the narratives into a class book. Make the book available in the classroom library.

Teacher Note

This is the last week of the unit. You will need to reassign partners before you begin the next genre unit.

Remind the students that after they have all shared their personal narratives from the Author's Chair, you will compile the narratives into a class book. This book will be available for the students to read during independent reading time.

EXTENSION

Write Letters Home About Personal Narratives

Provide letter-writing practice for the students by having them write letters home about what they learned about personal narrative writing. Stimulate their thinking by reviewing the "Notes About Personal Narratives" chart and discussing questions such as:

Q　*What's special about personal narrative writing?*

Q　*What steps did you go through to develop and publish your personal narrative?*

Q　*What is one thing that you're proud of about your published personal narrative?*

If necessary, review the elements of a letter (date, salutation, body, closing, and signature) by modeling or writing a shared sample letter with the class. Have the students write and proofread their letters; then attach each student's letter to a copy of her own published personal narrative and send it home.

Fiction

Genre

Fiction

Genre Fiction

During this six-week unit, the students explore fiction writing and draft, revise, and publish their own stories. Through reading different kinds of fiction stories and exploring the way authors put stories together, they learn how to integrate elements of character, setting, and plot into their own stories. They further their understanding of how characters are revealed through description, action, and speech, and they use interesting verbs and adverbs to make their writing dynamic. They cultivate a relaxed and creative attitude toward their writing and continue to be contributing members of the classroom writing community.

Development Across the Grades

Grade	Elements of Fiction	Language and Craft	Skills and Conventions
3	• Developing characters using actions and description	• Writing engaging openings • Using descriptive details to convey character	• Verbs • Adverbs • Listening for periods • Punctuating speech
4	• Describing settings that work within a story • Developing characters through speech and thoughts	• Writing engaging openings • Using descriptive details to convey setting	• Nouns • Adjectives • Punctuating speech • Listening for periods
5	• Developing interesting plots that make sense • Continuing to develop characters	• Using descriptive details to convey character and setting • Connecting things that happen in the plot to what comes before and after	• Pronouns • Past and present tense • First- and third-person points of view • Listening for periods
6	• Developing interesting plots that make sense • Building and resolving conflict in the plot	• Building suspense • Using dialogue to tell a story • Using humor in a story • Paying attention to character, setting, and plot	• Pronouns • Past and present tense • First and third person points of view • Listening for periods

UNIT OVERVIEW

WEEK	DAY 1	DAY 2	DAY 3	DAY 4
	Immersion and Drafting			
1	**Exploring Fiction:** *Tacky the Penguin* **Focus:** Imaginary characters	**Exploring Fiction:** *If You Were a Writer* (first half) **Focus:** Real or imaginary	**Drafting Fiction:** *If You Were a Writer* (second half) **Quick-Write:** Interesting people	**Drafting Fiction and Pair Conferring** **Quick-Write:** "What if?"
2	**Drafting Fiction:** *Cherries and Cherry Pits* **Focus:** Describing characters	**Drafting Fiction:** *Cherries and Cherry Pits* **Focus:** Describing characters	**Drafting Fiction:** *Julius, the Baby of the World* **Quick-Write:** Describing characters through actions	**Drafting Fiction and Pair Conferring** **Quick-Write:** Describing characters through speech
3	**Drafting Fiction:** *The Paper Bag Princess* **Focus:** Describing characters through actions and speech	**Drafting Fiction:** *Boundless Grace* **Focus:** Describing characters through action and speech	**Drafting Fiction:** *Scarecrow* **Quick-Write:** Creating a story around an object	**Drafting Fiction and Pair Conferring** **Quick-Write:** Describing characters through thoughts
	Revision, Proofreading, and Publication			
4	**Selecting Drafts** **Focus:** Kevin Henkes	**Analyzing, Completing, and Revising Drafts** **Focus:** Developing character	**Analyzing and Revising Drafts** **Focus:** Developing plot	**Pair Conferring** **Focus:** Character and plot
5	**Writing Second Drafts** **Focus:** Setting and descriptive language	**Writing Second Drafts** **Focus:** Interesting verbs	**Writing Second Drafts** **Focus:** Verbs and adverbs	**Self-Assessing and Pair Conferring** **Focus:** Character and descriptive language
6	**Completing Second Drafts and Proofreading** **Focus:** Punctuating speech	**Proofreading** **Focus:** Listening for periods. Dividing long sentences	**Publishing** **Focus:** Writing final versions	**Publishing** **Focus:** Author's Chair sharing

Week 1 Overview

GENRE: FICTION

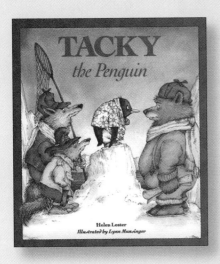

Tacky the Penguin
by Helen Lester,
illustrated by Lynn Munsinger
(Houghton Mifflin, 1988)

A one-of-a-kind penguin saves the day.

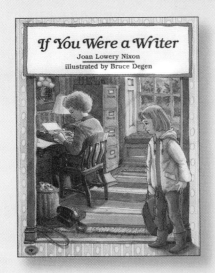

If You Were a Writer
by Joan Lowery Nixon,
illustrated by Bruce Degen
(Aladdin, 1995)

Melia wants to be a writer like her mother,
but she isn't sure what writers do.

Writing Focus

- Students hear and discuss fiction.

- Students informally explore elements of fiction.

- Students generate and quick-write ideas for fiction.

- Students draft fiction pieces.

Social Focus

- Students build the writing community

- Students cultivate a relaxed attitude toward writing.

- Students express interest in and appreciation for one another's writing.

DO AHEAD

- Prior to Day 1, decide how you will randomly assign partners to work together during this unit. See the front matter for suggestions about assigning partners randomly (page xiii) and for considerations for pairing English Language Learners (page xxviii).

- Consider prereading this week's read-aloud selection with your English Language Learners. Stop during the reading to discuss vocabulary and to check for understanding. You might have partners who speak the same native language turn and talk to each other in that language about what they see in the illustrations during a picture walk.

TEACHER AS WRITER

"My writing is full of lives I might have led. A writer imagines what could have happened, not what really happened."
— Joyce Carol Oates

The work of the fiction writer is to invent new worlds. This week imagine a life you might have led, and write your "memories" of this fictitious life. Perhaps you were born into a different culture, grew up in a different family, or chose a different profession. How do you imagine that these life experiences have shaped you? As you write, include your feelings and perspectives, and invent details to make that life seem real.

Day 1

Exploring Fiction

In this lesson, the students:

- Work with a new partner
- Hear and discuss fiction
- Informally explore the elements of fiction
- Write freely about things that interest them

Immersion in and Drafting of Fiction

In a fiction story, *something happens to someone somewhere in time*. In this unit, the students build this understanding in stages over a six-week period.

The first half of this unit immerses the students in stories, stimulating their imaginations and developing their dispositions for creativity and experimentation. The students hear, enjoy, and make observations about different examples of fiction. Having heard some examples, they begin drafting fiction and continue to learn about the genre. Skills and conventions are taught later in the unit so that the students can focus first on the big ideas: inventing interesting characters, describing believable settings, and building imaginative plots that make sense.

GETTING READY TO WRITE

▶1 Pair Students and Discuss Working Together

Randomly assign partners (see "Do Ahead" on page 257) and make sure they know each other's names. Ask the students to gather with partners sitting together, facing you.

Explain that over the next six weeks partners will work together to explore writing fiction. They will hear and discuss fiction stories and learn how to write engaging stories.

Have partners take a couple of minutes to talk about some of the things they have written so far this year. Signal for their attention and ask:

Q *What did you learn about the writing your partner has done this year?*

Materials

- *Tacky the Penguin*
- *The Pain and the Great One* from Unit 1
- *Grandpa's Face* from Unit 1
- *She Come Bringing Me That Little Baby Girl* from Unit 1
- *Oliver Button Is a Sissy* from Unit 1
- Chart paper and a marker

Making Meaning® Teacher

You can either have the students work with their current *Making Meaning* partner or assign new partners for this unit.

Teacher Note ▶

The partners you assign today will stay together for the unit. If necessary, take a few minutes at the beginning of today's lesson to let them get to know each other better by talking informally in a relaxed atmosphere.

Introduce Fiction

Show the covers of *The Pain and the Great One*, *Grandpa's Face*, *She Come Bringing Me That Little Baby Girl*, and *Oliver Button Is a Sissy*. Remind the students that they heard these fiction stories at the beginning of the year. Ask and briefly discuss:

Q *What do you think you know about fiction?*

> **Students might say:**
>
> "Fiction is made-up stories. They can seem like they are true."
>
> "Fiction has characters. Sometimes characters can be talking animals."
>
> "Fiction can be funny or serious or scary."
>
> "Some fiction stories are based on the author's life."

Record the students' ideas on a sheet of chart paper entitled "Notes About Fiction" and tell the students that you will continue to add ideas to the chart as they learn more about fiction in the coming weeks.

Point out that fiction writers try to tell stories that capture the interest and imagination of their readers. Explain that by the end of the unit the students will have learned and practiced different techniques for writing a good fiction story and will have published their own story for the class library.

Read *Tacky the Penguin* Aloud

Show the cover of *Tacky the Penguin* and read the title and the author's and illustrator's names aloud. Invite the students to think about what it might be like to write such a story themselves as they listen to it.

Read the story aloud slowly and clearly, showing the illustrations and clarifying vocabulary as you read.

Suggested Vocabulary

companions: friends (p. 3)

in the distance: far away (p. 14)

switch: branch or stick used for hitting something (p. 17)

Teacher Note

Your students may be familiar with some of the read-alouds in this program. Encourage them to listen to the read-alouds as ◀ writers, noticing what the author is trying to do and thinking about what they could try in their own writing.

◀ **Teacher Note**

To review the procedure for defining vocabulary during the read-aloud, see page 45.

Teacher Note

The discussion prompts are:

- "I agree with _____ because…"
- "I disagree with _____ because…"
- "In addition to what _____ said, I think…"

4 ▶ Discuss the Story

Ask and briefly discuss the questions that follow. Remind the students to use the discussion prompts to help them listen and build on one another's thinking. Be ready to reread from the text to help the students recall what they heard.

Q *What makes Tacky an amusing character to read about?*

Q *If you were going to create a character like Tacky for a story, what odd things might you have that character do?*

Students might say:

"Tacky is an odd bird. He doesn't do anything like anybody else."

"I agree with [Pete]. Instead of saying 'hello' politely, he says, 'What's happening?'"

"In addition to what [Kim] said, he does huge cannonballs in the water."

"I would make a character that blows giant bubbles with bubble gum."

Teacher Note ▶

Note that on Days 1 and 2 of this week, the students may write fiction or anything else they choose. On Day 3, after exposure to a couple more examples of fiction, all the students will be asked to begin writing in this genre.

Point out that in fiction stories some things can happen in real life while other things (like talking penguins) can happen only in the imagination. On the "Notes About Fiction" chart, write *some fiction could happen in real life, and some fiction could happen only in the imagination*. Invite the students to think about both kinds of events as they write freely today.

WRITING TIME

5 ▶ Write Independently

Ask the students to return to their seats and write silently for 20–30 minutes. During this time they may write about anything they choose. Remind them that they should write double-spaced in their notebooks and that there should be no talking, whispering, or walking around.

Join the students in writing for a few minutes; then walk around the room and observe.

Signal to let the students know when writing time is over.

SHARING AND REFLECTING

6 ▶ Briefly Share Writing and Reflect

Ask partners to talk briefly about what they wrote today. After a moment, signal for their attention and ask:

Q   *What did your partner write about today?*

Q   *What did you and your new partner do to work well together when you were talking and sharing your writing?*

ELL Note

English Language Learners may benefit from drawing their ideas before they write. Encourage them to draw what they want to write about and then talk quietly with you or a partner about their drawing. If necessary, write down key words and phrases they want to use so that they can copy them into their writing.

Teacher Note

Save the "Notes About Fiction" chart to use in Day 2 and throughout the unit.

Day 2

Materials

- *If You Were a Writer*
- *Assessment Resource Book*

Exploring Fiction

In this lesson, the students:

- Hear and discuss fiction
- Informally explore the elements of fiction
- Cultivate a relaxed attitude toward writing
- Write freely about things that interest them

The Importance of Attitude in Writing

To get enough practice with writing during their elementary school years, it is extremely important that students learn to start to write fairly quickly after they sit down and to write freely and abundantly, without fear. This requires a relaxed attitude, free from inhibitions, especially during the early drafting stages. In this lesson, the students hear a story about a silly, far-fetched situation. The intent is to inspire their imaginations and help them know that writing can be lighthearted and can be about *anything*.

Regularly remind the students that they are primarily writing for themselves. Encourage them to be willing to write something that's less than perfect. The important thing is to repeatedly practice getting their ideas on paper.

GETTING READY TO WRITE

▶1 Briefly Review and Discuss Writing Attitude

Gather the class with partners sitting together, facing you. Review that yesterday the students began exploring fiction, or invented stories. Today they will hear another example of fiction and do more writing.

Point out that learning to write is like learning any new sport, musical instrument, or skill; you must practice over and over to become good at it. Ask:

Q *What can be hard about starting to write, or continuing to write, for the whole writing time?*

Students might say:

"It's hard to start writing when I don't know what to write."

"I stop writing if I don't know how to spell something."

Explain that you expect the students' writing to have spelling errors and to be imperfect and incomplete. This is natural for young writers. Assure them that practicing by writing many, many imperfect pieces is more important than writing just a few perfect pieces.

Encourage the students to try to bring a fun, relaxed attitude to their writing today.

▶2 Read the First Half of *If You Were a Writer* Aloud

Show the cover of *If You Were a Writer* and read the title and the author's and illustrator's names aloud. Tell the students that you will read the first half of the book today and the second half tomorrow. Invite the students to think as they listen about what they learn about being a writer.

Read pages 5–13 of *If You Were a Writer* aloud, showing the illustrations and clarifying vocabulary as you read.

Suggested Vocabulary

fragrance: smell, aroma (p. 7)

wedge: slice (p. 7)

ELL Vocabulary

English Language Learners may benefit from discussing additional vocabulary, including:

typewriter: writing machine used before home computers became popular (p. 5; see illustration on p. 4)

Stop after:

p. 13   "'Then they could slip between the sheets to snore and
            sleep!' she said."

3 **Discuss the Story and Generate Ideas**

Ask and briefly discuss:

Q *What did you find out about being a writer?*

Q *In* Tacky the Penguin, *the events in the story could not happen in real life. Could the events in today's story happen in real life? Explain your thinking.*

Use "Think, Pair, Share" to have the students first think about and then discuss:

 Q *What real or imaginary things might you write about today?* [pause] *Turn to your partner.*

Students might say:

"I could write a funny story about when our new puppy ran around the house with my only clean pair of socks."

"I might be able to write about how our car had a flat tire today."

"It might be fun to write about a kid who can fly."

Explain that the students may write about real or imaginary situations, or anything else they choose, during writing time today. Encourage them to relax and write as freely and imaginatively as possible.

WRITING TIME

4 **Write Independently**

Ask the students to return to their seats and write silently for 20–30 minutes. They may write about real or imaginary situations or anything else they choose. Join the students in writing for a few minutes; then walk around the room and observe.

CLASS ASSESSMENT NOTE

Observe the students and ask yourself:

Q *Are the students staying in their seats and writing silently?*

Q *Are they double-spacing their writing?*

Q *Do they seem to be writing with a relaxed and free attitude (or do they seem overly cautious and inhibited)?*

If necessary, remind student to double-space their writing. If you notice many students having difficulty starting to write, call for the class's attention and have partners talk to each other about what they might write. Have a few volunteers share their ideas with the class, then have them resume silent writing.

Record your observations in the *Assessment Resource Book*.

Signal to let the students know when writing time is over.

SHARING AND REFLECTING

5 ▶ Reflect on Writing Attitude

Talk briefly as a class about the students' attitude as they wrote today. Ask:

Q *Were you able to relax and write freely today without getting stuck? If so, what happened? If not, what made you feel stuck? What did you do to try to get unstuck?*

Explain that the students will continue to focus on developing a relaxed attitude toward their writing.

Day 3

Materials

- *If You Were a Writer*
- "Notes About Fiction" chart from Day 1

Drafting Fiction

In this lesson, the students:

- Hear, discuss, and draft fiction
- Generate and quick-write ideas for fiction
- Cultivate a relaxed attitude toward writing

GETTING READY TO WRITE

1 ▶ Read the Second Half of *If You Were a Writer* Aloud

Gather the class with partners sitting together, facing you. Have them bring their notebooks and pencils with them.

Review that the students are hearing examples of fiction and thinking about what fiction can be. Explain that today they will hear the second half of *If You Were a Writer* and begin drafting a fiction story.

Tell the students that you will stop several times during today's reading to have partners talk about what they heard. Read pages 15–30 of *If You Were a Writer* aloud slowly and clearly, showing the illustrations and stopping as described below. Clarify vocabulary as you read.

Suggested Vocabulary

alley: a narrow street or passageway, usually between two buildings (p. 22)

ELL Vocabulary

English Language Learners may benefit from discussing additional vocabulary, including:

in disguise: in a costume to hide who you are (p. 17)

Stop after:

> **p. 17**   "What if the boy is really a detective in disguise? What could happen then?"

Ask:

 Q   *What could happen then? Turn to your partner.*

Have partners discuss the question for a few moments; then signal for their attention. Without stopping to discuss as a class, reread the last sentence and continue reading to the next stopping point:

> **p. 22**   "'What dog?' Veronica asked. 'What monster? Tell me!'"

Ask:

 Q   *What could happen in this story? Turn to your partner.*

Have partners discuss the question for a few moments; then signal for their attention. Without stopping to discuss as a class, reread the last sentence and continue reading to the end of the story.

2 ▶ Discuss the Story and Quick-Write: Interesting People We Know

Ask and briefly discuss:

Q   *What more did you find out about being a writer?*

Q   *What are some things that happen to Melia that give her ideas for writing?*

Students might say:

"Melia sees the boy running with the dog, and she makes up a story from that."

"She also makes up a story about the missing jar of honey. A bear comes in and eats it."

Point out that Melia uses people and situations in her own life to help her make up stories. Add *making up stories about people and situations in our own lives* to the "Notes About Fiction" chart, and add any other ideas about fiction that the students heard in the reading.

◀ **Teacher Note**

To review the procedure for "Turn to Your Partner," see pages 26–27.

Use "Think, Pair, Share" to have the students first think about and then discuss:

 Q *What interesting people do you know about whom you could make up a story?* [pause] *Turn to your partner.*

Without discussing the question, have the students open their writing notebooks to the next blank page of the writing ideas section, label it "Interesting People I Know," and write a list of interesting people they know outside of school about whom they could write a story. Stop them after 3–4 minutes and have partners share and discuss their lists with each other. Then have them resume listing for a few more minutes.

Explain that today you would like all of the students to try writing a fiction story. They may make up a story about one of the interesting people on their list, or they may write any other made-up story. Remind them to look at the "Notes About Fiction" chart to help them get more ideas.

> **Teacher Note ▶**
>
> The students are just beginning to generate ideas for fiction. They are not expected to know or incorporate specific features of the genre into their writing at this point. They will build their understanding as they explore the genre over the coming weeks.

WRITING TIME

▶3 Begin Drafting Fiction Pieces

Ask the students to return to their seats. Write the following choices on the board and have the students write silently for 20–30 minutes.

> **Teacher Note ▶**
>
> The students will write all first drafts, double-spaced, in their notebooks. In Week 4, they will select one of the drafts to develop and publish. Double-spacing now allows space for revision later. The students will write their final versions in Week 6 on loose, lined paper (or on the computer, if available).

- Make up a story about one of the interesting people on your list.

- Continue a fiction story you started earlier.

- Start any new fiction story.

Join the students in writing for a few minutes and then walk around the room and observe.

Signal to let the students know when writing time is over.

SHARING AND REFLECTING

 Reflect on Writing Process and Attitude

Ask and briefly discuss:

Q *Were you able to make up a story about an interesting person you know? Tell us about it.*

Q *What other fictional ideas did you write about today?*

Q (Point to the "Notes About Fiction" chart.) *Which notes did you think about as you started writing today?*

Q *How did you feel as you wrote today? If you got stuck, what happened? What do you want to try tomorrow to help you in your writing?*

Explain that the students will continue to read and draft fiction for the next couple of weeks. They will eventually select one of their fiction drafts to develop and publish as a book for the class library.

EXTENSION

Real and Imaginary Fiction Stories

Give the students more experience distinguishing between real and imaginary stories in fiction by having them share about fiction stories they are reading independently. As a class, discuss questions such as:

Q *What's happening in your story?*

Q *Could that story happen in real life? Why or why not?*

Day 4

Drafting Fiction and Pair Conferring

In this lesson, the students:

- Review the story they heard on Day 3
- Quick-write "What if?" questions
- Draft fiction pieces
- Cultivate a relaxed attitude toward writing
- Express interest in and appreciation for one another's writing

GETTING READY

 Review *If You Were a Writer*

Gather the class with partners sitting together, facing you. Have them bring their notebooks and pencils with them. Review that they heard *If You Were a Writer* and began drafting fiction stories. Show pages 14–15 of the story and remind the students that Melia's mother suggests asking the question, "What if?" to get ideas for stories.

Reread the following passages from the story and ask the students to think about "What if?" questions they could ask as they listen:

p. 15 "'Maybe the dog and the boy could turn into an idea,' Mother said. 'Ask yourself, "What if?"'

'What if what?' Melia wondered.

'What if a diamond necklace has caught on the dog's collar? What if the necklace has been stolen by a pirate? What if the boy is really a detective in disguise? What would happen then?'"

p. 18 "'What if we were all in the backyard and a bear squeezed into the house through the front window? What if the bear were under the dining room table, eating the honey, but none of us knew he was there until we sat down at the table for dinner? What would happen then?'"

2 ▶ Generate "What If?" Questions

Explain that authors commonly get ideas for stories by asking themselves "What if?" questions. Direct the students' attention to the "Notes About Fiction" chart and add *What if?* to it. Ask:

Q *What "What if?" questions can you think of that might lead to an interesting story?*

As the students report their ideas, record them on a sheet of chart paper entitled "What If?"

> ***Students might say:***
>
> "What if a monkey got loose from the zoo and ended up in my backyard?"
>
> "What if I became the president of the United States?"
>
> "What if someone finds out she can read people's minds?"
>
> "What if a boy's parents forgot who he was?"

◀ **Teacher Note**

If the students have difficulty generating ideas, suggest some like those in the "Students might say" note.

3 ▶ Quick-Write: What If?

Ask the students to select one of the charted "What if?" questions and write in their notebooks for a few minutes about imaginative ways to answer it. Encourage them to imagine things that could happen in real life, as well as things that could not. Stop them after 3–4 minutes of silent writing and have partners discuss their thinking; then have them write silently for a few more minutes.

Signal for the students' attention and ask several volunteers to share the "What if?" question they selected and the ideas they wrote.

Explain that during writing time today the students may continue the "What if?" story they started, list other "What if?" questions, or work on any other fiction story. Assure them that it is perfectly fine to leave drafts incomplete and start new ones. Encourage them to relax and use their imaginations as they write today.

◀ **Teacher Note**

If you notice many students having difficulty quick-writing about a "What if?" question, stop the class and model writing a few sentences together. Elicit the students' suggestions to add to the piece. (An example might be, *What if a monkey got loose from the zoo and ended up in the backyard? We heard screeching and got up from our dinner to see what was happening. We found the monkey swinging wildly from the swing set. We decided he was hungry, so we brought him inside and fed him a plate of spaghetti.*)

WRITING TIME

Teacher Note ▶

You may want to shorten today's writing time to leave more time for the pair conferences in Step 5.

4 ▶ Draft Fiction Pieces

Ask the students to return to their seats. Write the following choices on the board and have them write silently for 20–30 minutes.

- Continue the "What if?" story you started during the quick-write.

- Start a new "What if?" story.

- List "What if?" questions in your writing ideas section.

- Work on any other fiction story.

Join the students in writing for a few minutes; then begin conferring with individual students.

TEACHER CONFERENCE NOTE

Over the coming three weeks, confer with individual students to get an idea of their thinking as they write fiction drafts. Ask each student to show you a piece of her writing and read some of it aloud to you. Hold off on any feedback about grammar or spelling, and instead focus on clarifying the student's ideas about the story she wants to write. Ask questions such as:

Q *What is this story about?*

Q *Who [is/are] the character(s)? What's interesting about [him/her/them]?*

Q *What do you imagine might happen to [him/her/them]?*

Q *Where do you imagine this story takes place?*

Q *What part are you going to work on next?*

Document your observations for each student using the "Conference Notes" record sheets (BLM1). Use the "Conference Notes" record sheets during conferences throughout the unit.

Signal to let the students know when writing time is over.

SHARING AND REFLECTING

5 ▶ Confer in Pairs About Fiction Drafts

Explain that the students will read one of their fiction drafts to their partner and confer about it today. Briefly review the procedure you established for pair conferring (see Unit 1, Week 4, Day 4, on pages 76–77) and remind the students that conferring means not only reading their writing to each other but talking about it as well. Explain that today partners will tell each other one think they like about the other's draft. Ask and briefly discuss:

Q *What would you like your partner to do to show that he's interested in your writing and your creative ideas?*

Students might say:

"I would like my partner to listen as I read my story."

"I would like my partner to ask me questions about the story."

"I would like my partner to tell me the part he likes."

"I would like my partner to say something nice about my story, like 'I really want to read your story.'"

Have partners share their writing. Scan the class without intervening, providing sufficient time for both partners to share their writing before you signal for their attention.

6 ▶ Reflect on Pair Conferences

Help partners reflect on their work together by asking:

Q *What did your partner do to show interest in your writing and creative ideas?*

Q *What did you like about your partner's writing?*

Explain that the students will continue to write fiction drafts during the coming two weeks.

ELL Note

You might provide the prompt "I would like my partner to…" to your English Language Learners to help them verbalize their answers to this question.

◀ **Teacher Note**

Consider having pairs spread out so that partners can better hear each other. If necessary, signal about halfway through sharing time so that partners can switch roles if they have not yet done so.

EXTENSION

Repeat Quick-Write: "What If?"

You might have the students repeat the "What if?" writing activity they did in today's lesson. You can have them start or add to a list of their own "What if?" questions in their writing notebooks, or you might assign one "What if?" question for all of the students to write a story about. The "What if?" technique can be very effective in getting creative juices flowing.

Week 2   Overview

GENRE: FICTION

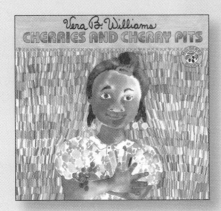

Cherries and Cherry Pits
by Vera B. Williams
(Greenwillow Books, 1986)

Bidemmi draws stories about her life.

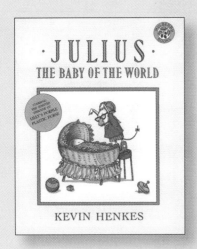

Julius, the Baby of the World
by Kevin Henkes
(Greenwillow Books, 1990)

Lilly is jealous of her little brother Julius.

Writing Focus

- Students hear, discuss, and draft fiction.

- Students explore how character is developed in stories.

- Students generate and quick-write ideas for fiction.

- Students cultivate creativity in their writing.

Social Focus

- Students cultivate a relaxed attitude toward writing.

- Students express interest in and appreciation for one another's writing.

- Students help one another improve their writing.

DO AHEAD

- Consider prereading this week's read-aloud selection with your English Language Learners. Stop during the reading to discuss vocabulary and to check for understanding. You might have partners who speak the same native language turn and talk to each other in that language about what they see in the illustrations during a picture walk.

TEACHER AS WRITER

"Don't say the old lady screamed—bring her on and let her scream."
— Mark Twain

Twain, like most fiction writers, found ways to "show, not tell" a story. What might happen in a passage in which the old lady is "brought on and screams?" How might that compare to a passage in which we're simply told that she screams? This week experiment with writing a passage in which a reader can see, hear, smell, taste, or feel what's happening.

Day 1

Materials

- *Cherries and Cherry Pits*
- "Notes About Fiction" chart from Week 1

Drafting Fiction

In this lesson, the students:

- Hear, discuss, and draft fiction
- Become familiar with plot, character, and setting
- Cultivate a relaxed attitude toward writing

GETTING READY TO WRITE

▶1 Briefly Review the Purpose of Fiction

Gather the class with partners sitting together, facing you. Have them bring their writing notebooks and pencils with them. Review that the students heard fiction stories last week and began drafting their own stories. This week they will continue to draft fiction pieces. Remind them that they will eventually select one of their drafts to develop and publish for the class library.

Direct the students' attention to the "Notes About Fiction" chart and review the items on it. Explain that in fiction stories, *something happens to someone somewhere in time.* The terms *plot*, *character*, and *setting* are used to describe the different features of stories.

Add *something happens (plot) to someone (character), somewhere in time (setting)* to the chart. Encourage the students to try to notice things about the plot, characters, and setting as they listen to a story today.

▶2 Read Parts of *Cherries and Cherry Pits* Aloud

Show the cover of *Cherries and Cherry Pits* and read the title and author's name aloud. Explain that you will read parts of this book aloud today and tomorrow. Ask the students to try to get pictures in their minds as they listen, and tell them you will not show the illustrations today so that they can make their own mental pictures.

Making Meaning® Teacher

Cherries and Cherry Pits is introduced in *Making Meaning* Unit 2, Week 1. If the students have heard the story very recently, explain that they will listen to parts of it again as writers, thinking about how authors can describe characters in interesting ways.

Read pages 4–11 of *Cherries and Cherry Pits* slowly and clearly without showing the illustrations. Clarify vocabulary as you read.

Suggested Vocabulary

subway: underground train (p. 7)

ELL Vocabulary

English Language Learners may benefit from discussing additional vocabulary, including:

pit: hard seed found in the center of some fruits (p. 10)

3 ▶ **Briefly Discuss the Story**

Facilitate a class discussion using the question that follows and be ready to reread from the story to help the students recall what they heard. Ask:

Q *What is this story about so far?*

Students might say:

"The story is about a girl named Bidemmi. She draws pictures."

"In addition to what [Maxine] said, it's about a man who brings cherries home to his children."

"I agree with [Deborah]. All his children have names that start with 'D.'"

4 ▶ **Visualize a Character in the Story**

Point out that Vera B. Williams includes a lot of details to help readers make pictures of the characters in their minds. Tell the students that you will reread passages that describe the man in the story. Have them close their eyes and imagine as they listen.

Reread the following passage aloud:

p. 8 "THIS is the door of the subway and THIS is the man leaning on the door…. His face is a nice face. But it is also not so nice. He has a fat wrinkle on his forehead. It's like my mother's wrinkle. It's from worrying and worrying, my mother says."

FACILITATION TIP

During this unit, we invite you to practice **asking facilitative questions** during class discussions to help the students respond directly to one another, not just to you. After a student comments, ask the class questions such as:

Q *Do you agree or disagree with [Deborah]? Why?*

Q *What questions can we ask [Deborah] about what she said?*

Q *What can you add to what [Deborah] said?*

Ask:

Q *What does this man look like in your mind so far? Turn to your partner.*

Repeat this procedure with the following passage:

> **p. 8** "And his neck is thick and his arms are thick with very big, strong muscles. His shirt is striped blue and white and his skin is dark brown and in his great big hands he has a small white bag. This man looks so strong I think he could even carry a piano on his head. But he is only carrying this little white bag."

Explain that today the students will continue to write fiction stories. Encourage them to include details to help the reader imagine their characters. Remind them that they can look at the "Notes About Fiction" chart to help them get ideas.

WRITING TIME

5 ▶ Draft Fiction Pieces

Write the following choices on the board and have the students write silently for 20–30 minutes.

- Work on a story you started earlier.

- Start a new story.

- Include details to help a reader imagine the characters.

Join the students in writing for a few minutes; then confer with individual students.

TEACHER CONFERENCE NOTE

Continue to confer with individual students as they write fiction drafts. Ask each student to show you a piece of his writing and read some of it aloud to you. Hold off on any feedback about grammar and spelling, and instead focus

continues

TEACHER CONFERENCE NOTE *continued*

on clarifying the student's ideas about the story he wants to write. Ask questions such as:

Q *What is this story about?*

Q *Who [is/are] the character(s)? What's interesting about [him/her/them]?*

Q *What do you imagine might happen to [him/her/them]?*

Q *Where do you imagine this story takes place?*

Q *What part are you going to work on next?*

Document your observations for each student using the "Conference Notes" record sheet (BLM1).

Signal to let the students know when writing time is over.

SHARING AND REFLECTING

 Reflect on Writing Process and Attitude

Help the students reflect on their work together by discussing the questions that follow. Invite them to read passages of their writing aloud to the class as they respond.

Q *What ideas came out of your imagination in your writing today?*

Q *Did you write an interesting description of a character? If so, tell us about it.*

Q *How did you feel as you wrote today? If you got stuck, what happened? What do you want to try tomorrow to help you in your writing?*

Explain that the students will continue to hear, discuss, and draft fiction tomorrow.

Day 2

Materials

- *Cherries and Cherry Pits* from Day 1
- Transparency of "Excerpts from *Cherries and Cherry Pits*" (BLM8–BLM9)
- *Student Writing Handbook* pages 5–6

Drafting Fiction

In this lesson, the students:

- Hear, discuss, and draft fiction
- Visualize characters
- Reflect on creativity in their own writing
- Ask one another questions about their writing

The Importance of Creativity in Writing

It is important for students to understand that fiction writing requires reaching into their imaginations and telling things in their own way. Children come to school with vivid imaginations, full of possibilities. Nurture these possibilities by consistently showing interest in their ideas, actively asking them questions, and encouraging them to develop their ideas further.

The lessons in this program help to build a safe classroom environment in which students can take the risks necessary to develop their creativity. Further nurture their creativity by regularly sharing your own creative writing and ideas with them.

GETTING READY TO WRITE

1 ▶ Gather and Briefly Review

Gather the class with partners sitting together, facing you. Have them bring their *Student Writing Handbooks* and pencils with them.

Remind the students that they heard the beginning of *Cherries and Cherry Pits* and thought about how the man in the story is described. Explain that you will read more from the story today. Encourage the students to try to get pictures in their minds of the characters as they listen.

2 ▶ Read More from *Cherries and Cherry Pits*

Read pages 13–24 of *Cherries and Cherry Pits* aloud without showing the illustrations. Stop during the reading as described below, clarifying vocabulary as you read.

Suggested Vocabulary

escalator: moving staircase (p. 23)
beret: flat hat made of soft cloth (p. 27)

ELL Vocabulary

English Language Learners may benefit from discussing additional
vocabulary, including:

pocketbook: purse (p. 13)

Stop after:

p. 13 "In the pocketbook is a bag."

Ask:

 Q *What do you see in your mind? Turn to your partner.*

Have partners discuss their mental images for a few moments;
then signal for their attention. Without stopping to share as a class,
reread the last line and continue reading to the next stopping point.
Follow the same procedure at the next two stopping points:

p. 18 "They are both eating cherries and spitting out the pits,
eating cherries and spitting out the pits."

p. 24 "Don't forget to spit out the pit."

3   Analyze Passages from the Story

Ask the students to open to *Student Writing Handbook* pages 5–6
as you place the transparency of "Excerpts from *Cherries and Cherry
Pits*" on the overhead projector. Explain that several passages from
today's reading are reproduced here. Ask partners to read through
the passages in the *Student Writing Handbook* together and underline
words or phrases that helped them imagine the characters.

After several minutes, signal for the students' attention. Ask and
briefly discuss as a class:

Q *What words or phrases did you underline? What do those words
tell us about this character?*

Students might say:

"I underlined 'old, old shoes.' Those words tell us that she might
be poor."

"We underlined 'there's your own little cherry tree.' This sentence
tells us that she has a good sense of humor."

"My partner and I underlined 'jumping on and off the stoops.'
We could imagine this boy jumping all over the place. It tells
us he's energetic."

Teacher Note ▶

Physical descriptions in the
excerpts include: "On her
head is a black hat with a pink
flower, like a rose flower" and
"And when he smiles you can
see the space between his big
front teeth like my brother's."

Actions include: "She laughs and
dumps all of the cherries onto the
geranium plant in front of her" and
"he's hollering to his little sister."

Speech includes: "'You like it?'
asks the lady. 'You like cherries,
honeybird?'" and "'Hey come on
out here. See what I got for you.'"

The students explore character
development in more depth
during the later weeks of this unit.

Point out that authors use physical descriptions, actions, and speech
to make their characters real for the reader. Underline examples of
each of these on the transparency.

Explain that the students will continue to write fiction today.
Encourage them to think of ways to make their characters come
alive by describing their physical appearance, actions, and speech.

WRITING TIME

4 **Draft Fiction Pieces**

Write the following choices on the board and have the students
write silently for 20–30 minutes.

- Work on a story you started earlier.

- Start a new story.

- Try to include physical descriptions, actions, or speech to make
  your characters come alive.

Join the students in writing for a few minutes; then confer with
individual students.

TEACHER CONFERENCE NOTE

Continue to confer with individual students, asking them
questions such as:

Q *What is this story about?*

continues

> **TEACHER CONFERENCE NOTE** *continued*
>
> **Q** *Who [is/are] the character(s)? What is interesting about [him/her/them]?*
>
> **Q** *What do you imagine might happen to [him/her/them]?*
>
> **Q** *Where do you imagine this story takes place?*
>
> **Q** *What part are you going to work on next?*
>
> Document your observations for each student using the "Conference Notes" record sheet (BLM1).

Signal to let the students know when writing time is over.

SHARING AND REFLECTING

5 ▶ **Share One Sentence and Reflect on Creativity**

Explain that one of the most important things fiction writers do is tap into their creativity—their ability to use their imaginations to create something new or to recreate something familiar in their own way.

Ask the students to review the writing they did today and choose one sentence to share with the class. Encourage them to choose a sentence that they like or that they believe shows their creativity. After a moment, go around the room and have each student read her sentence aloud, without comment.

After the students have shared their sentences, facilitate a discussion by asking:

Q *What sentence did you hear that got you interested in someone else's writing?*

Q *What questions do you want to ask a classmate about his or her writing?*

Explain that everyone is creative and can become more creative by writing and doing other creative things, such as drawing, playing

◀ **Teacher Note**

The intention in this activity is to hear one sentence from every student in the class. This lets the students hear what their classmates are writing and builds their accountability. After they underline their sentences, have them put their pencils away. Have them read their sentences in a loud voice, one after another, without stopping to comment. In the discussion afterward, they are not expected to remember every sentence they heard.

musical instruments, and solving interesting problems in their own way. Explain that the students will continue to develop their creativity throughout the year.

EXTENSION

Read and Discuss the Rest of *Cherries and Cherry Pits*

Read the rest of *Cherries and Cherry Pits* aloud and encourage the students to visualize the characters. The students might be interested in seeing the illustrations and talking about how they compare to the mental images they formed.

Day 3

Drafting Fiction

In this lesson, the students:

* Review character, plot, and setting
* Hear, discuss, and draft fiction
* Describe characters' actions
* Reflect on creativity in their own writing
* Ask one another questions about their writing

GETTING READY TO WRITE

1 ▸ Gather and Briefly Review

Gather the class with partners sitting together, facing you. Have the students bring their notebooks and pencils with them. Refer to the "Notes About Fiction" chart and remind the students that in a fiction story something happens to someone somewhere in time and that the terms *plot*, *character*, and *setting* are used to describe these features of fiction.

Remind the students that they are focusing on developing interesting characters using physical description, actions, and speech. Add *describing characters through physical description, actions, and speech* to the "Notes About Fiction" chart.

Explain that you will read another story with interesting characters today. Encourage the students to think about how the author makes the characters come to life.

2 ▸ Read *Julius, the Baby of the World* Aloud

Show the cover of *Julius, the Baby of the World* and read the title and author's name aloud. Read the story aloud slowly and clearly, showing the illustrations and clarifying vocabulary as you read.

Materials

* *Julius, the Baby of the World*
* *Cherries and Cherry Pits* from Day 1
* "Notes About Fiction" chart

Making Meaning® Teacher
Julius, the Baby of the World is introduced in *Making Meaning* Unit 3, Week 2. If your students have heard this story recently, use the questions in Step 3 to review the story briefly and continue with the lesson from there.

Suggested Vocabulary

beady: small, round, and shiny, like a bead (p. 7)

nifty: very good (p. 12)

dazzled: amazed (p. 16)

restrain: control (p. 17)

verbal exuberance: loud, cheerful talking and singing (p. 18)

niceties: nice things, such as toys or new clothing (p. 24)

quivered: trembled (p. 28)

ELL Vocabulary

English Language Learners may benefit from discussing additional vocabulary, including:

insulting: meant to hurt a person's feelings (p. 6)

disgusting: very unpleasant (p. 7)

extraordinary: wonderful (p. 10)

babbled and gurgled: made baby sounds (p. 16)

quite a spread: lots of tasty foods and drinks (p. 26)

3 Discuss the Characters in the Story

Ask and briefly discuss the questions that follow, and be ready to reread from the story to help the students recall what they heard.

Q *What is Lilly like? What does she do in the story that makes you think that?*

Students might say:

"Lilly is a mean sister until her cousin says something mean about Julius."

"I agree with [Emily]. She puts on costumes and makes him cry."

"She also tried to make him disappear."

"In addition to what [Aiden] said, I think she's jealous. She keeps saying 'disgusting' whenever they call him the baby of the world."

Point out that one way Kevin Henkes shows us what Lilly is like is by describing things she does (her actions). Authors often use actions to show their characters' personalities.

4 **Quick-Write: Showing Character Through Actions**

Have the students open their writing notebooks to the piece of writing that they worked on most recently. Ask them to think to themselves for a moment about the following questions:

Q *Who is the main character in this story?*

Q *What kind of person is this character? What makes him or her unique, or different from everyone else?*

After a moment, have the students open to the next blank page in the writing ideas section of their notebook and write the character's name (or a temporary name, if they don't have one) at the top of the page. Tell them that they will do a 5-minute quick-write in which they will write actions their character might do, based on his or her personality.

After several minutes, signal for the students' attention and ask volunteers to share what they wrote with the class.

Explain that today the students may continue what they started during the quick-write, work on a fiction story they started earlier, or begin a new story. Encourage them to include actions in their story to help readers imagine their characters.

WRITING TIME

 5 **Draft Fiction Pieces**

Ask the students to return to their seats. Write the following choices on the board and have the students write silently for 20–30 minutes.

- Write more about the character you thought about during the quick-write.

- Work on a story you started earlier.

- Start a new story.

- Try to include descriptions of characters' actions.

Join the students in writing for a few minutes; then confer with individual students.

> **Teacher Note**
>
> If the students have difficulty writing ideas for characters' actions, call for their attention and model an example together as a class. You might say, "I'm writing about a character who is very nervous. What are some things that a nervous person might do?" Elicit ideas from the class and write these where everyone can see them (for example, *a nervous person might bite his fingernails, pace around, and talk very quickly*). After modeling some examples, have the students resume the quick-write for a few more minutes.

TEACHER CONFERENCE NOTE

Continue to confer with individual students as they write fiction drafts, asking them questions such as:

Q *What is this story about?*

Q *Who [is/are] the character(s)? What is interesting about [him/her/them]?*

Q *What do you imagine might happen to [him/her/them]?*

Q *Where do you imagine this story takes place?*

Q *What part are you going to work on next?*

Document your observations for each student using the "Conference Notes" record sheet (BLM1).

Signal to let the students know when writing time is over.

SHARING AND REFLECTING

 Share One Sentence and Reflect on Creativity

As you did yesterday, ask the students to review the writing they did today and choose a sentence that they like or that shows their creativity. Give the students a moment to select their sentences; then go around the room and have each student read his sentence aloud to the class, without comment.

After the students have shared their sentences, facilitate a class discussion by asking:

Q *What sentence did you hear that got you interested in someone else's writing?*

Q *What questions do you want to ask a classmate about his or her writing?*

Day 4

Drafting Fiction and Conferring in Pairs

Materials

- *Julius, the Baby of the World*
- *Assessment Resource Book*

In this lesson, the students:

- Review the story they heard on Day 3
- Describe characters' speech
- Draft fiction
- Express interest in and appreciation for one another's writing
- Ask for and receive feedback about their writing
- Give feedback in a helpful way

GETTING READY TO WRITE

1 **Review *Julius, the Baby of the World***

Gather the class with partners sitting together, facing you. Have them bring their writing notebooks and pencils with them.

Remind the students that they heard *Julius, the Baby of the World* yesterday and thought about how the author shows Lilly's personality, or what she is like, through her actions. Point out that the author also uses speech in the story to show personality.

Briefly review the story by reading the following lines from the story aloud and calling on a couple of volunteers to say which character spoke that line and what they remember about the story:

p. 7 "'Disgusting.'"

p. 17 "'Lilly, let's restrain ourselves, please.'"

p. 29 "'And for your information, his nose is shiny, his eyes are sparkly, and his fur smells like perfume.'"

2 ▶ **Quick-Write: Showing Character Through Speech**

Point out that what a character says and how he or she says it can show a lot about that character. Explain that the students can also use speech in their stories to show character. Today they will do a quick-write and practice writing things one of their characters might say.

Have the students open their notebooks to the quick-write they did yesterday. Ask them to think to themselves for a moment about:

Q *What is a typical thing this character might say? How would he or she say it?*

After a moment, have the students open to the next blank page in the writing ideas section of their notebook and brainstorm and write several typical things their character might say, based on his or her personality.

After several minutes, signal for the students' attention and ask volunteers to share what they wrote with the class.

Explain that during writing time today the students may continue to work on this piece or a story they started earlier, or they may start a new story. Remind them that it is perfectly fine to leave drafts incomplete and start new ones. Encourage them to use speech in their stories if they can and to relax and use their imaginations in their writing today.

Teacher Note ▶

If the students have difficulty writing ideas for what their characters might say, call for their attention and model an example together as a class. You might say, "What are some things that my nervous character from yesterday might say?" Elicit ideas from the class and write these where everyone can see them (for example, "I don't know. Don't ask me anything," "I can't think about that right now," "I have butterflies in my stomach"). After modeling some examples, have the students resume the quick-write for a few more minutes.

WRITING TIME

3 ▶ **Draft Fiction Pieces**

Teacher Note ▶

You may want to shorten today's writing time to leave more time for the pair conferences in Step 4.

Write the following choices on the board and have the students work on them for 20–30 minutes.

- Write more about the character you thought about during the quick-write.

- Work on a story you started earlier.

- Start a new story.

- Include descriptions of characters' actions and speech.

Join the students in writing for a few minutes; then walk around and observe.

CLASS ASSESSMENT NOTE

Observe the students and ask yourself:

* Do the students seem to be writing with a relaxed and free attitude, inspired by their own thoughts?

* If they seem overly cautious or inhibited, do they eventually start writing freely?

Support any student who is still struggling to start after about 10 minutes by asking him questions such as:

Q *What are you thinking about right now?*

Q *Who is the character you are writing about? What is she like?*

Q *What interesting thing happens to this character?*

Q *What might this character say or do in this situation? Why would that make sense for her personality?*

As the student responds to the questions, have him write his responses in his notebook and continue to write what happens.

Record your observations in the *Assessment Resource Book*.

Signal to let the students know when writing time is over.

SHARING AND REFLECTING

4 ▶ **Confer in Pairs About Fiction Drafts**

Gather the class with partners sitting together. Explain that the students will read one of their fiction drafts to their partner and confer about it today. If necessary, briefly review the procedure for pair conferring and remind the students that conferring means not only reading their writing to each other but talking about it as well. Ask and briefly discuss:

Teacher Note ▶

If the students have difficulty answering this question, suggest some ideas like those in the "Students might say" note; then ask, "What else could you ask your partner to listen for?"

Q *What would you like to ask your partner to listen for as you read your story today?*

Students might say:

"I want to ask my partner to listen for her favorite part."

"I want to ask my partner to tell me if any parts are confusing."

"I want to ask my partner if he can imagine my story happening."

Teacher Note ▶

If necessary, signal about halfway through sharing time so partners can switch roles if they have not yet done so.

Have partners take a moment to talk about what they will listen for; then have them share their writing. Scan the class, without intervening, providing sufficient time for both partners to share their writing before signaling for their attention.

FACILITATION TIP

Continue to practice **asking facilitative questions** to help the students respond to one another during class discussions. When students direct their responses to you, redirect them toward the class by asking questions like:

Q *Do you agree or disagree with what [Travis] just said, and why?*

Q *What questions can we ask [Travis] about what he said?*

Q *Why does what [Travis] said make sense?*

Much learning in this program relies on creating a dynamic discourse among the students. Facilitative questions teach them that their comments contribute to a class discussion and that they are responsible for listening to one another and responding.

5 ▶ Reflect on Pair Conferences and Writing Attitude

Help partners reflect on their work together by asking:

Q *What questions did you ask your partner about your story? What did your partner say?*

Q *What did you do to show interest in your partner's writing?*

Q *Why is it important that we ask other people questions about our own writing?*

Explain that the students will continue to explore and draft fiction next week.

Overview

GENRE: FICTION

The Paper Bag Princess
by Robert Munsch, illustrated by Michael Martchenko
(Annick Press, 2002)

A feisty princess sets out to rescue her betrothed from a dragon.

Boundless Grace
by Mary Hoffman, pictures by Caroline Binch
(Scholastic, 1995)

Young Grace gets to know her father's new family in Africa.

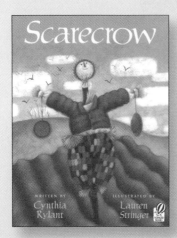

Scarecrow
by Cynthia Rylant, illustrated by Lauren Stringer
(Voyager Books, 1998)

A scarecrow witnesses the life around him.

Writing Focus

- Students hear, discuss, and draft fiction.

- Students explore how character is developed in stories.

- Students generate and quick-write ideas for fiction.

- Students cultivate creativity in their writing.

Social Focus

- Students cultivate a relaxed attitude toward writing.

- Students express interest in and appreciation for one another's writing.

- Students help one another improve their writing.

DO AHEAD

- Consider prereading this week's read-aloud selection with your English Language Learners. Stop during the reading to discuss vocabulary and to check for understanding. You might have partners who speak the same native language turn and talk to each other in that language about what they see in the illustrations during a picture walk.

TEACHER AS WRITER

"A young woman with long hair and a short white halter dress walks through the casino at the Riviera in Las Vegas at one in the morning…. I know nothing about her…. How exactly did she come to this?"
                                                    — Joan Didion

An entire novel can be inspired by an author's glimpse of a stranger in a curious situation. This week look for an opportunity to sit in a public place with your notebook. Observe people who intrigue you and wonder about them. Ask yourself:

- What are they doing?

- What brought them to this moment?

- What do they love? Hate? Hope for? Fear?

Write short character sketches in your notebook as you imagine their lives.

Day 1

Materials

- *The Paper Bag Princess*
- "Notes About Fiction" chart

Drafting Fiction

In this lesson, the students:

- Hear, discuss, and draft fiction
- Explore how characters are developed in stories
- Cultivate a relaxed attitude toward writing

GETTING READY TO WRITE

▶1 Gather and Briefly Review

Gather the class with partners sitting together, facing you. Have them bring their writing notebooks and pencils with them.

Review that the students heard fiction stories over the past two weeks and drafted their own stories. This week they will continue to draft fiction pieces. Remind them that they will eventually select one of their drafts to develop and publish for the class library.

Direct the students' attention to the "Notes About Fiction" chart and review the items on it. Ask:

Q *What else are you learning about fiction that we could include on this chart?*

Add the students' ideas and encourage them to keep these things in mind as they listen to stories and write them this week.

▶2 Read *The Paper Bag Princess* Aloud

Show the cover of *The Paper Bag Princess* and read the title and name of the author aloud. Invite the students to think as they listen about what it might be like to write such a story themselves.

Read the story aloud slowly and clearly, showing the illustrations.

Making Meaning® Teacher

The Paper Bag Princess is introduced in *Making Meaning* Unit 3, Week 1. If the students have heard the story recently, skip the introduction and the reading and continue with Step 4.

3 ▶ Briefly Discuss the Story

Facilitate a class discussion using the questions that follow and be ready to reread from the story to help the students recall what they heard.

Q *Who is the main character in this story? Why do you think so?*

Q *What happens to the character?*

Q *Where does this story take place? How would you describe the place?*

4 ▶ Visualize a Character in the Story

Tell the students that you will reread passages that describe Elizabeth. Ask them to close their eyes and imagine as they listen. Reread the following passage aloud:

p. 8 "Elizabeth decided to chase the dragon and get Ronald back. She looked everywhere for something to wear, but the only thing she could find that was not burnt was a paper bag. So she put on the paper bag and followed the dragon."

Ask:

 Q *What might we guess about Elizabeth from this description? Turn to your partner.*

Repeat this procedure with the following passages:

p. 14 "'Is it true,' said Elizabeth, 'that you can burn up ten forests with your fiery breath?'"

p. 26 "'Ronald,' said Elizabeth, 'your clothes are really pretty and your hair is very neat. You look like a real prince, but you are a bum.' They didn't get married after all."

Explain that today the students will continue to write fiction stories. Encourage them to include details to help the reader imagine their characters. Also remind them to look at the "Notes About Fiction" chart to help them get ideas.

FACILITATION TIP

Continue to **ask facilitative questions** to build accountability for listening and participation during class discussions. Redirect students' comments to the class by asking:

Q *Do you agree or disagree with [Ricki]? Why?*

Q *What questions can we ask [Ricki] about what she said?*

Q *What can you add to what [Ricki] said?*

WRITING TIME

5▶ Draft Fiction Pieces

Ask the students to return to their seats. Write the following choices on the board and have the students write silently for 20–30 minutes.

● Work on a story you started earlier.

● Start a new story.

● Include details to help a reader imagine the characters.

Join the students in writing for a few minutes; then confer with individual students.

TEACHER CONFERENCE NOTE

Continue to confer with individual students, asking them questions such as:

Q *What is this story about?*

Q *Who [is/are] the character(s)? What is interesting about [him/her/them]?*

Q *What do you imagine might happen to [him/her/them]?*

Q *Where do you imagine this story takes place?*

Q *What part are you going to work on next?*

Document your observations for each student using the "Conference Notes" record sheet (BLM1).

Signal to let the students know when writing time is over.

SHARING AND REFLECTING

6▶ Reflect on Writing Process and Attitude

Help the students reflect on their work together by discussing the questions that follow. Invite them to read passages of their writing aloud to the class as they respond.

Q   *What writing ideas came out of your imagination today?*

Q   *How did you feel as you wrote today? If you got stuck, what happened? What do you want to try tomorrow to help you in your writing?*

Explain that the students will continue to hear, discuss, and draft fiction tomorrow.

EXTENSION

Write in Response to Literature

Facilitate a discussion about *The Paper Bag Princess* by asking:

Q   *Why does Elizabeth change her mind about marrying the prince?*

Q   *What do you admire about Elizabeth?*

Have the students choose one of the following prompts to write about in their notebooks:

- In what ways are you like Elizabeth?

- In what ways is Elizabeth different from other storybook princesses?

Day 2

Materials

- *Boundless Grace*

Drafting Fiction

In this lesson, the students:

- Hear, discuss, and draft fiction
- Explore how characters are developed in stories
- Reflect on creativity in their own writing
- Ask one another questions about their writing

GETTING READY TO WRITE

Making Meaning® Teacher

Boundless Grace is introduced in *Making Meaning* Unit 3, Week 3. If the students have heard the story recently, skip the introduction and the reading. Instead, use the questions in Step 2 to help the students review the story, and continue the lesson from there.

1▶ Read *Boundless Grace* Aloud

Gather the class with partners sitting together, facing you. Remind them that they heard *The Paper Bag Princess* and thought about how the main character in the story is described. Explain that you will read another story today. Encourage the students to try to create pictures in their minds of the characters as they listen.

Show the cover of *Boundless Grace* and read the title and names of the authors aloud.

Read the story aloud slowly and clearly, showing the illustrations and clarifying vocabulary as you read.

> **Suggested Vocabulary**
>
> **particularly:** especially (p. 2)
> **speechless:** unable to speak (p. 5)
> **The Gambia:** a country in Africa (p. 6)
> **compound:** enclosed area containing a group of buildings (p. 8)
> **cross:** angry; not pleased (p. 10)
> **tame:** gentle; not wild (p. 22)

ELL Vocabulary

English Language Learners may benefit from discussing additional vocabulary, including:

nana: grandmother (p. 2)

split up: separated; divorced (p. 2)

wicked: very bad; cruel (p. 10)

stepmother: father's new wife (p. 10)

shopping: things that were bought (p. 14)

homesick: missing home (p. 19)

holy place: place set aside for worship (p. 22)

2 Briefly Discuss the Story

Ask and briefly discuss:

Q　*What do we find out about Grace in this story?*

Q　*What does she say or do in the story to make you think that?*

Remind the students that authors use physical descriptions, actions, and speech to make their characters real for the reader. Encourage them to think of ways to make their characters come alive by describing their physical appearance, actions, and speech as they work on their fiction drafts today.

◀ **Teacher Note**

The students will explore character development in more depth during the later weeks of this unit.

WRITING TIME

3 Draft Fiction Pieces

Ask the students to return to their seats. Write the following choices on the board and have the students write silently for 20–30 minutes.

● Work on a story you started earlier.

● Start a new story.

● Include physical description, actions, and speech to make your characters come alive.

Join the students in writing for a few minutes; then confer with individual students.

> ### TEACHER CONFERENCE NOTE
>
> Continue to confer with individual students as they write fiction drafts, asking them questions such as:
>
> **Q** *What is this story about?*
>
> **Q** *Who [is/are] the character(s)? What is interesting about [him/her/them]?*
>
> **Q** *What do you imagine might happen to [him/her/them]?*
>
> **Q** *Where do you imagine this story takes place?*
>
> **Q** *What part are you going to work on next?*
>
> Document your observations for each student using the "Conference Notes" record sheet (BLM1).

Signal to let the students know when writing time is over.

SHARING AND REFLECTING

 Share and Reflect on Writing

As you did last week, ask the students to review the writing they did today and choose one sentence to share with the class. Encourage them to choose a sentence that they believe shows their creativity. After a moment, ask each student to read her sentence aloud, without comment.

After the students have shared their sentences, facilitate a class discussion by asking:

Q *What sentence did you hear that got you interested in someone else's writing?*

Q *What questions do you want to ask a classmate about his or her writing?*

Day 3

Drafting Fiction

In this lesson, the students:

- Review character, plot, and setting
- Hear, discuss, and draft fiction
- Describe characters' thoughts
- Reflect on creativity in their own writing
- Ask one another questions about their writing

Materials

- *Scarecrow*
- "Notes About Fiction" chart

GETTING READY TO WRITE

1 Gather and Briefly Review

Gather the class with partners sitting together, facing you. Have them bring their notebooks and pencils with them. Refer to the "Notes About Fiction" chart and remind the students that in a fiction story something happens to someone somewhere in time, and that the terms *plot*, *character*, and *setting* are used to describe these features of fiction.

Explain that in addition to physical description, actions, and speech, authors also use thoughts to show what a character is like. Tell the students that you will read a story with an interesting character today. Encourage the students to listen for the character's thoughts and think about what this tells us about the character.

2 Introduce and Read *Scarecrow* Aloud

Show the cover of *Scarecrow* and read the title and the author's and illustrator's names aloud. Briefly discuss what a scarecrow is and why a farmer might want to scare crows and other birds away from a field.

Read the story aloud slowly and clearly, showing the illustrations and clarifying vocabulary as you read.

Suggested Vocabulary

grackle: kind of blackbird (p. 8)

starling: kind of short-tailed, dark bird (p. 8)

mammoth: very large (p. 15)

lapel: part of a collar on the front of a coat (p. 20)

3▶ Discuss the Characters in the Story

Ask and briefly discuss the questions that follow and be ready to reread from the story to help the students recall what they heard.

Q *Who is the main character in this story? Why do you think so?*

Q *What thoughts does this character have? What do these thoughts tell us about his personality?*

4▶ Quick-Write: Stories Around Objects

Point out that, in *Scarecrow*, the author creates an entire story around a single object, a scarecrow. She imagines that the scarecrow is alive and describes its thoughts and experiences over time.

Ask the students think about other objects like the scarecrow that they might create a story around. Invite them to imagine those objects alive, thinking, and having experiences. Brainstorm a few ideas as a class (for example, a musical instrument, a shoe, a chair). Then ask the students to quick-write other objects they might be able to create a story around.

Explain that today the students may continue what they started during the quick-write, work on a fiction piece they started earlier, or begin a new story. Encourage them to include characters' thoughts in their story to help readers get to know the characters.

WRITING TIME

 Draft Fiction Pieces

Ask the students to return to their seats. Write the following choices on the board and have the students write silently for 20–30 minutes.

- Add to what you started in the quick-write.

- Work on a story you started earlier.

- Start a new story.

- Try to include characters' thoughts.

Join the students in writing for a few minutes; then confer with individual students.

> ### TEACHER CONFERENCE NOTE
>
> Continue to confer with individual students as they write fiction drafts, asking them questions such as:
>
> **Q** *What is this story about?*
>
> **Q** *Who [is/are] the character(s)? What is interesting about [him/her/them]?*
>
> **Q** *What do you imagine might happen to [him/her/them]?*
>
> **Q** *Where do you imagine this story takes place?*
>
> **Q** *What part are you going to work on next?*
>
> Document your observations for each student using the "Conference Notes" record sheet (BLM1).

Signal to let the students know when writing time is over.

SHARING AND REFLECTING

 Share One Sentence and Reflect on Creativity

As you did yesterday, ask the students to review the writing they did today and choose a sentence they like or that shows their creativity.

Give the students a moment to select their sentences; then go around the room and have each student read his sentence aloud to the class, without comment.

After the students have shared their sentences, facilitate a class discussion by asking:

Q *What sentence did you hear that got you interested in someone else's writing?*

Q *What questions do you want to ask a classmate about his or her writing?*

Day 4

Drafting Fiction and Pair Conferring

In this lesson, the students:

- Describe characters' thoughts
- Draft fiction
- Express interest in and appreciation for one another's writing
- Ask for and receive feedback about their writing
- Give feedback in a helpful way

Materials

- *Scarecrow* from Day 3
- *Assessment Resource Book*

GETTING READY TO WRITE

1 Briefly Review *Scarecrow*

Gather the class with partners sitting together, facing you. Have them bring their writing notebooks and pencils with them.

Remind the students that they heard *Scarecrow* yesterday and thought about the way the author shows the scarecrow's personality through its thoughts. Facilitate a brief discussion about the question that follows, and be ready to reread from the story to help the students recall it.

Q *In the book, the author writes, "it takes a liking for long, slow thoughts" to be a scarecrow. What are some of this scarecrow's long, slow thoughts?*

2 Quick-Write: Showing Character Through Thoughts

Have the students choose a character they have created in their recent writing. Ask them to do a quick-write on a blank page in the writing ideas section of their notebooks about some thoughts that character might have. If you notice them struggling to write the character's thoughts, call them together and model some examples as a class (see the Teacher Note on Week 2, Day 4, page 292).

After a few moments, signal for the students' attention and have a few volunteers share some characters' thoughts with the class.

Explain that during writing time today the students may continue to work on this piece, another story they started earlier, or a new story. Encourage them to include thoughts, as well as physical description, actions, and speech, to show who their characters are.

If necessary, remind the students that it is perfectly fine to leave drafts incomplete and start new ones.

WRITING TIME

3▶ Draft Fiction Pieces

Write the following choices on the board and have the students write silently for 20–30 minutes.

- Write more about the character you thought about during the quick-write.

- Work on a story you started earlier.

- Start a new story.

- Include descriptions of characters' thoughts, actions, and speech.

Join the students in writing for a few minutes; then walk around and observe.

Teacher Note ▶

You may want to shorten today's writing time to leave more time for the pair conferences in Step 4.

CLASS ASSESSMENT NOTE

Observe the students and ask yourself:

- Do the students seem to be writing with a relaxed and free attitude, inspired by their own thoughts?

- If they seem overly cautious or inhibited, do they eventually start writing freely?

continues

CLASS ASSESSMENT NOTE *continued*

Support any student who is still struggling to start after about 10 minutes by asking him questions such as:

Q *What are you thinking about right now?*

Q *Who is the character you are writing about? What is she like?*

Q *What interesting thing happens to this character?*

Q *What might this character say or do in this situation? Why would that make sense for her personality?*

As the student responds to the questions, have him write his responses in his notebook and continue to write what happens.

Record your observations in the *Assessment Resource Book*.

Signal to let the students know when writing time is over.

SHARING AND REFLECTING

▶**4**▶ **Confer in Pairs About Fiction Drafts**

Gather the class with partners sitting together. Explain that the students will read one of their fiction drafts to their partner and confer about it today. If necessary, briefly review the procedure for pair conferring and remind the students that conferring means not only reading their writing to each other but talking about it as well. Ask and briefly discuss:

Q *What would you like to ask your partner to listen for as you read your story today?*

Have partners take a moment to talk about what they will listen for; then have them share their writing. Scan the class, without intervening, providing sufficient time for both partners to share their writing before signaling for their attention.

◀ **Teacher Note**

If necessary, signal about halfway through sharing time so partners can switch roles if they have not yet done so.

Reflect on Pair Conferences and Writing Attitude

Help partners reflect on their work together by asking:

Q *What questions did you ask your partner about your story? What did your partner say?*

Q *What did you do to show interest in your partner's writing?*

Q *Were you able to relax and write freely today without getting stuck? If so, what happened? If not, what made you feel stuck? What did you do to try to get unstuck?*

Explain that the students will continue to explore and draft fiction next week.

GENRE: FICTION

"About Kevin Henkes"
excerpted from www.kevinhenkes.com

Kevin Henkes shares about his life as an author.

Writing Focus

- Students review their fiction drafts and select one to develop, revise, proofread, and publish.

- Students learn about a professional author's writing process.

- Students analyze their drafts and think of ways to develop characters and plot.

- Students cultivate creativity in their writing.

- Students confer with one another and the teacher.

Social Focus

- Students listen respectfully to the thinking of others and share their own.

- Students help one another improve their writing.

- Students express interest in and appreciation for one another's writing.

- Students make decisions and solve problems respectfully.

DO AHEAD

- (Optional) Prior to Day 2, review the fiction pieces you have written and select a single page to use to model adding details to a draft. Make a transparency of the page. Alternatively, you can make a transparency of the "Sample Fiction Draft" (BLM10–BLM12).

TEACHER AS WRITER

"Before I write down one word, I have to have the character in mind through and through. I must penetrate into the last wrinkle of his soul…down to the last button, how he stands and walks, how he conducts himself, and what his voice sounds like. Then I do not let him go until his fate is fulfilled."
— Henrik Ibsen

Review the characters you have created in your drafts and select one who intrigues you. Write a detailed description of that character. Ask yourself:

- What was this character like as a youngster?

- How does he or she dress?

- What physical movements does he or she do subconsciously?

- What is he or she unusually good or bad at?

Day 1

Materials

- *Julius, the Baby of the World* from Week 2
- "About Kevin Henkes" (see page 334)

Selecting Drafts

In this lesson, the students:

- Learn about a professional author's writing process
- Review their fiction drafts and select one to develop and publish
- Reread their writing critically
- Ask one another questions about their writing
- Share their partner's thinking with the class

Developing and Publishing Fiction Stories

In Weeks 4–6 of this unit, the students select one fiction draft they've written in the prior three weeks to develop for publication for the class library. They take this piece through guided analysis (in which you help them look for specific ways to improve their stories) and revision, writing a second draft before publication. They learn important writing skills and conventions as they proofread their drafts.

While students usually select pieces that are appropriate for class publication, you may occasionally have students who want to publish a piece containing content you feel is questionable (such as excessive violence or inappropriate language). Work with these students individually to help them understand that they may write about whatever they wish in their notebooks, but they should select pieces for publication that everyone will want to read and that will be appropriate for the class library.

GETTING READY TO WRITE

▶1 Introduce the Writing Focus for the Coming Three Weeks

Gather the class with partners sitting together, facing you. Remind them that over the past three weeks they have been drafting fiction pieces. Explain that today they will review their drafts and select one piece to develop into a published story for the classroom library.

Remind the students that so far this year they have learned about several professional authors and how they devote a lot of time to rethinking, revising, and improving their books. Explain that the students will learn about another professional author's writing process before they begin their work today.

 2 Learn About Kevin Henkes

Remind the students that they heard *Julius, the Baby of the World* by Kevin Henkes earlier in the unit. Ask and briefly discuss:

Q *What other books by Kevin Henkes have you read?*

Q *Based on his stories, what kind of person do you think he might be? Why?*

Explain that you will read an excerpt from Kevin Henkes's website. Read "About Kevin Henkes" aloud slowly and clearly.

Ask and briefly discuss:

Q *What did you find out about Kevin Henkes?*

> **Students might say:**
>
> "He wanted to be an artist even when he was a kid."
>
> "In addition to what [James] said, I learned that he lives with his wife and son and daughter."
>
> "He also loved to read as a child."

Explain that the students will create their own fiction book for the class library and that they will begin rewriting it today to make it the best story it can be. Like Kevin Henkes, they will make sure to include their strong mental images and vivid descriptions of their characters and environments.

3 Prepare to Review Fiction Drafts

Explain that during writing time the students will reread all of their fiction drafts and select one to revise and publish as a book. The draft can be a piece they've started but not finished. Encourage

FACILITATION TIP

Continue to practice **asking facilitative questions** during class discussions to help the students respond directly to one another.

them to select a piece that they can imagine making changes to and that they think their classmates will enjoy. Ask:

Q *As you're looking through your drafts, what might you want to look for to help you decide on one to develop?*

Students might say:

"I want to look for a draft that I really like or have some strong feelings about."

"I will look for drafts that have characters I like."

"I want my story to be different from everyone else's, so I'm going to look for a draft that is really unique."

Teacher Note ▶

If the students have difficulty answering this question, offer some ideas like those in the "Students might say" note; then ask, "What else might you look for?"

WRITING TIME

▶4 Reread Drafts and Select One to Develop

Have the students return to their seats, reread all their drafts, and select one to develop and publish. Students who select a draft before the time is up can start thinking about what they can add to, change, or improve in the draft.

As the students review their drafts, circulate around the room and support students by asking them questions such as:

Q *Why did you choose this piece to revise?*

Q *What can you imagine adding or changing in this piece to make it more interesting?*

Teacher Note ▶

If a student wants to publish a piece that is already very long, encourage her to identify one section of it to develop and publish for the class library. She may continue to work on other parts of the story on her own at another time.

If you notice the students selecting pieces with limited potential for revision (for example, pieces they feel are already "perfect," very long or very short pieces, pieces not double-spaced), gently guide them toward a more workable piece.

SHARING AND REFLECTING

5▶ Confer in Pairs About Selected Drafts

Explain that pairs will confer about the drafts they selected and talk about why they chose those drafts. Ask:

Q *What questions can you ask your partner about the draft he or she chose?*

Students might say:

"I could ask my partner why he chose that draft to publish."

"I could ask my partner how she's thinking of revising her draft."

Alert the students to listen carefully to each other because you will ask them to share what their partner said in the whole-class discussion. Ask partners to start conferring.

After several minutes of pair sharing, signal for the students' attention. Have several students share what their partner said. Follow up with questions such as:

Q *Why did your partner select that draft?*

Q *What is interesting to you about your partner's draft?*

Q *What else did your partner tell you about the draft he is going to work on to publish?*

6▶ Reflect on Pair Conferences

Help the students reflect on their partner work by briefly discussing:

Q *What did you do today to make sure you could accurately share what your partner said with the class?*

EXTENSION

Read About Other Authors

If your students enjoyed learning about Kevin Henkes, encourage them to search the Internet to find out about other authors they like. Many authors have their own websites. The students can enter an author's name on any search engine to find websites with information about that author.

Day 2

Analyzing, Completing, and Revising Drafts

In this lesson, the students:

- Reread their writing critically
- Mark places in their drafts where characters are revealed through actions, thoughts, or speech
- Complete and begin revising their drafts
- Reflect on creativity in their own writing

GETTING READY TO WRITE

1 Facilitate Guided Rereading of Drafts

Have the students stay at their seats today. Ask them to open their writing notebooks to the fiction draft they selected yesterday. Explain that today you will help them think about how they might revise and improve their draft in preparation for publishing it.

Ask the students to reread their draft quietly and look up when they are finished. Distribute a pad of self-stick notes to each student. Explain that you will ask the students to look for and think about several specific things in their draft.

Say the following prompts one at a time, giving the students several minutes between each prompt to review their drafts and mark passages with the self-stick notes.

- *Find one place in your story that you really like. This might be a place where you used words that you like or one where you wrote a sentence you like. Put a self-stick note in the margin next to that place and write "I like" on it.*

Materials

- Pad of small (1½" x 2") self-stick notes for each student
- Transparency of your own fiction writing (see "Do Ahead" on page 315) OR transparency of "Sample Fiction Draft" (BLM10–BLM12)
- Overhead pen
- *Assessment Resource Book*

Teacher Note

The purpose of the guided rereading is to give the students experience reading their drafts critically *before* they begin to revise. Note that some students will not be finished with their piece and will need time this week to both complete and revise their drafts.

Teacher Note

If necessary, model attaching a self-stick note to the outer margin of a notebook page so that it marks the text without covering it up.

Teacher Note

If the students have difficulty identifying places that reveal, or could reveal, a character's personality, call for their attention and show the transparency of your own fiction writing (or the "Sample Fiction Draft") on the overhead projector. Read the passage aloud and model marking places where a character's actions, speech, or thoughts are or could be described. (You might say, "I think the first sentence tells something about Larry the Lizard by describing his actions. I might want to add some information about what he looks like, so I'll mark that.")

Teacher Note

You might say, "I want to add information about what Larry the Lizard looks like. I will add a sentence that says *He was green and bumpy and had a long, shiny tail.*"

● *Find a place in your draft where you describe, or could describe, your character's appearance. Put a self-stick note in the margin next to that place and write "looks" on it.*

● *What is your main character like? Find a place in your draft where you describe, or could describe, your main character's actions. Put a self-stick note in the margin next to that place and write "actions" on it.*

2 ▶ **Model Revising to Develop Characters**

Explain that during writing time today the students will look at the places they marked with self-stick notes and begin making revisions. Explain that they will incorporate these revisions into a second draft next week.

Show the transparency of your own writing (or the "Sample Fiction Draft") on the overhead projector. Ask the students to watch as you model adding information about a character's appearance or his or her actions, thoughts, or speech. Read the passage aloud and think aloud about a place you want to revise. Model using an arrow (caret) to insert new text and crossing out text to delete.

Sample Fiction Draft

Larry the Lizard lounged on a rock and flicked his long

He was green and bumpy and had a long, shiny tail.
tongue in and out of his mouth. ▲He spent his days in the

backyard, eating bugs and slithering beneath the plants.

He was friendly with almost all the backyard creatures,

including the bees and the butterflies and the worms, but

he wasn't friendly with Chacha the Cat.

"Where's that cat?" Larry asked Bertha the Bee.

"Beats me," said Bertha, who buzzed on by. Bertha

didn't care, but Larry sure did, since the cat's favorite

activity was to sneak up on small lizards and pounce on

Looks

WRITING TIME

③ Revise First Drafts

Write the following tasks on the board and have the students work silently on them for 20–30 minutes.

- Complete your draft.

- Add descriptions, actions, thoughts, and speech to tell about your character.

- Remove the self-stick notes when you finish revising.

Join the students in writing for a few minutes; then walk around the class and observe.

CLASS ASSESSMENT NOTE

Observe the students and ask yourself:

- Do the students seem engaged in thinking of ways to develop their drafts?

- Are they focusing on developing their characters?

- Do they have ideas for actions, speech, and thoughts they could write to reveal character?

Support students who are having difficulty by asking them questions such as:

Q *What were you thinking about when you marked this place on your draft?*

Q *What kind of person is your character? How might a person like that act? What might a person like that say or think?*

Q *What could your character do or say at this point to show his or her personality?*

Record your observations in the *Assessment Resource Book.*

Signal to let the students know when writing time is over. Explain that they will continue to work on their drafts tomorrow.

SHARING AND REFLECTING

4▶ Reflect on Writing and Creativity

Help the students reflect on their work by asking:

Q *What ideas did you have for describing your character today?*

Q *What ideas did you have that you feel were creative or original today? Tell us about them.*

Remind the students how important it is to use their imaginations, both in writing drafts and in revision. Encourage them to strive to make their stories as creative and interesting as they can.

Day 3

Analyzing and Revising Drafts

In this lesson, the students:

- Reread their writing critically
- Mark places in their drafts where interesting things happen in the plot
- Think about both adding and deleting text
- Revise their drafts
- Reflect on creativity in their own writing

GETTING READY TO WRITE

1 ▶ Briefly Review Purpose of Revision

Have the students stay at their desks today. Ask them to open their writing notebooks to the story they are developing. Review that they began to analyze and revise their drafts yesterday. Remind them that the purpose of revision is to make their piece as interesting and readable as possible before they publish it for their classmates.

Explain that today you will ask them to think about a couple more ways they might improve their drafts.

2 ▶ Continue Guided Rereading of Drafts

Have the students quietly reread their draft and look up when they are finished. Have them get out their self-stick notes and get ready to think about the following prompts. Say the prompts one at a time, giving the students several minutes between each prompt to review their draft and mark passages with the self-stick notes.

- *What happens to your character(s) in this story? Find places in your draft where interesting things happen, or could happen, to*

Materials

- Pad of small (1½" x 2") self-stick notes for each student
- Revised transparency of your own fiction writing (or of the "Sample Fiction Draft") from Day 2
- Overhead pen

Teacher Note

Developing the plot of a story is a focus of fiction study at grade 5 of the program and thus is treated with a lighter touch in grade 3 (see "Development Across the Grades" on page 254).

your character. Put self-stick notes in the margin next to those places and write "interesting" on them.

Q *Will your reader be able to follow what happens from the beginning to the end of your story? If you think a place might be confusing, mark that place with a self-stick note and write "confusing" on it.*

▶ 3 Model Revising to Develop the Plot

Explain that, as they did yesterday, the students will look at the places they marked with self-stick notes and make revisions to their stories. Remind them that they will incorporate these revisions into a second draft next week.

Show the transparency of your own writing (or the "Sample Fiction Draft") on the overhead projector. Ask the students to watch as you model revising your draft to make your story as clear and interesting as possible. Read the story and think aloud about a place you might clarify information. Model adding and, if necessary, deleting text on the transparency.

Teacher Note

If the students have difficulty identifying places where interesting things happen to their character(s), call for their attention and show the transparency of your own writing (or the "Sample Fiction Draft") on the overhead projector. Read the passage aloud and model marking places where interesting things happen. (You might say, "I think it's interesting that the lizard, the cat, and the dog all ask the bee the same question. I will mark those places.")

Teacher Note

You might say, "I don't think it's clear who's talking at the end of the story, so I'm going to add the phrase, *grumbled Bertha.* I also think it would make the story more interesting if Bertha was also afraid of somebody, so I'm going to have her say, *By the way, where's that bird?* at the very end."

Sample Fiction Draft *continued*

wide yawn. Then, out of the corner of his eye, he saw a tiny shape go scurrying under a bush. Duffel yelped and jumped back. Larry the Lizard!

"Where's that lizard?" he asked Bertha the Bee.

"Beats me," said Bertha, who buzzed on by. Bertha didn't care, but Duffel sure did, since the lizard's favorite activity was to sneak up on napping dogs and bite them on the toes.

"Hmph, if everyone would learn to leave each other alone, I wouldn't have to answer so many silly
grumbled Bertha. "By the way, where's the bird?"
questions!"

[Interesting]

[Confusing]

WRITING TIME

4 ▶ Continue Revising Drafts

Write the following tasks on the board and have the students work silently on them for 20–30 minutes.

* Add information or make changes so your story is as interesting and clear as possible.

* Remove the self-stick notes when you finish revising.

* Continue adding to your story until it is finished.

Join the students in writing for a few minutes; then confer with individual students.

TEACHER CONFERENCE NOTE

Over the coming two weeks, confer again with individual students, this time talking with them about the draft they selected to develop. As you listen to them read their writing aloud, ask yourself:

* Does this student's story have a character with distinct traits that are shown through action, speech, or thought?

* Does something interesting or important happen to the character?

* Does the story make sense? Is it easy to follow what is happening, when, and to whom?

Support students in integrating the elements of fiction by asking questions such as:

Q *What kind of person is your main character?*

Q *What actions, thoughts, or dialogue [have you added/ could you add] to show who the character is?*

Q *What interesting or important thing happens to your character?*

Q *What happens to the character before and after this event?*

Document your observations for each student using the "Conference Notes" record sheets (BLM1).

Signal to let the students know when writing time is over.

SHARING AND REFLECTING

5 ▶ Reflect on Writing and Creativity

Help the students reflect on their work during writing time today by asking:

Q *How did you add to or revise your story to make it more interesting?*

Q *What ideas did you have that you feel were creative or original today? Tell us about them.*

Explain that partners will confer about their stories tomorrow.

Day 4

Pair Conferring

In this lesson, the students:

- Ask for and receive feedback about their writing
- Give feedback in a helpful way
- Ask one another questions about their writing
- Anticipate and solve problems that arise in their work together
- Share their partner's thinking with the class

Materials

- Chart paper and a marker
- Revised transparency of your own fiction writing (or of the "Sample Fiction Draft") from Day 3
- Overhead pen
- *Assessment Resource Book*

GETTING READY TO WRITE

1 **Prepare for Pair Conferences**

Gather the class with partners sitting together, facing you. Have them bring their writing notebooks and pencils with them. Explain that today partners will meet to confer about their drafts. Remind the students that in the writing community the goal of giving feedback is to help each person create the best possible piece of writing. Ask and briefly discuss:

Q *What have you learned about giving feedback respectfully?*

Q *What problems can arise when you are conferring with a partner? How will you avoid those problems today?*

2 **Prepare to Give Feedback About Character and Plot**

Explain that during pair conference time today partners will read and tell each other about their stories, including their revisions, and receive feedback about character and plot.

Explain that as they listen to their partner's story you would like them to ask themselves three questions. Write the following questions on a sheet of chart paper as you say them aloud:

> - Am I getting to know the character's personality? How?
>
> - Does something interesting or important happen to the character?
>
> - Can I follow what's happening in the story? Am I confused at any point?

Have the students practice giving you feedback about the questions. Show the transparency of your own fiction writing (or the "Sample Fiction Draft") and read it aloud, along with any revisions. Use "Think, Pair, Share" to have the students first think about and then discuss your draft using the charted questions.

After a few moments, signal for the students' attention and have several volunteers give you feedback about your draft using the three questions.

◤3 Confer in Pairs

Encourage the students to listen carefully to their partner and be ready to report to the class what their partner said.

Give the students ample time to confer in pairs.

CLASS ASSESSMENT NOTE

Circulate among conferring pairs and observe without intervening. Ask yourself:

● Are pairs staying on task, reading and discussing their writing?

continues

When most pairs have had time to discuss their drafts, call for the class's attention.

4 ▶ Reflect on Feedback

Gather the class and briefly discuss:

Q *What was helpful about the way your partner talked to you today?*

Q *What problems, if any, did you have during pair conferences? What will you do to avoid those problems next time?*

Share any problems you noticed and discuss what the students will do to avoid those problems next time. Ask:

Q *What is one thing your partner told you about your piece?*

Remind the students that authors take feedback very seriously, although they may not always agree with the feedback. Authors need to decide for themselves what will result in the best possible piece.

Explain that during writing time today the students will revise their draft based on their partner's feedback.

WRITING TIME

▶5 Revise Drafts Based on Conference Feedback

Write the following tasks on the board and have the students work silently on them for 20–30 minutes.

- Revise your draft based on partner feedback.

- Finish writing and revising your story.

- If you finish, work on another piece of writing.

During the writing time, confer with individual students about their writing.

TEACHER CONFERENCE NOTE

Continue to confer individually with students about the drafts they have selected to develop. As you listen to them read their writing aloud, ask yourself:

- Does this student's story have a character with distinct traits that are shown through action, speech, or thought?

- Does something interesting or important happen to the character?

- Does the story make sense? Is it easy to follow what is happening, when, and to whom?

Support the students in integrating the elements of fiction by asking questions such as:

Q *What kind of person is your main character?*

Q *What actions, thoughts, or dialogue [have you added/ could you add] to show who the character is?*

Q *What interesting or important thing happens to your character?*

Q *What happens to the character before and after this event?*

Document your observations for each student using the "Conference Notes" record sheet (BLM1).

Signal to let the students know when writing time is over.

SHARING AND REFLECTING

6 ▶ **Reflect on Writing**

Help the students reflect on their work today by briefly discussing:

Q *What feedback from your partner did you incorporate into your revision today? Tell us about it.*

Explain that the students will start writing a second draft of their story in the coming week.

About Kevin Henkes

excerpted from www.kevinhenkes.com

Some quotes from Kevin Henkes:

"I grew up desperately wanting to be an artist. That desire was a huge part of my identity for as far back as I can remember. It wasn't until I was in high school that writing became as important to me. During my junior year of high school I decided I wanted to write and illustrate children's books for a career."

"I also loved books, and the ones I was lucky enough to own were reread, looked at over and over, and regarded with great respect. To me 'great respect' meant that I took them everywhere, and the ones I still own prove it. They're brimming with all the telltale signs of true love: dog-eared pages, fingerprints on my favorite illustrations, my name and address inscribed on both front and back covers in inch-high crayon lettering, and the faint smell of stale peanut butter on the bindings. I wondered about authors and illustrators back then—What did they look like? Where did they live? Did they have families? How old were they?—but I never imagined that one day I would be one myself."

"…because I'm a visual person, I do have very strong images in my head as I work. I love describing my characters and their environments. Setting a scene—providing proper lighting, the colors and textures of things, sounds—is one of my favorite things…."

"I used to live with my parents and brothers and sister and work at a card table in my bedroom. Now I live with my wife and son and daughter in our own house and work at a drawing table in my own studio. I never thought I'd be lucky enough to be a real author and illustrator. I wouldn't trade it for anything."

Week 5 Overview

GENRE: FICTION

Writing Focus

- Students assess their own writing.

- Students analyze their drafts and think of ways to develop the setting.

- Students develop a second draft of their story, integrating revisions.

- Students explore verbs and adverbs.

- Students confer with one another and the teacher.

Social Focus

- Students listen respectfully to the thinking of others and share their own.

- Students help one another improve their writing.

- Students make decisions and solve problems respectfully.

DO AHEAD

- Prior to Day 4, create a chart labeled "Self-Assessment Questions" with the following questions written on it:

  Q *In the story, does something interesting happen to someone, somewhere in time?*

  Q *Does the main character act, think, and speak in a way that shows what he or she is like?*

  Q *Is everything that happens connected to what happens before and after?*

  Q *Does every sentence of the story make sense?*

- (Optional) If computers are available, you might have some students type and print out their drafts. You can also recruit parent volunteers to help the students do so.

TEACHER AS WRITER

"The plot is the line on which I hang the wash, and the wash is what I care about."
— *Robert B. Parker*

Reread the description of the character you wrote in Week 4. Explore plot this week by having something interesting, important, or challenging happen to your character. Describe what happens to the character before and after the event. Ask yourself:

- What makes the experience interesting, important, or challenging to my character?

- What is this character like before the situation? After?

- What does the character learn by going through this experience?

Day 1

Materials

- *Scarecrow* from Week 3
- Pad of small (1½" x 2") self-stick notes for each student
- Lined chart paper and a marker
- Revised transparency of the page of your own fiction writing (or of the revised "Sample Fiction Draft") from Week 4
- Loose, lined paper for second drafts

Teacher Note

Developing the setting of a story is a focus of the fiction unit in grade 4 of the program and thus is treated with a lighter touch in grade 3 (see "Development Across the Grades" on page 254). ▶

Teacher Note ▶

If necessary, repeat this discussion with other books with noteworthy settings from this unit:

- *Tacky the Penguin*
- *Cherries and Cherry Pits*
- *The Paper Bag Princess*
- *Boundless Grace*

Writing Second Drafts

In this lesson, the students:

- Mark places in their drafts to develop setting and descriptive language
- Review their revisions and begin writing second drafts
- Ask one another questions about their writing

GETTING READY TO WRITE

▶ 1 Briefly Review and Discuss Setting in Fiction

Have the students stay at their seats today. Explain that this week they will write second drafts of their stories, incorporating their revisions. Explain that today they will think about the setting of their story and begin writing their second drafts.

If necessary, remind the students that the setting of a story is the place and time in which the story occurs. Ask the students to think quietly for a moment about where and when their story occurs.

Show the cover of *Scarecrow* and briefly discuss the place described in the story, using the question that follows. Be ready to reread from the text to help the students remember the story. Ask:

Q *What do you remember about the setting of this story? What did it look like? Sound like? Smell or feel like?*

Students might say:

"The setting is on a farm. There are birds and sunflowers and other growing things."

"There's all kinds of weather—rain, snow, sunshine."

"I remember it said that it was silent sometimes."

2 Continue Guided Rereading of Drafts

Have the students quietly reread their draft and look up when they are finished. Have them get out their self-stick notes and get ready to think about the following prompts. Say the prompts one at a time, giving the students several quiet minutes between each prompt to review their draft and mark passages with the self-stick notes.

- *Where and when does your story take place? Find a place in your draft where you describe, or could describe, the setting. Put a self-stick note in the margin next to that place and write "setting" on it.*

- *What might someone see or hear in your setting? Find places where you could add words to describe how it looks or sounds. Put a self-stick note in the margin next to that place and write "looks" or "sounds" on it.*

- *What might someone smell or feel in your setting? Find places where you could add words to describe how it smells or feels. Put a self-stick note in the margin next to that place and write "smell" or "feel" on it.*

◀ **Teacher Note**

If the students have difficulty identifying places where they can describe the setting, use the transparency of your own writing (or the "Sample Fiction Draft") to model (for example, "I could add description about what the backyard is like. I might use words like *sunny* and *grassy*. I will mark that").

3 Prepare to Write Second Drafts

Tell the students that during writing time they will make revisions to the places they marked with self-stick notes and then begin writing their second drafts on loose, lined paper. Remind them to write on every other line, as this will give them space to make corrections as they get ready to write a final version later on.

Point out that a second draft should be an improved, more interesting, and more complete version of the story they began in their first draft. If the students find themselves copying their first draft onto the lined paper without any revisions, they are probably not writing a true second draft and should ask for help.

◀ **Teacher Note**

If necessary, model beginning to write a second draft using the transparency of your revised writing from last week. Read the first sentence aloud and model writing that sentence, with revisions, on every other line on lined chart paper.

Teacher Note

If the students use a word-processing program to write their second drafts, they should double-space the drafts and print them out.

WRITING TIME

4 ▶ Begin Writing Second Drafts

Distribute the lined paper and have the students work silently on their revisions and second drafts for 20–30 minutes.

Join the students in writing for a few minutes, then walk around and observe.

CLASS ASSESSMENT NOTE

Observe the students and ask yourself:

* Do the students incorporate their revisions into a second draft?

* Are the second drafts improvements on their first drafts?

Support students who are having difficulty by asking them questions such as:

Q *I notice that you marked this part of your draft for revision. What were you thinking about when you marked it?*

Q *Read this passage aloud with the new sentence you want to add. Does that make sense? If not, how can you change it so it does make sense?*

Record your observations in the *Assessment Resource Book*.

Signal to let the students know when writing time is over.

SHARING AND REFLECTING

5 ▶ Share Revisions and Reflect

Have several volunteers share passages they revised by reading the original and the revised passages. As the students share, probe their thinking by asking:

Q *[John], how do you think your revision improves your piece?*

Q *What questions can we ask [John] about his revision?*

Help the students reflect on their participation in this discussion by asking:

Q *What did you do during the sharing time today to show you were interested in what your classmates said and wrote?*

Explain that the students will continue to work on their second drafts in the coming days.

Day 2

Materials

- *Julius, the Baby of the World* from Week 2
- Transparency of "Excerpts from *Julius, the Baby of the World*" (BLM13–BLM14)
- *Student Writing Handbook* pages 7–8
- Loose, lined paper for second drafts
- *Assessment Resource Book*

ELL Note

You might provide the prompt "I remember that…" to your English Language Learners to help them verbalize their answers to this question.

Writing Second Drafts

In this lesson, the students:

- Continue to write second drafts
- Explore using interesting verbs to make writing descriptive
- Ask one another questions about their writing

GETTING READY TO WRITE

▶1 Introduce Interesting Verbs

Ask the students to stay at their desks today. Have them get out their writing notebooks, *Student Writing Handbooks*, and pencils.

Explain that the students will continue to work on their second drafts today and that they will make their writing as descriptive as possible so readers will be able to imagine what's happening in their stories. Explain that one way writers make their writing descriptive and communicate exactly what they want to say is by using interesting *verbs*, or action words.

▶2 Analyze Verbs in *Julius, the Baby of the World*

Show the cover of *Julius, the Baby of the World* and remind the students that they heard this story earlier in the unit. Briefly review the story using the question that follows, and be ready to reread from the text to help the students remember the story. Ask:

Q *What do you remember about this story?*

Have the students open to *Student Writing Handbook* pages 7–8, "Excerpts from *Julius, the Baby of the World*" as you place the same transparency on the overhead projector. Explain that these are several passages from the story in which the author uses interesting verbs.

Read the passages aloud to the class and ask:

 Q *What verbs, or action words, does the author use in these passages? Turn to your partner.*

Have partners discuss the question for a moment; then signal for their attention. Call on a few volunteers to share the verbs they found. Underline these on the transparency. As the students report, ask the class follow-up questions such as:

Q *How is the verb* exclaim *different from* said? *Why might the author have chosen to use* exclaim *here?*

Q *What do the verbs* twitched *and* quivered *tell us about how Lilly might be feeling?*

Students might say:

"My partner and I underlined *exclaimed*. We could imagine the parents saying that in a high, happy voice."

"I agree with [Petra]. They 'exclaimed' about Julius but they only 'said' about Lilly."

"The words *twitched* and *quivered* tell us that Lilly is getting ready for a fight!"

 Review Drafts for Verbs

Ask the students to look closely at their own drafts and find places where they used, or could use, interesting verbs in their stories. After a few moments, ask:

Q *Did you find a verb you like? If so, read us the sentence with that verb.*

Q *Did you find a verb that you might be able to replace with a more interesting one? Give us an example.*

Explain that you would like the students to think about interesting verbs they could add to make their stories more descriptive as they write today.

WRITING TIME

4 Continue to Write Second Drafts

Have the students work silently on their second drafts for 20–30 minutes, paying attention to using interesting verbs in their stories. Make sure they have access to more lined writing paper, if they need it.

Join them in writing for a few minutes; then walk around the class and observe.

CLASS ASSESSMENT NOTE

Observe the students and ask yourself:

* Are the students able to use verbs to enrich the descriptions?

* Are they able to incorporate their revisions into a second draft?

* Does their writing communicate clearly? If not, what's unclear?

Support students who are having difficulty by asking them to reread their writing and asking questions and offering suggestions such as:

Q *Does your story make sense? What part doesn't make sense? How can you rewrite it so it makes sense?*

Q *Can you find a place in your story where you used a verb you liked? Let's read the rest of your story and see whether we can find places to use more interesting verbs.*

Q *What verb could you use to help us imagine how the [snake] in your story is moving?*

Record your observations in the *Assessment Resource Book*.

Signal to let the students know when writing time is over.

SHARING AND REFLECTING

5 ▶ Share Revisions and Reflect

Have several volunteers share passages they revised by reading the original and revised passages. As the students share, probe their thinking by asking:

Q *[Karina], how do you think your revision improves your piece?*

Q *What questions can we ask [Karina] about her revision?*

Ask and briefly discuss:

Q *Did you make any revisions today to the verbs in your story? Tell us about it.*

Explain that the students will continue to work on their second drafts tomorrow.

FACILITATION TIP

Continue to practice **asking facilitative questions** during class discussions and notice the effect this has on the students' listening and participation. Encourage them to look at one another, address their comments directly to their classmates, and use the discussion prompts they have learned.

Day 3

Materials

- *Tacky the Penguin* from Week 1
- *Student Writing Handbook* pages 9–10
- Transparencies of "Excerpts from *Tacky the Penguin*" (BLM15–BLM16)
- Overhead pens in two colors
- Loose, lined paper for second drafts

Writing Second Drafts

In this lesson, the students:

- Continue to write second drafts
- Explore using interesting verbs and adverbs to make writing descriptive
- Ask one another questions about their writing

GETTING READY TO WRITE

▶ 1 Review Verbs

Have the students stay at their desks today. Remind them that they explored interesting verbs to make writing more descriptive. Ask and briefly discuss:

Q *What did you learn about interesting verbs yesterday?*

Remind the students that yesterday they looked at an excerpt from *Julius, the Baby of the World* and talked about the interesting verbs Kevin Henkes uses to help us imagine what is happening. Explain that today the students will look at another excerpt to see how the author uses verbs.

▶ 2 Analyze Verbs in *Tacky the Penguin*

Show the cover of *Tacky the Penguin* and remind the students that they heard this story earlier in the unit. Briefly review the story using the question that follows and be ready to reread from the text to help the students remember the story. Ask:

Q *What do you remember about this story?*

Have the students open to *Student Writing Handbook* pages 9–10, "Excerpts from *Tacky the Penguin*," as you place the same transparency on the overhead projector. Using the same procedure and questions you used yesterday, have the students identify interesting verbs in the passages and underline them.

Explain that while verbs describe actions, *adverbs* describe how the actions are done. Adverbs often end in "-ly" and give more information about the verbs. For example, "quietly and politely" describe how the penguins "greeted" each other. Underline *quietly* and *politely* on the transparency using a second color pen; then ask:

Q   *What other adverbs could be used to describe the way characters in a story greet each other?*

> **Students might say:**
>
> "Characters might greet each other happily."
>
> "Loudly."
>
> "Rudely."
>
> "Nervously."

Ask partners to spend a few minutes looking for and underlining adverbs in the excerpts. After sufficient time, signal for their attention and have volunteers share their thinking as you underline the adverbs they report on the transparency.

Encourage the students to try to include interesting verbs and adverbs in their writing today.

◀ **Teacher Note**

If the students have difficulty answering this question, suggest some ideas like those in the "Students might say" note; then ask, "What other adverbs could be used?"

WRITING TIME

▶3 **Continue to Write Second Drafts**

Have the students work silently on their second drafts for 20–30 minutes. Make sure they have access to more lined writing paper.

Join the students in writing for a few minutes; then confer with individual students.

TEACHER CONFERENCE NOTE

Continue to confer individually with students about the drafts they have selected to develop. As you listen to them read their writing aloud, ask yourself:

* Does something interesting happen to a distinct character in this story?

* Is there attention to developing the main character through descriptions, actions, speech, or thoughts?

* Does the student use verbs and adverbs?

* Does the story make sense? Is it easy to follow what's happening, when, where, and to whom?

Support the students by asking them questions such as:

Q *Who is your main character? What happens to [him/her]?*

Q *What kind of person is your main character? What does [he/she] look like?*

Q *What does your main character say or do to show what [he/she] is like?*

Q *What verb could you use beside* [walked] *here? What adverb might make it more descriptive?*

Document your observations for each student using the "Conference Notes" record sheet (BLM1).

Signal to let the students know when writing time is over.

SHARING AND REFLECTING

 Share Revisions and Reflect

Ask and briefly discuss:

Q *Did you include any interesting verbs or adverbs in your story today? Tell us about it.*

Have several volunteers share passages they revised by reading the original and the revised passages. As the students share, probe their thinking by asking:

Q *[Alexei], how do you think your revision improves your piece?*

Q *What questions can we ask [Alexei] about his revision?*

Explain that partners will confer about their stories tomorrow.

EXTENSION

Continue to Explore Interesting Verbs and Adverbs

Give the students more experience with verbs and adverbs by occasionally having them share verbs and adverbs they come across in books they are reading independently. Ask questions such as:

Q *What other verbs could the author have used there?*

Q *What does that adverb tell us about the verb?*

Day 4

Materials

- "Notes About Fiction" chart
- "Self-Assessment Questions" chart, prepared ahead (see "Do Ahead" on page 335)
- Revised transparency of your own fiction writing (or of the "Sample Fiction Draft" from Week 4)
- *Assessment Resource Book*

Self-Assessing and Pair Conferring

In this lesson, the students:

- Assess their own writing
- Initiate pair conferences about their drafts
- Ask for and receive feedback about their writing
- Give feedback in a helpful way
- Use writing and pair conference time responsibly

GETTING READY TO WRITE

1▶ Prepare to Self-Assess

Have the students stay at their desks today. Have them get their writing notebooks and pencils.

Remind the students that over the past few weeks they have learned about fiction. Briefly review the "Notes About Fiction" chart from earlier in the unit and ask:

Q *What else have you learned about fiction that we can record on this chart?*

Add any suggestions to the chart; then direct the students' attention to the "Self-Assessment Questions" chart, and explain that you would like the students to ask themselves these questions as they reread their drafts today. Read the questions aloud.

Show the transparency of your revised fiction writing from Day 1 (or the "Sample Fiction Draft") and briefly model rereading your draft, asking yourself the questions, and thinking aloud about the answers.

Self-Assess

Ask the students to reread their own draft and ask themselves the "Self-Assessment Questions." After most students have had time to finish, signal for their attention and have a few volunteers share their thinking with the class. As they share, follow up by asking:

Q *What will you add to or change in your story to make your [character] more [real/interesting/believable]?*

Q *What will you add or change to make your story make sense?*

Prepare to Write and Initiate Pair Conferences

Explain that today the students will make the revisions they are thinking about and then work on finishing their second drafts. When they finish their second drafts, they will initiate a conference with a partner to get some feedback before starting to work on their final version.

Remind the students of the procedure for initiating their own pair conferences by reviewing that you will give a signal about halfway through the writing time, after which the students may confer in pairs if they are ready. The students should ask their assigned partner first. If their own partner is busy writing and would rather not stop to confer, they may ask another student. Ask and briefly discuss:

Q *If someone asks you to confer, but you would rather keep writing, how will you respond to the person respectfully?*

Q *What problems can arise when you are initiating a pair conference? What will you do to avoid those problems today?*

Redirect the students' attention to the "Self-Assessment Questions" and explain that you would like partners to discuss each piece of writing during the pair conferences.

WRITING TIME

4 ▶ Write Independently and Confer

Have the students work silently on their second drafts. After about 15 minutes of writing, signal that the students may confer in pairs if they are ready. Remind them to discuss the "Self-Assessment Questions" during the conference. Assure students who are still working on their second drafts that they will have other opportunities in the coming week to confer with a partner.

CLASS ASSESSMENT NOTE

Observe the students as they initiate and participate in pair conferences, and ask yourself:

* Are the students able to find a partner and begin pair conferences with minimal disruption to the class?

* What problems are they having initiating pair conferences?

* Are they giving each other feedback about the questions on the chart?

Support partners who are having difficulty by asking them questions such as:

Q *What difficulties are you having in your conference?*

Q *What are you trying to accomplish during this conference? What is preventing you from accomplishing that?*

Q *What can you do to solve that problem? If that doesn't work, what else can you try?*

Record your observations in the *Assessment Resource Book.*

Signal to let the students know when writing time is over.

Teacher Note

Not all the students will be ready to confer today. Those who need to should continue to work on their second drafts during writing times into Week 6 and confer about the draft when it is finished.

SHARING AND REFLECTING

 5 **Reflect on Writing and Pair Conference Time**

Gather the students to discuss how they did during writing and pair conference time today. Remind them that in the writing community the goal of giving feedback is to help each person create the best possible piece of writing. Ask:

Q *If you participated in a pair conference today, what feedback did you receive from your partner that was helpful to you?*

Q *If you continued to write while pair conferences were happening, were you able to concentrate? Why or why not?*

Q *What problems arose today during the pair conference time? What effect did those problems have on our writing community? How can we avoid those problems next time?*

Explain that the students will complete their second drafts next week and proofread and publish their stories.

EXTENSION

Technology Tip: Publishing Student Writing Online

Next week the students will publish their fiction for the class library. Some students might also be interested in publishing their writing online. There are a number of websites where students can publish their writing online; search for them using the keywords "publishing children's writing." Publishing online allows family members and friends to easily access and enjoy students' writing.

Teacher Note

Save the "Self-Assessment Questions" chart to use in Week 6.

Week 6 # Overview

GENRE: FICTION

Writing Focus

- Students proofread their second drafts for spelling and punctuation.

- Students learn how to punctuate speech.

- Students write their final version and publish it as a book.

- Students present their books to the class from the Author's Chair.

- Students confer with one another and the teacher.

Social Focus

- Students work in a responsible way.

- Students help one another improve their writing.

- Students act in fair and caring ways.

- Students express interest in and appreciation for one another's writing.

DO AHEAD

- Prior to Day 3, decide on how you would like the students to make their books, and gather any materials they will need (for example, construction paper for covers, drawing paper for illustrations, markers, staples).

- (Optional) If computers are available, you might have some students type and print out their final versions.

TEACHER AS WRITER

"By the time I am nearing the end of a story, the first part will have been reread and altered and corrected at least one hundred and fifty times. I am suspicious of both facility and speed. Good writing is essentially rewriting. I am positive of this."

— Roald Dahl

Reread the drafts you have written and select one to develop. Ask yourself:

- Who is telling this story?

- What actions, thoughts, or dialogue could I add to reveal character traits or relationships among characters?

- What event or action that is both surprising and believable can I add to this plot?

- Where and when does this story take place? What descriptive language could I add to help the reader see, hear, smell, or feel this setting?

Day 1

Materials

- *Student Writing Handbook* page 11
- Transparency of "Speech Punctuation in Two Stories" (BLM17)
- "Self-Assessment Questions" chart from Week 5
- *Assessment Resource Book*

Completing Second Drafts and Proofreading

In this lesson, the students:

- Explore and practice punctuating speech
- Begin proofreading their drafts
- Initiate pair conferences about their drafts
- Ask for and receive feedback about their writing
- Use writing and pair conference time responsibly

GETTING READY TO WRITE

1 ▶ Explore Speech Punctuation

Have the students stay at their seats today. Have them get out their writing notebooks, *Student Writing Handbooks*, and pencils.

Remind the students that earlier in the unit they talked about how authors often tell us more about a character in their story by writing what they say. Ask the students to open to *Student Writing Handbook* page 11, as you place the transparency of "Speech Punctuation in Two Stories" on the overhead projector. Together, read the first excerpt, from *Tacky the Penguin*. Ask:

Q *Who are the characters who are speaking in this passage? How can you tell?*

Q *How can you tell the difference between the words they are actually saying and the other words in the story?*

Students might say

"Tacky and the hunters are speaking because it says 'blared Tacky' and 'they growled.'"

"The words they are saying have quotation marks around them."

Underline words and quotation marks on the transparency as the students report them. Point out that authors use quotation marks to let readers know which words the characters are saying or thinking. Quotation marks open and close what the characters say.

Explain that the second excerpt is from *The Paper Bag Princess*. Read the excerpt together as a class and ask:

Q *Who is speaking in this passage? How can you tell?*

Q *What do you notice about the way speech is punctuated in this passage?*

> **Students might say:**
>
> "I notice that the sentence with the quotation marks can start at the beginning of a paragraph or in the middle of it."
>
> "I notice that the part that tells who's speaking can come before or after the part in quotation marks."

Again, underline words and quotation marks on the transparency as the students report them.

▶2 Review Drafts for Speech Punctuation

Ask the students to look closely at any speech they included in their own drafts to make sure they have used quotation marks around spoken language and indicated who is speaking. Have them use the passages on *Student Writing Handbook* page 11 as a reference for the way to use quotation marks.

Explain that the students will continue working on their second drafts today. Those who have completed their second draft and conferred with a partner may begin proofreading their story to get it ready for publication. Remind the students to use their word bank and proofreading notes, which they learned to use at the beginning of the year, to check spelling and correctness in their drafts.

◀ **Teacher Note**

At grade 3, the students learn to use quotation marks to distinguish spoken language from narrative. They will learn additional conventions of punctuating speech in grade 4 of the program.

◀ **Teacher Note**

If the students have difficulty answering this question, suggest the ideas in the "Students might say" note.

◀ **Teacher Note**

You will review using the word bank and proofreading notes with the whole class tomorrow. If any of your students need help using these today, review briefly with individual students or with a small group.

WRITING TIME

3 ▶ **Write Independently and Confer in Pairs**

Write the following tasks on the board and have the students work silently on them for 20–30 minutes.

● Try to finish your second draft.

● Check to make sure you use quotation marks to show speech.

● Begin proofreading your second draft for publication.

Remind the students that you will signal after 10–15 minutes of silent writing to indicate that they may confer in pairs about their drafts. Direct their attention to the "Self-Assessment Questions" chart and remind partners to give each other feedback using these questions today.

Join the students in writing for a few minutes; then walk around and observe.

CLASS ASSESSMENT NOTE

Observe the students and ask yourself:

● Are the students able to use quotation marks to distinguish speech from their stories?

● Do they incorporate their revisions into a second draft?

● Does their writing communicate clearly? If not, what's unclear?

Support students who are having difficulty by asking questions and offering suggestions such as:

Q *What are some of the things your character says in your story?*

Q *Do you use quotation marks to show speech? Show me.*

Q *How can you change the word* said *to a more interesting word?*

Record your observations in the *Assessment Resource Book.*

After 10–15 minutes, signal to indicate that the students may confer in pairs.

Signal to let the students know when writing time is over.

SHARING AND REFLECTING

4 ▶ **Share Revisions and Reflect**

Have several volunteers share passages they revised by reading the original and revised passages. As the students share, probe their thinking by asking:

Q *[Anita], how do you think your revision improves your piece?*

Q *What questions can we ask [Anita] about her revision?*

Ask and briefly discuss:

Q *Did you make any revisions today to the speech in your story? Tell us about it.*

Day 2

Materials

- *Student Writing Handbooks*
- "Self-Assessment Questions" chart
- Transparency of "Unpunctuated Fiction Samples" (BLM18)
- Loose, lined paper for final versions

Proofreading

In this lesson, the students:

- Review speech punctuation
- Listen for periods as they read their drafts aloud
- Proofread their second drafts for spelling and conventions
- Ask for and receive feedback about their writing
- Give feedback in a helpful way

GETTING READY

1 ▶ Briefly Review Speech Punctuation and Record in Proofreading Notes

Have the students stay at their seats today. Remind them that they learned about punctuating speech yesterday and thought about the speech in their own stories. Ask and briefly discuss:

Q *What did you learn about some of the ways to punctuate speech correctly?*

Ask the students to open their *Student Writing Handbooks* to the proofreading notes section. Write the notes in the diagram below where everyone can see them, and have the students copy them into their proofreading notes.

Teacher Note ▶

To provide your students with more practice using quotation marks to punctuate speech, do the related activity in the *Skill Practice Teaching Guide* with them.

Rule	Example	Notes
Using quotation marks to punctuate speech.	"What's happening?" blared Tacky.	See examples on handbook page 10.

Encourage the students to refer to their proofreading notes and other *Student Writing Handbook* pages to remind them about speech punctuation and to help them use it correctly in their stories.

2 ▸ Proofreading: Listening for Periods

Explain that the students will proofread their second drafts today to make sure they have corrected all errors before publishing the story. In addition to using their word bank and proofreading notes, they will pay attention to how they are beginning and ending their sentences. Point out that very long sentences should be divided into shorter sentences.

Show the first passage on the transparency of the "Unpunctuated Fiction Samples" on the overhead projector. Ask the students to listen as you read it aloud, pausing only at the comma and the period at the end. Ask:

Q *What's strange about the way I read this passage?*

Point out that right now the passage is one long sentence that doesn't sound right when read aloud. Ask the students to reread the passage slowly with you and stop when it feels natural to do so. At each stop (and as appropriate), model writing a period and capitalizing the next letter to begin a new sentence.

Write the words *and*, *so*, and *then* in the margin and point out that these words are sometimes used when a period would be better. With the students, look for these words in the passage and replace them with a period (capitalizing the first letter of the next sentence).

Follow this same procedure with the second passage on the "Unpunctuated Fiction Samples."

Explain that you would like the students to read their draft aloud to make sure they have used periods where their voices stop, and to check whether they want to replace *and*, *so*, and *then* with periods.

◀ **Teacher Note**

To provide your students with more practice with dividing long sentences, do the related activity in the *Skill Practice Teaching Guide* with them.

3 Briefly Review Proofreading for Spelling and Conventions

Teacher Note ▶

You may have students who have not yet finished their second draft. Assure them that they will have time to finish the draft and confer with a partner before moving on to proofreading. Ask all the students to pay attention as you review proofreading, so they will be able to do this step when they are ready.

Remind the students that they learned how to use the word bank and proofreading notes to help them proofread their drafts for spelling and correctness (see Unit 2, Week 3, Days 1 and 2, on pages 156–163 for review). Briefly review these procedures by reminding the students to:

- Circle words that they are unsure how to spell and look them up in the word bank. If necessary, they will add words to their word bank after looking up the correct spelling in a dictionary or other resource.

- Use their proofreading notes as a checklist of things to look for in their draft. They will correct errors in the draft by crossing them out and writing the corrections next to them.

Teacher Note ▶

You will review the procedures for publishing stories with the whole class tomorrow. Support students who are ready to begin publishing today by reviewing procedures briefly with individuals or with a small group.

Explain that the students will work toward finishing their second draft and proofreading it today. Students who have completed their proofreading may begin writing the final version of their story by copying their revised second draft in their best handwriting on loose, lined paper. They may single-space their final versions.

WRITING TIME

4 Complete Second Drafts and Confer in Pairs

Write the following tasks on the board and have the students work silently on them for 20–30 minutes.

- Read your draft aloud and check for periods.
- Check whether to replace *and*, *so*, and *then* with periods.
- Proofread your draft for spelling and other conventions.
- Begin writing your final version on loose, lined paper.

Remind the students that you will give them a signal after 10–15 minutes of silent writing to indicate that they may confer in pairs when they are ready. Remind them to give feedback using the questions on the "Self-Assessment Questions" chart.

Join the students in writing for a few minutes; then confer with individual students.

TEACHER CONFERENCE NOTE

Confer with individual students who seem to need extra support in preparing their second drafts for publication. Ask yourself:

- What does this student need to work on to be ready to publish his story?

Discuss questions such as:

Q *What are you working on right now?*

Q *Do you have any long sentences? Let's reread them and see whether they need to be divided into shorter sentences.*

Q *What else do you need to do to be ready to write your final version?*

Document your observations for each student using the "Conference Notes" record sheet (BLM1).

Signal to let the students know when writing time is over.

SHARING AND REFLECTING

▶5 **Reflect as a Class**

Gather the students to discuss how they did during writing and pair conference time today. Discuss:

Q *If you worked on proofreading your draft for spelling today, how did that go? What words did you find in your word bank? How did you check on words that were not in the word bank?*

Q *If you participated in a pair conference today, how did you help your partner? How did your partner help you?*

Q *What did you do to take responsibility for yourself during writing time today?*

EXTENSION

Continue to Explore Speech and Dialogue in Fiction

Continue to raise the students' awareness of speech and dialogue in fiction by occasionally having them share dialogue in books they are reading independently. Discuss questions such as:

Q *Who is speaking in the passage you read? What do you find out about the characters from this [speech/dialogue]?*

Q *What other words does the author use to mean* said*? Why might the author have chosen to use those words instead of* said*?*

Day 3

Publishing

In this lesson, the students:

- Finish writing and proofreading their second drafts
- Write their final versions and make them into books
- Share materials and equipment fairly
- Handle materials and equipment responsibly
- Act considerately toward others

Materials

- Loose, lined paper for final versions
- Materials for publishing stories (see "Do Ahead" on page 353)
- (Optional) Computers for word processing

GETTING READY TO WRITE

1 Prepare to Publish Stories

Have the students stay at their desks today. Explain that they will finish writing and proofreading their second drafts and then begin writing their final versions and making them into books today. Review any procedures you would like the students to follow to make their books (for example, how to handle art supplies, how to share computers, and where to place published stories for Author's Chair sharing tomorrow).

Briefly discuss how the students will share materials and equipment fairly and act considerately toward one another as they work on their books. Ask:

Q *What will you do today to take care of our book-making materials? Why is that important?*

Q *If you want to use something that someone else is using, like the computer or the hole-punch, what can you do to share it fairly?*

Q *If you're using something that someone else wants to use, what can you do to share it fairly?*

Q *What else can we do to act considerately toward one another as we publish our books today?*

Explain that you will check in with the students at the end of the lesson to see how they did sharing the materials fairly and acting considerately toward one another.

WRITING TIME

2 **Write Final Drafts and Confer in Pairs**

Write the following tasks on the board and have the students work silently on them for 20–30 minutes.

- Finish proofreading your draft for spelling and other conventions.

- Write your final version on loose, lined paper.

- Gather your final pages into a book with cover (and include illustrations, if you wish).

Remind the students that you will signal after 10–15 minutes of silent writing to indicate that they may confer in pairs about their second drafts. Join them in silent writing for a few minutes; then confer with individual students.

TEACHER CONFERENCE NOTE

Confer with individual students who seem to need extra support in preparing their second drafts for publication. Ask yourself:

- What does this student need to work on to be ready to publish his story?

Discuss questions such as:

Q *What are you working on right now?*

Q *Do you have any long sentences? Let's reread them and see whether they need to be divided into shorter sentences.*

Q *What else do you need to do to be ready to write your final version?*

Document your observations for each student using the "Conference Notes" record sheet (BLM1).

Signal to let the students know when writing time is over.

SHARING AND REFLECTING

3 ▶ **Reflect on Sharing Materials Fairly and Being Considerate**

Help the students reflect on how they did sharing materials fairly and acting considerately toward one another by discussing:

Q *What did you do today to use our materials fairly? What problems did you have? How can we avoid those problems next time?*

Q *What other considerate behaviors did you notice today? How did those help our writing community?*

Explain that the students will begin sharing their published books from the Author's Chair tomorrow.

Day 4

Materials

- (Optional) "Notes About Fiction" chart
- A chair to use as the Author's Chair
- Loose, lined paper for final versions
- Materials for publishing stories from Day 3
- *Assessment Resource Book*

Publishing

In this lesson, the students:

- Reflect on writing fiction
- Write their final versions and make them into books
- Present their books from the Author's Chair
- Express interest in and appreciation for one another's writing
- Ask one another questions about their writing

GETTING READY TO WRITE

1 Reflect on Writing Fiction

Gather the class with partners sitting together, facing you. Remind the students that over the past six weeks they learned about fiction and took a piece of fiction through the writing process, from a first draft to a published book. Ask:

Q *What have you learned about how to write a good fiction story?*

Teacher Note ▶

If necessary, refer the students to the "Notes About Fiction" chart.

Students might say:

"I learned that a good fiction story has an interesting character."

"I learned that something happens to the main character in the story."

"I learned that you can tell a story using an 'I' narrator."

"I learned about verb tenses."

Use "Think, Pair, Share" to have partners first think about and then discuss each of the following questions. For each question, have 2–3 volunteers share their thinking with the class.

Q *What is one way your final story has turned out better than your first draft?* [pause] *Turn to your partner.*

Q *What is one thing you are glad you learned about writing fiction?* [pause] *Turn to your partner.*

Q *What did you find challenging about writing fiction?* [pause] *Turn to your partner.*

Remind the students that writers become better writers as they practice writing over and over. Encourage students who feel particularly drawn to fiction to continue to write fiction during their free time and during the open weeks of this program.

Explain that the students will continue to work on publishing their stories today and begin sharing their stories from the Author's Chair.

WRITING TIME

2 ▶ Write Independently and Confer in Pairs

Ask the students to return to their seats. Have them finish writing their final versions and making them into books. Remind them that you will signal after 10–15 minutes of silent writing that they may confer in pairs. Join them in writing for a few minutes; then walk around and observe.

CLASS ASSESSMENT NOTE

Observe the students without intervening and ask yourself:

* Have most students had time to complete, or nearly complete, a fiction story for the class library?

* If not, do I need to plan an open week or some other time next week so the students can finish?

* Have I conferred once or twice during this unit with every student?

continues

FACILITATION TIP

Reflect on your experience over the past three weeks with **asking facilitative questions**. Does this technique feel comfortable and natural for you? Do you find yourself using it throughout the school day? What effect has using this technique had on your students' listening and participation in discussions? We encourage you to continue to use and reflect on this technique throughout the year.

> ### CLASS ASSESSMENT NOTE *continued*
>
> - Which students would benefit from another conference with me to help them finish their story?
>
> - What evidence do I see that the students have learned something about character, plot, point of view, and verb tense?
>
> - Are the students bringing a relaxed, creative attitude to their writing?
>
> Record your observations in the *Assessment Resource Book*.

Signal to let the students know when writing time is over.

SHARING AND REFLECTING

3 **Review Sharing Writing from the Author's Chair**

Gather the class with partners sitting together, facing the Author's Chair. Explain that in the coming days they will read their published stories aloud and hear and enjoy one another's stories.

Teacher Note ▶

If necessary, refer to Unit 2, Week 3 to review.

Remind the students of the procedure you have established for presenting books from the Author's Chair.

4 **Review Speaking Clearly and Expressing Interest in One Another's Writing**

Before asking a student to share from the Author's Chair today, discuss how the students will act, both as presenting authors and as members of the audience. Ask and discuss:

Q *Why is it important to speak in a loud, clear voice when you're sharing your book with the class?*

Q *If you're in the audience and you can't hear the author, how can you politely let him or her know?*

Q *How will you let the author know that you're interested in his or her story? Why is it important to express interest in one another's writing?*

Encourage the students to be attentive audience members, and tell them that you will check in with them afterward to see how they did.

5 Conduct Author's Chair Sharing

Ask a student who has completed her story to read it aloud from the Author's Chair. At the end of the reading, facilitate a discussion using questions like the ones that follow, and give the author an opportunity to respond to the class's comments and questions.

Q *What was interesting to you about [Janaya's] story? Turn to your partner.*

Q *What kind of character has [Janaya] created? What clues did you hear that told you that?*

Q *What did you hear in the story that was creative?*

Q *What sensory details did you hear as you listened to the story? What did they make you imagine?*

Q *What questions can we ask [Janaya] about her story?*

Follow this same procedure to have other students share from the Author's Chair, as time permits.

6 Reflect on Audience Behavior During Author's Chair Sharing

Ask and briefly discuss:

Q *What did we do well as an audience today? What might we want to work on the next time authors share their work?*

Q *If you shared a book today, how did the audience make you feel? What did they do that made you feel [relaxed/nervous/proud]?*

Assure the students that everyone will have a chance to share their
published stories from the Author's Chair in the coming days. After
they are read aloud, the stories will be placed in the class library so
the students can read them during independent reading time.

EXTENSION

Write Letters Home About Fiction

Provide letter-writing practice for the students by having them
write a letter home about what they learned about fiction writing.
Stimulate their thinking by reviewing the "Notes About Fiction"
chart and discussing questions such as:

Q   *What's special about fiction writing?*

Q   *What steps did you go through to develop and publish your own
fiction story?*

Q   *What is one thing you're proud of about your published fiction story?*

If necessary, review the elements of a letter (date, salutation, body,
closing, and signature) by modeling or writing a shared sample
letter with the class. Have the students write and proofread their
letters; then attach each student's letter to a copy of her own
published story and send it home.

Blackline Masters

Conference Notes

Student's Name: _____

Date	Observations	Suggestions

Sample First Draft

One Saturday last year, my parents drove my brother and me to the home of their friends George and Patty. I didn't want to go. I wanted to be home riding my shiny red bike.

George and Patty met us at the door with beaming smiles. We followed them through their house and out to the backyard. I heard some tiny barks and some loud barks. Four small puppies came running up to us! There also was a big dog that turned out to be the puppies' mother.

continues

Sample First Draft *continued*

My brother and I played with the puppies for a while.

They were all good dogs. Then my father said something I

still can't believe.

"Which puppy do you want, kids?" he said. "That is, if

you even want one."

Did we ever! It only took us a minute to agree on the

smallest puppy of the group. And that's how we got Beck,

the best dog in the world.

 Being a Writer™ | **BLM3**

from **"Candy"**

in *Childtimes* by Eloise Greenfield and Lessie Jones Little

Sometimes we had candy pullings. We'd put sugar and a little vinegar in a brass kettle and set it on the stove, and as soon as the sugar got hot, the vinegar would dissolve it. Then we cooked it until it hardened some, just a little, not too much, and we'd pour it in a platter that had been greased with butter. When the candy cooled enough, two of us would put butter on our hands and we'd pick up the candy, one of us at one end and one at the other, and we'd pull it, kind of easy like. When we started pulling, it would be brown, but after we had stretched it enough, it looked right silvery. Then we'd lay it all around on the platter and break it into sticks. It used to look so pretty, I almost didn't want to eat it.

Childtimes: A Three-Generation Memoir copyright © 1979 by Eloise Greenfield and Lessie Jones Little. Used by permission of HarperCollins Publishers and the Herman Agency.

Sample Personal Narrative

One summer, my mom packed up the car with suitcases, sandwiches, and my brother Mike and me, and we drove all night to visit my grandparents.

We pulled into a gas station. It was the middle of the night when Mike and I were sound asleep, me in the front, and him in back.

I didn't wake up until my mom slammed the door and said, "That should do it. We won't need to stop again for 100 miles."

She drove out of the gas station and pulled up to a stoplight. Just then, I heard a loud bang on my window

continues

Sample Personal Narrative *continued*

and I looked up to see a dark shape standing next to the car.

"There's someone trying to get in the car!" I screamed.

The traffic light turned green, and my mom took off.

"Wait!" I yelled. In an instant, I recognized that the person outside the car was my brother!

My mom pulled over, and Mike got in.

"I told Eddie I was running to the bathroom," he said, looking at me accusingly. He probably did tell me that, but I was sound asleep!

Excerpts

Opening Sentences from Four Personal Narratives

Every year, right after the last day of school, I'd pack a suitcase with my cool summer clothes, my favorite toys, and a sketchbook. Then my dog, Daisy, and I were off to Grandma's apartment in El Barrio.

— from *Grandma's Records*

We had right much work to do. In the house and out in the garden, too. We planted and weeded, and dug up sweet potatoes, and picked butter beans.

— from **"Chores"**
(*Childtimes*)

A terrible thing happened to my brother John in the schoolyard one day.

— from **"John and the Snake"**
(*Childtimes*)

When I first started going to school, I was scared that the other kids might laugh at me.

— from **"First Day of School"**
(*Kids Write Through It*)

Excerpts

from ***Cherries and Cherry Pits***
by Vera B. Williams

THIS is the train seat. THIS is a tiny white woman sitting on the train seat. She is almost as short as I am, but she is a grandmother. On her head is a black hat with a pink flower, like a rose flower. It has shiny green leaves, like the leaves in my uncle's florist shop. On her feet are old, old shoes. These are the buckles. And in her lap is a big black pocketbook.

"You like it?" asks the lady. "You like cherries, honeybird?"

She laughs and dumps all of the cherries onto the geranium plant in front of the parrot. "There's your own little cherry tree," she says to the parrot. She stands next to the geranium in her stocking feet, eating cherries with the parrot.

----

continues

And this boy is tall like my brother. And he has glasses like my brother. And the same kind of cap. And the same green and black jacket, too. It has the orange letters from his team. And when he smiles you can see the space between his big front teeth like my brother's.

When he gets off his train at his station, he just runs right up the escalator. He runs right along the streets, jumping on and off the stoops to his house. Before he even gets up the stairs, and he can take them in just two steps, he's hollering to his little sister, "Hey, come on out here. See what I got for you."

Sample Fiction Draft

Larry the Lizard lounged on a rock and flicked his long tongue in and out of his mouth. He spent his days in the backyard, eating bugs and slithering beneath the plants. He was friendly with almost all of the backyard creatures, including the bees and the butterflies and the worms, but he wasn't friendly with Chacha the Cat.

"Where's that cat?" Larry asked Bertha the Bee.

"Beats me," said Bertha, who buzzed on by. Bertha didn't care, but Larry sure did, since the cat's favorite activity was to sneak up on small lizards and pounce on their tails.

continues

Sample Fiction Draft *continued*

Before long, Chacha appeared at the top of the stairs, nose and ears twitching. She glanced around for the lizard, feeling in the mood for a nice game of pounce-on-the-tail. Suddenly she smelled something that made her fur stand on end. Duffel the Dog!

"Where's that dog?" she asked Bertha the Bee.

"Beats me," said Bertha, who buzzed on by. Bertha didn't care, but Chacha sure did, since the dog's favorite activity was to chase cats and run them out of the yard.

Soon Duffel the Dog wandered into the yard. He stretched his big paws in front of him as he yawned a

continues

Sample Fiction Draft *continued*

wide yawn. Then, out of the corner of his eye, he saw a tiny shape go scurrying under a bush. Duffel yelped and jumped back. Larry the Lizard!

"Where's that lizard?" he asked Bertha the Bee.

"Beats me," said Bertha, who buzzed on by. Bertha didn't care, but Duffel sure did, since the lizard's favorite activity was to sneak up on napping dogs and bite them on the toes.

"Hmph, if everyone would learn to leave each other alone, I wouldn't have to answer so many silly questions!"

Excerpts

from *Julius, the Baby of the World*
by Kevin Henkes

After Julius was born, it was a different story.

Lilly took her things back.

She pinched his tail.

And she yelled insulting comments into his crib.

But her parents loved him.

They kissed his wet nose.

They admired his small black eyes.

And they stroked his sweet white fur.

----

continues

Lilly's parents were dazzled when Julius babbled and gurgled.

"Such a vocabulary!" they exclaimed.

But if Lilly did the exact same thing, they said, "Lilly, let's act our age, please."

Lilly's nose twitched.

Her eyes narrowed.

Her fur stood on end.

And her tail quivered.

Excerpts

from ***Tacky the Penguin***
by Helen Lester

Every day Goodly, Lovely, Angel, Neatly, and Perfect greeted each other quietly and politely.

Tacky greeted them with a hearty slap on the back and a loud "What's happening?"

----

continues

"PENNNNGUINS?" said Tacky. "Do you mean those birds that march neatly in a row?"

And he marched, 1-2-3, 4-2, 3-6-0, 2½, 0. The hunters looked puzzled.

"Do you mean those birds that dive so gracefully?" Tacky asked.

And he did a splashy cannonball.

The hunters looked wet.

"Do you mean those birds that sing such pretty songs?"

Tacky began to sing, and from behind the block of ice came the voices of his companions, all singing as loudly and dreadfully as they could.

"HOW MANY TOES DOES A FISH HAVE? AND HOW MANY WINGS ON A COW?

I WONDER. YUP, I WONDER."

Excerpts

Speech Punctuation in Two Stories

"What's happening?" blared Tacky, giving one hunter an especially hearty slap on the back.

They growled, "We're hunting for penguins. That's what's happening."

— from ***Tacky the Penguin***

Elizabeth said, "Dragon, is it true that you can fly around the world in just ten seconds?"

"Why, yes," said the dragon and jumped up and flew all the way around the world in just ten seconds.

He was very tired when he got back, but Elizabeth shouted, "Fantastic, do it again!"

— from ***The Paper Bag Princess***

Excerpt from *Tacky the Penguin* by Helen Lester. Text copyright © 1988 by Helen Lester. Reprinted by permission of Houghton Mifflin Company. All rights reserved. Excerpts from *The Paper Bag Princess* by Robert Munsch. Copyright © by Robert Munsch. Published by Annick Press Ltd. 1980. Reprinted with permission.

Unpunctuated Fiction Samples

Larry the Lizard lounged on a rock and flicked his long

tongue in and out of his mouth He spent his days in the

backyard eating bugs and slithering beneath the plants

He was friendly with almost all the backyard creatures

including the bees and the butterflies and the worms but

he wasn't friendly with Chacha the Cat.

Where's that cat Larry asked Bertha the Bee

Beats me said Bertha who buzzed on by Bertha didn't

care but Larry sure did since the cat's favorite activity was

to sneak up on small lizards and pounce on their tails.

Proofreading Notes

✔	Rule	Example	Notes
☐			
☐			
☐			
☐			
☐			
☐			
☐			
☐			

Being a Writer™   Reorder Information

Grade 3

Additional Units

Poetry Genre Unit (Teacher's Manual and CD-ROM Reproducible Materials)	BWA-GU3-1
Letter Writing Genre Unit (Teacher's Manual, 2 trade books, and CD-ROM Reproducible Materials)	BWA-GU3-2
Additional Genre Units Package (Poetry Genre Unit and Letter Writing Genre Unit)	BWA-GUP3-1
Preparing for a Writing Test, Grades 3–5 (Teacher's Manual and CD-ROM Reproducible Materials)	BWA-PWT35

Classroom Package — **BW-CP3**

Contents: Teacher's Manual (2 volumes), Skill Practice Teaching Guide, Assessment Resource Book, 25 Student Writing Handbooks, 25 Student Skill Practice Books, and 33 trade books.

Available separately

Teacher's Manual, vol. 1	BW-TM3-V1
Teacher's Manual, vol. 2	BW-TM3-V2
Skill Practice Teaching Guide	BW-STG3
Assessment Resource Book	BW-AB3
Student Writing Handbook pack (5 books)	BW-SB3-Q5
Student Skill Practice Book pack (5 books)	BW-SSB3-Q5
CD-ROM Grade 3 Reproducible Materials	BW-CDR3
Trade book set (33 books)	BW-TBS3

Grade 4

Additional Units

Persuasive Nonfiction Genre Unit (Teacher's Manual and CD-ROM Reproducible Materials)	BWA-GU4-1
Letter Writing Genre Unit (Teacher's Manual and CD-ROM Reproducible Materials)	BWA-GU4-2
Additional Genre Units Package (Persuasive Nonfiction Genre Unit and Letter Writing Genre Unit)	BWA-GUP4-1
Preparing for a Writing Test, Grades 3–5 (Teacher's Manual and CD-ROM Reproducible Materials)	BWA-PWT35

Classroom Package — **BW-CP4**

Contents: Teacher's Manual (2 volumes), Skill Practice Teaching Guide, Assessment Resource Book, 30 Student Writing Handbooks, 30 Student Skill Practice Books, and 25 trade books.

Available separately

Teacher's Manual, vol. 1	BW-TM4-V1
Teacher's Manual, vol. 2	BW-TM4-V2
Skill Practice Teaching Guide	BW-STG4
Assessment Resource Book	BW-AB4
Student Writing Handbook pack (5 books)	BW-SB4-Q5
Student Skill Practice Book pack (5 books)	BW-SSB4-Q5
CD-ROM Grade 4 Reproducible Materials	BW-CDR4
Trade book set (25 books)	BW-TBS4

Grade 5

Additional Units

Letter Writing Genre Unit (Teacher's Manual, 1 trade book, and CD-ROM Reproducible Materials)	BWA-GU5-1
Functional Writing Genre Unit (Teacher's Manual and CD-ROM Reproducible Materials)	BWA-GU5-2
Additional Genre Units Package (Letter Writing Genre Unit and Functional Writing Genre Unit)	BWA-GUP5-1
Preparing for a Writing Test, Grades 3–5 (Teacher's Manual and CD-ROM Reproducible Materials)	BWA-PWT35

Classroom Package — **BW-CP5**

Contents: Teacher's Manual (2 volumes), Skill Practice Teaching Guide, Assessment Resource Book, 30 Student Writing Handbooks, 30 Student Skill Practice Books, and 25 trade books.

Available separately

Teacher's Manual, vol. 1	BW-TM5-V1
Teacher's Manual, vol. 2	BW-TM5-V2
Skill Practice Teaching Guide	BW-STG5
Assessment Resource Book	BW-AB5
Student Writing Handbook pack (5 books)	BW-SB5-Q5
Student Skill Practice Book pack (5 books)	BW-SSB5-Q5
CD-ROM Grade 5 Reproducible Materials	BW-CDR5
Trade book set (25 books)	BW-TBS5

Grade 6

Additional Units

Letter Writing Genre Unit (Teacher's Manual, 1 trade book, and CD-ROM Reproducible Materials)	BWA-GU6-1
Functional Writing Genre Unit (Teacher's Manual, 1 trade book, and CD-ROM Reproducible Materials)	BWA-GU6-2
Additional Genre Units Package (Letter Writing Genre Unit and Functional Writing Genre Unit)	BWA-GUP6-1

Classroom Package — **BW-CP6**

Contents: Teacher's Manual (2 volumes), Skill Practice Teaching Guide, Assessment Resource Book, 30 Student Writing Handbooks (2 volumes), 30 Student Skill Practice Books, and 14 trade books.

Available separately

Teacher's Manual, vol. 1	BW-TM6-V1
Teacher's Manual, vol. 2	BW-TM6-V2
Skill Practice Teaching Guide	BW-STG6
Assessment Resource Book	BW-AB6
Student Writing Handbook pack (5 books)	BW-SB6-Q5
Student Skill Practice Book pack (5 books)	BW-SSB6-Q5
CD-ROM Grade 6 Reproducible Materials	BW-CDR6
Trade book set (14 books)	BW-TBS6

The *Being a Writer* program is also available at grades K–2. Visit www.devstu.org for more information.

Ordering Information:

To order call 800.666.7270 * fax 510.842.0348 * log on to www.devstu.org * e-mail pubs@devstu.org

Or Mail Your Order to:

Developmental Studies Center * Publications Department * 2000 Embarcadero, Suite 305 * Oakland, CA 94606-5300

DEVELOPMENTAL STUDIES CENTER™